# CORPORATE
# STRATEGIC
# COMMUNICATION

# RICHARD STANTON

# CORPORATE STRATEGIC COMMUNICATION

## A GENERAL SOCIAL AND ECONOMIC THEORY

 macmillan education    palgrave

First published 2017 by
PALGRAVE

Palgrave in the UK is an imprint of Macmillan Publishers Limited, registered in England, company number 785998, of 4 Crinan Street, London, N1 9XW.

Palgrave Macmillan in the US is a division of St Martin's Press LLC, 175 Fifth Avenue, New York, NY 10010.

Palgrave is a global imprint of the above companies and is represented throughout the world.

Palgrave® and Macmillan® are registered trademarks in the United States, the United Kingdom, Europe and other countries.

ISBN 978–1–137–54407–0 paperback

This book is printed on paper suitable for recycling and made from fully managed and sustained forest sources. Logging, pulping and manufacturing processes are expected to conform to the environmental regulations of the country of origin.

A catalogue record for this book is available from the British Library.

A catalog record for this book is available from the Library of Congress.

# CONTENTS

# LIST OF FIGURES

# LIST OF TABLES

# PREFACE

## Approach

This book focuses on publicly listed corporations: how they communicate and where they fit in the structure of western societies. It provides a fresh perspective and brings together a range of different ideas. Its objective is to assist professional communicators and students, particularly those in business and management schools, to advance their knowledge of social and communication theories and practices. It provides *a new theory of corporate strategic communication* and a new formula, a *differential transmission of communication*, for engagement with stakeholders. It offers a new approach to understanding and categorizing *corporate strategy selection*.

Significantly, the book imagines a new way to interpret corporate communication through *reverse engineering*. The reverse engineering model explores forensically below the surface of corporate strategic communication and what it really looks like if it is done well. The book is driven by case studies which are presented as exemplifications of corporate strategic communication. It takes into account the major challenges facing corporations in the twenty-first century. There are six outstanding case studies from important corporations around the world. Additionally, examples of corporate communication that support the book's overall design are embedded throughout the text.

The book is designed to support students and professional communicators through a narrative arc that demonstrates why corporations communicate, how they make a contribution to societal goals and objectives, and what motivates them to remain sustainable. It takes account of the dynamic nature of technological and regulatory change under which corporations operate and it looks closely at the ways in which corporations adapt to those changes while remaining relevant.

The content of each chapter is followed by a conclusion and discussion questions. The questions are designed to encourage readers to reflect on and contextualize the various theories, models and cases within the book. In setting out each chapter the book attempts to provide a strong overview of the body of knowledge and to assist students and professional practitioners to develop a concise understanding of the field of corporate strategic communication.

While research has demonstrated that strategies can be emerging rather than planned as part of a traditional structure (see, for example, Mintzberg, 1994) and that disruptive upstarts work to create emerging strategies (see the FireEye case study, Chapter 2), the basic concept of strategic communication in this book is taken to mean communication which has direction and scope over the longer term.

The book is a scholarly work that explores the basis of corporate strategic communication, its theories, its strategy and practice, and its place within reporting mechanisms inside corporate entities. Drawing on important theories of communication, the book explores multiple facets of the ways in which public companies communicate with different stakeholders in wider society.

While the book takes a sophisticated view of the issues and concepts of corporate strategic communication it is written in a style which is accessible to undergraduate students as well as postgraduates. The book gets away from the simplistic view of corporate communication by deliberately not including chapters around standard subjects such as corporate identity, planning, internal communications, issues and crisis management. All of this is touched on in a more general discussion of important concepts. The key tenets of corporate communications – in particular the wider discussion around stakeholder engagement and empowerment – are dealt with in depth as are issues around the organizational narrative and relationship between reputation, image and brand – the corporate RIB.

The book introduces the important work of Leon Mayhew and brings his thinking and arguments about publics into the corporate communication mainstream. In this, the book is concerned with thinking about corporations from a rhetorical standpoint and reflecting upon a world of complexity.

From a teaching standpoint it attempts to break down disciplinary boundaries and to invent a new way to approach the subject. It is supported by examples and contemporary reflection of the world around us. It is designed to be disruptive and to move thinking forward so that students and professionals might engage differently. The book's exploratory breadth and critical tone are designed to situate corporate strategic communication in a wider societal context.

## Organization of the text

The chapters are arranged sequentially so that they can form part of a lecture programme.

The Introduction is intended as a broad overview of the topic of corporate strategic communication.

Chapter 1 provides an overview of corporate communication history in the west from the earliest recorded communication strategy that, in 1710, transformed the Sword Blade Company into the global financial South Sea Corporation. It pinpoints a number of historically important corporate communications culminating in the communication strategies of global entities such as Bank of America at the time of the Global Financial Crisis (GFC). From the patterns that formed during the past three hundred years it offers a glimpse beyond the GFC to the future of strategic corporate communication.

Chapter 2 provides a detailed prescription for analysing strategic corporate communication. It presents a *reverse engineering* process similar in shape to that which is used by manufacturers to discover competitor secrets. It presents a step-by-step guide to the reverse engineering of strategic corporate communication that underpins the following chapters. It is thus an analytical tool focused on the various tactics required to reverse engineer strategic corporate communication. The reverse engineering process works by examining the components of the strategy in the same way a product is broken down into its component parts including examination of public documents, analysis of media matter and engagement with stakeholders through surveys, focus groups and other informational reception channels.

Chapter 3 provides an overview of the theories that drive corporate communication and presents a new theory for understanding corporations in society. It presents an overview of how corporate image and branding connect to reputation and how all three are underpinned by effective strategic corporate communication. It argues that strategic corporate communication is imbued with rhetoric and acts in a one-way asymmetrical sense without considering the requirements of the location of the corporate entity in society. The chapter outlines the idea of corporate social responsibility for deeper consideration in a later chapter.

Chapter 4 explains the significance of stakeholders, stakeholder engagement and stakeholder management as core elements within strategic corporate communication. It provides an overview of all conceivable stakeholders and teases out their relative relationships with corporate entities and with themselves. It examines different stakeholders in different contexts. Once a stakeholder is defined in these wider terms the relative importance of effective strategic corporate communication becomes clearer.

Chapter 5 provides practical explanations of the various methods available to analyse stakeholders including focus groups and surveys. It develops an understanding of how the reverse engineering tool is employed once surveys and focus groups are completed. It demonstrates how to best interpret the raw data into stakeholder profiles. It provides a calculus of corporate contemplation on stakeholders and presents evidence of how corporations create stakeholder hierarchies. It explains the processes in the development of a stakeholder map and what functions it might serve in the conceptualization of an effective strategy.

Chapter 6 explains the concepts of grand strategy and narrative theory as they apply to corporate communication. It explains the various aspects of narrative theory. It describes the historical narrative of the corporation as one which has led to a contemporary asymmetrical approach to corporate communication strategy. It provides a brief outline of other theories that play out in corporate communication including discourse theory and content analysis. It extends Carl Botan's definition of grand strategy which is interpreted as policy-level decisions being made about goals, alignments, ethics and relationships with publics and other forces in the environment. It explains Vincent Hazleton's work in developing a taxonomy of corporate strategy selection. It argues that while there are other models available, Hazleton's taxonomies provide an important underpinning from which to investigate and analyse corporate stakeholder communication and engagement. It provides an extensive evaluation of Hazleton's taxonomies and adds a significant dimension to them by demonstrating ways in which additional categories are conceptualized and function.

Chapter 7 argues the importance of Leon Mayhew's theories of a *New Public* in which professional communicators have the means of social influence. It analyses Mayhew's rhetorical practices as they apply to strategic corporate communication. It develops an argument that places Mayhewian theory as a central tenet of future strategic corporate communication. While Mayhew's theory and his rhetorical practices were derived from political observations, this book reworks and adapts them for the corporate environment. They are particularly relevant given that the western political sphere has shifted in recent years more into alignment with societal mores while the corporate sphere has drifted almost to the point of uncoupling from society.

Chapter 8 explains the notion of corporate responsibility, contextualizing it socio-economically and socioculturally. It presents evidence of existing corporate responsibility models and argues that most operate without recourse to a balanced engagement with stakeholders. It provides an outline for a new corporate responsibility through strategic stakeholder communication. It examines the notion of *social licence to operate* exerted upon corporations by community groups.

Chapter 9 looks closely at corporate accountability in relation to regulators in different countries. It explains the various regulatory frameworks that operate and how they function. It explains the value in parliamentary committees such as the Leveson Inquiry in Britain. It links regulatory frameworks to the case study country chapters. It also presents the various functions of strategic corporate communication that are linked to other forms of communication. In this it expands on the linkages between employee relations, media relations, investor relations – all internal and external communications.

Chapter 10 provides a conclusion and practical recommendations for the conceptualization and operationalization of strategic corporate communication that resonate with western societies. It recommends the development and application of a reverse engineering tool to reveal the core communication competences that drive the communication strategies of successful local and global corporate entities. It concludes by arguing the relevance of adopting Mayhewian argument within the corporate structure so that successful strategic corporate communication is aligned seamlessly within an ever-changing societal framework.

# ACKNOWLEDGEMENTS

To write is to share a communicative desire. It is not an isolated activity and when a work is published it is done so with the support and encouragement of many.

The book *Corporate Strategic Communication* emerged from an eponymously named masters subject that I created at Western Sydney University. That subject was followed by a more complex programme of corporate strategic communication that I created at the University of Sydney and taught at Sydney and at Temple University, Philadelphia. So it is to my former students at these institutions that I owe a debt of gratitude as the subjects and programmes were framed, argued over, examined and agreed upon. The book is a tribute to them all, but particularly to those former students and friends who are now directing corporate strategic communication around the globe, most notably those who contributed vigorous case studies to the book – Peter Arkle, Anna Friedrich and Elin Wibel.

From the beginning, the work of particular scholars contributed to my thinking, but they were pursuing questions of societal meaning in fields other than corporate communication. Leon Mayhew had investigated the impact of the political campaign on society. Vincent Hazleton had analysed aspects of society from a public relations standpoint. I am eternally grateful to them both for presenting me with the underpinnings of my arguments. I am also grateful to Donald Snooks for his work on the long-run dynamics of societies and for leading me towards a theory of societal dynamics.

I am grateful to my friend and former journalistic colleague Philippa Yelland for providing an important Australian case study, to my friend and former student Daniela de Silva for her contribution on South American corporate communication and to Julia Szatar for introducing me to Vitor Souza, who provided the North America standpoint.

For their valuable analysis of the draft I thank the anonymous referees. Without a publisher there would be no book so I sincerely thank Ursula Gavin for steering it to completion. I also thank Linsey Hague for her insightful and elegant editing – much appreciated.

Throughout my enjoyable time researching and writing the book one person provided unconditional support and encouragement – my wife Lorraine Margaret Stanton. Her no-fuss Scottish outlook kept me on track. To her I am eternally grateful.

# INTRODUCTION
# A GRAND STRATEGY FOR PROFITABLE CORPORATE COMMUNICATION

Effective corporate strategic communication is communication which has direction and scope over the long term. It should be viewed as integral to aligning seamlessly with the overarching grand strategy of a corporation. It must be dynamic and functional. It creates a competitive advantage for a corporate entity through its configuration of tactics and resources in constantly changing internal and external environments and through the dissemination of information to its stakeholders and to the societies in which it exists.

## CORPORATIONS IN SOCIETIES

Generally speaking, a corporation exists in perpetuity or has what is called perpetual existence. In some cases, shareholders create a corporation with a limited life. A corporation is defined as an artificial creation of the law existing as a voluntary chartered association of individuals that has most of the rights and duties of natural persons but with perpetual existence and limited liability. Sovereign states invoke legislation that governs how corporations are allowed to act within their jurisdictions. The traditional view of a corporate entity is that its directors have a duty to maximize profit for shareholders; social and other issues do not come into play in the discharge of those duties. The only parties they may consider, other than shareholders, are the interests of creditors if the entity is insolvent. Contemporarily, however, corporate entities are subject to the diverse and often whimsical expectations of the communities in which they are embedded. In 2005 John McFarlane, chief executive officer of one of Australia's largest banks, said three challenges faced today's corporations. Staying alive was the biggest challenge, followed closely by the ability to produce value for shareholders. Knowing how to build an enterprise that would survive and succeed over the longer term was third. McFarlane did not define longer term but he pointed to a number of statistics that assisted in identifying it as fewer than three hundred years but more than a financial quarter. As a guide he highlighted the invention of the *Financial Times* Stock Exchange (FTSE) 100 Index in 1984 which lists the most important corporations on the London Stock Exchange by market capitalization. Throughout the western world market capitalization is used most frequently as a reference point for corporate worth. It is more important than sales revenue or income. Many other countries have developed a similar index (a gauge of prosperity for regulated businesses); the United States has the Standard & Poor's 500 (widely referred to as the S&P 500) which was invented in 1957. These indices begin with a base level and fluctuations over time represent value. In speaking of relative longevity McFarlane was keen to point out that corporate entities do not last long. Twenty years after the FTSE began, 67 of the original 100 companies had gone from the list. Forty-five years after S&P began, 426 of the original 500 had not made the cut. That is not to say all those corporations had died in that time – some had simply not stayed as profitable as they had originally been while others had been acquired or merged. McFarlane provided this glimpse of corporate history as a backdrop to a specific reference to the duties of corporate directors towards shareholders and as a rhetorical reference to duties to other stakeholders.

In specifying what it was that corporate entities would be required to do in the future, McFarlane pointed to three things:

1 the nature of risk as it related to capital investment;
2 the potential for erosion of competitive advantage; and
3 the capacity of the corporation to balance long-term shareholder value with the 'short term desires of the market'.

(McFarlane, 2005, p. 5)

He pointed to a reality that today's corporations must look to meet the expectations of government but they must also look to meet those of the community. We know corporations have legislative responsibilities and therefore their conceptual and operational futures depend upon fulfilling those duties to governments as stakeholders. But what of the idea of fulfilment of duties to more diffuse stakeholders such as employees, customers, suppliers or distributors? Should such fulfilment be enshrined in legislation in the various corporations acts? In the past fifteen years a great deal of academic work has been published reflecting the virtue in private (non-government) enterprise displaying social responsibility. Much of the corporate investment on the presentation of a good social profile was applauded yet a substantial proportion of it surfaced as a counter-measure to the bad profiles that private activity got away with during the twentieth century. There was no shortage of case studies of private activity that had caused social and environmental problems and disasters across the world – perhaps more so in countries where there were historically low levels of government regulation and monitoring. Documented cases demonstrate that for much of their history corporate entities have shown enormous fidelity to their shareholders with little regard for the societies in which the corporations themselves reside. Part of the problem for corporate entities is the separation of ownership and control. For governments, the separation of powers was invented as a mechanism to check and balance political power – the separation of the legislature from the judiciary and the executive in the Westminster model allowed judges to make decisions independent of lawmakers and executive government. In the corporate sense, the separation of ownership and control does not create a model of checks and balances. It creates a model in which management controllers focus singularly on the creation of wealth for owners. Other stakeholders are perceived to inhibit wealth creation.

A famous position taken against a diversity of stakeholder engagement was that of US economist Milton Friedman. Friedman argued very simply that the social responsibility of business was to increase profits (Friedman, 1970). He rejected out of hand that businesses should have a social conscience and be involved in 'socialist' ideas such as providing employment, eliminating discrimination and avoiding pollution. To Friedman these were catchphrases used by businessmen who were 'unwitting puppets of the intellectual forces that have been undermining the basis of a free society these past decades' (Friedman, 1970). From a perspective almost two generations on, given the serious work and investment that corporations have made in presenting themselves as being socially responsible, Friedman's argument conjures an opaque image. Freidman referred to the idea as 'the doctrine of the social responsibility of business' (Friedman, 1970) in which he postulated that a corporate executive with social responsibility would act in some way that was not in the best interests of his employer (the shareholders of the corporation). The executive might not increase the price of a product to prevent inflation; it might spend money on reducing pollution beyond that specified under legislation as a contribution to the social objective of environmental improvement; or it might employ out-of-work people rather than qualified people to contribute to a reduction in poverty. These measures are agencies of society rather than agencies of corporations. In other words, they act as agencies upon the corporation for the benefit of society rather than for the benefit of shareholders. Shareholders, through their executives as agents, look to agencies that will maximize their profits. These include reduced prices for resources, better access to raw materials, lower wages and cheaper energy inputs. Corporate entities seek globally for these inputs. They look for the best opportunities for increasing their market capital and thus their profits. In 2015 Monsanto, a publicly listed US-based multinational agrochemical corporation, set about attempting to acquire a competing Swiss corporation, Syngenta. Among the rhetorical flourishes written by Monsanto and published in the news media were two vital pieces of information that were most attractive to Monsanto shareholders: administrative and general cost cuts were estimated to be between $US500 million and $US1 billion. Additionally, re-incorporation in Switzerland would have saved Monsanto $US500 million in taxes it paid each year to the US Treasury. This was not unprecedented. James Hardie, an Australian industrial building products corporation best known in recent years for its association with disease-causing asbestos, relocated from Australia to the Netherlands where, it claimed, it could take advantage of significant tax advantages. The advantages that looked good in 2001 must have deteriorated because James Hardie later headquartered in Ireland. Paradoxically, it was listed on the Australian Stock Exchange and the New York Stock Exchange.

## DEFINING CORPORATIONS IN SOCIETIES

In an attempt to define corporations in terms of the societies in which they are located we need to critically consider ontological and epistemological differences in qualitative or quantitative engagement. Throughout this book we engage with qualitative practices – identifying matter and analysing it by way of a set of assumptions brought together as a model underpinned by narrative theory. Following Goertz and Mahoney (2012b) we are concerned with the issue of ontology as it relates to the concept of what a corporation is and how it fits into a society. We are interested in the 'intrinsic defining attributes' (Goertz and Mahoney, 2012b, p. 206) of this concept. When we attempt a definition of the concept of corporations in society we are confronted with an array of attributes and characteristics. When we analyse and interpret strategic corporate communication we also seek to define attributes and characteristics and thus present a qualitative framework for making recommendations and drawing conclusions. It would be equally worthy to undertake a quantitative analysis of strategic corporate communication whereby we analysed a given amount of corporate matter using a latent variable and identified causal relationship indicators. Important quantitative work has been achieved using indices and other data capture, notably the FTSE and S&P mentioned above. Others include the Hang Seng Index, Fortune 500 and Moody's. Qualitative analysis, however, provides us with the freedom to discuss concepts and attributes precisely because it does not require large amounts of numeri-cal data. Thus we are able to re-tool US strategist Vincent Hazleton's (Page and Hazleton, 1999) attributes of stakeholders so that they become identifiable for twenty-first-century use (for a complete evaluation, see Chapter 6).

Epistemologically, we are interested in the way a corporation identifies itself – its beliefs (usually represented as mission statements and statements of value) and its justification – and through these how it seeks to communicate strategically. A corporation is defined and imagined by its strategic communication. Additionally, it is identified by its core compe-tences or, in epistemological terms, what it knows and how it knows what to do with what it knows. We are also interested in the *value problem* and in the identification of knowledge that produces value for a corporation. Corporations describe their abilities as *core com-petences*. These core competences drive the activities of corporations. Core competences combined with innovation provide corporations with competitive and comparative advantages and fulfil the requirements of usable capacity. They are in effect the sum of the knowledge and beliefs a successful corporation holds that derive its value. A value placed on a corporation most often applies to the financial stability of the entity or of its market capitalization. Value ought to be derived from a corporation's inherent knowledge base which in turn forces the *epistemic commodity* – true belief. Corporations are sometimes attracted to the idea of belief without a concomitant commitment to knowledge. There is a tendency to act in the short term to satisfy market and shareholder requirements. We will see in the following chapters, however, that successful entities, while presenting a rhe-torical public face, do so as an overlay to long-term strategy. In this we will later examine the nature of value relative to profit-seeking and rent-seeking.

## THE DIFFUSE NATURE OF CORPORATIONS

Corporations are more diverse than humans. Different human races occupy a variety of global spaces but corporate entities exist across human activity. Global corporations produce goods and services across all sectors of a country's economy. They are responsible for primary, secondary and tertiary activity. Primary activity includes the extraction and production of raw materials, with their bases in agriculture, mining and fishing. Secondary activity transforms raw materials into manufactured goods such as motor vehicles, cloth-ing, footwear, food and computers. Tertiary activity services all primary and secondary phases of the economy and includes the provision of other activities such as education, banking and finance. Activity in all three sectors is not the sole province of corporations. Private and public businesses which are not incorporated flourish across all three sectors. Service providers such as restaurants and cafés, dentists, medical practitioners, plumb-ers and electricians most often exist outside the corporate framework. Corporations have what is known as an advantage in *economies of scale* when involved in primary and secondary activity. Motor vehicle manufacturers, for example, rely on parts suppliers for the production of cars and trucks. Motor vehicle corporations such as Toyota, Fiat and Tata do not manufacture each and every component that is bolted together to create their vehicles – they source parts and accessories globally. Equally, motor vehicle manufacturers do not always build their products in their country of origin. Tata Motors, for example, the first Indian corporation to be listed on the New York Stock Exchange, manufactures in India but also in Argentina, Thailand, South Africa and the United Kingdom. It is the world's seventeenth largest automobile manufacturer. Tata does not confine itself to manufacturing small cars for its very large Indian home market. It also owns Jaguar Land Rover, which manufactures luxury automotive brands Range Rover, Land Rover and Jaguar. In 2008 Tata produced the world's cheapest motor car, the Nano, which in 2015 sold for around Rs. 200,000, the equivalent of £2,000. Such a possibility is non-existent for small businesses that do not have economies of scale. If we look at other products and services that have been invented or conceptualized outside the corporate frame we see that they come to market but that they do so for different reasons to the large-scale production required to satisfy corporate yields, or returns on investments. It is possible and profitable to invent and manufacture successfully without the support of global corporate listed investment. For example, the British inventor of the Dyson vacuum cleaner, James Dyson, founded the private company Dyson in 1993. Dyson makes vacuum cleaners, hand dryers and fans and claimed in 2013 to have revenue (sales) of £6 billion, profit of £800 million and by 2015 to have employed more than 4500 people.

## BUSINESS IN SPACE

A relatively new way that corporations do business is in what is known as cyberspace. It is also referred to as e-commerce. Companies operate online rather than in the tangible world of factories and shops. Most corporations offer their products and services with an online component. In other words, one may purchase goods and services directly from a shopfront or indirectly, online, without the need to leave home. Such has been the retail face of goods and service providers for some time. We may choose to visit a bank but we may choose the alternative – to do all our banking online using passwords and electronic funds transfers. Corporations also operate at this level with each other when providing and supplying goods and services. One such operator is the Chinese corporation Alibaba. The Alibaba Group, which is listed on the New York Stock Exchange and the Hong Kong Exchange, operates what it refers to as a 'leading online and mobile marketplace in retail and wholesale trade as well as cloud computing and other services'. Alibaba claims to provide technology and services to enable its business partners to 'conduct commerce in our ecosystem' (Alibaba Group, 2016). It also, intriguingly, has a vision which it reveals 'aims to build the future infrastructure of commerce [where] our customers will meet, work and live at Alibaba and that we will be a company that lasts at least one hundred and two years'. The relevance of the one hundred and two years is also intriguing. Alibaba was founded in 1999 so its mission as a corporation is to span three centuries 'an achievement that few companies can claim' (Alibaba Group, 2016). In the same year that Alibaba began operations a French-based corporation, PPR, began investing in luxury goods. PPR was born in 1962 as Etablissements Pinault, a wood trade negotiator. It went through a number of transformations before 1999 but since then it has repositioned itself as a lifestyle business which in 2013 was renamed Kering. By 2014 Kering owned world-renowned brands Gucci, Saint Laurent Paris, Sergio Rossi, Boucheron, Bottega Veneta and Balenciaga. It owned controlling interests in Stella McCartney and Alexander McQueen, Puma and Cobra Golf and its market capitalization was more than €17 billion, with group revenue of €11.5 billion (Kering, 2015). But global corporations do not always live harmoniously. The invention of the World Trade Organization (WTO) reflected global disharmony among countries and the corporations that live within their borders. The WTO is a dispute resolution mechanism that is driven by its member states. Not all countries in the world are members and not all abide by the governing principles. Corporations, however, are not represented by the WTO, as a dispute between Alibaba and Kering revealed in 2015. Kering filed a claim in the US federal court, alleging that Alibaba had, without permission, manufactured and sold counterfeit products bearing Kering trademarks (China Daily, 2015). In its defence Alibaba argued it had spent more than 1 billion yuan (the equivalent of $US160 million) protecting intellectual property and fighting counterfeiting (China Daily, 2015). Alibaba claimed it was poised to become the world's largest retail 'platform' a position held by Walmart, a US-based retail corporation. Walmart, coincidentally founded in 1962, was, according to Fortune Global 500, the world's largest corporation based on revenues (Fortune 500, 2014) and the eighteenth largest global public corporation based on market capitalization (Forbes Global, 2000). When we consider that most of Walmart's revenue is generated from within the United States we have an intriguing perspective on the ability of corporations to create strategic communication campaigns. In terms of its engagement and positioning within American society – its place of origin – its founder Sam Walton argued that the company was required to make a contribution to society by operating efficiently and thus lowering the cost of living for its customers (Fishman, 2006).

Economies of scale allow public and private activity in all three sectors to extract, produce, construct and deliver goods and services across large and complex societies with enormous urban populations coupled with vast rural and regional distances where populations are thinner but require the same levels of involvement. In circumstances where corporations provide high levels of products and services to complex societies they do so within a framework of government policy. Government policy serves to regulate the activity of corporations but at the same time governments grasp the significance of private sector investment and activity in their societies, without which those societies would cease to function. At the beginning of the twenty-first century more people lived in large urban precincts such as cities and towns than at any other time in history (United Nations, 2014). The United Nations forecasts that the 54 per cent who now live in urban areas will increase to 66 per cent by the midpoint of the twenty-first century. The world's urban population is expected to reach 6 billion within the next thirty years (United Nations, 2014). Thus governments setting out with a duty to house, feed, clothe and transport such vast numbers of urban dwellers must acknowledge an investment beyond their own capabilities – one which may be provided by global corporations. As we will see below there are a variety of organizations that are directly opposed to the public–private partnerships that this scenario creates. We will also see how these organizations use strategic communication as a countervailing measure.

The scale of such urban development is unprecedented. The United Nations estimates that what it refers to as 'mega cities' – those with populations of 10 million or more – are increasing in number. In 1990 the world had ten mega cities in which 153 million people lived. Twenty-five years later – a generation – there exist twenty-eight mega cities housing 453 million or 12 per cent of the world's urban population. Tokyo is the largest with 38 million, followed by Delhi, 25 million; Shanghai, 23 million; Mexico City, 21 million; São Paulo, 21 million; Mumbai, 21 million; Osaka, 20 million; and Beijing, 20 million (United Nations, 2014). While we may find a causal link between population flows and the production of goods and services during the twentieth century, it is important to grasp the significance of the shift relative to the present requirements to sustain such large urban populations. The question is whether large-scale production, especially in agriculture and energy generation, provides a balance for corporations and governments between shareholder profit and sociopolitical obligations. An example might be a broad-acre farm which cultivates thousands of acres (or hectares). It is owned by a global agribusiness. Across the farm are planted a variety of crops, all of which might have a harvest deadline of early spring. While all the crops have a specific yield and while all may have potential markets, in reality only one or two of the crops will 'top the market' at that particular time and in that particular place. The remainder, possibly thousands of tons (or tonnes) of harvested matter, will be ploughed back in. Those crops were unprofitable in that current market.

## DEFINING CORPORATE STRATEGIC COMMUNICATION

As illustrated earlier, effective corporate strategic communication is communication which has direction and scope over the long term. It should be viewed as integral to aligning seamlessly with the overarching *grand strategy* of a corporation. It must be dynamic and functional. It creates a *competitive advantage* for a corporate entity through its configuration of tactics and resources in constantly changing internal and external environments and through the dissemination of information to stakeholders. Corporate strategic communication is communication that provides a corporate entity with a competitive advantage. It functions as an integral component of a corporate entity's grand strategy. It influences stakeholder, public and political opinion on issues, and policies within the global public sphere.

The fields of business management studies and game theory identify strategy as a device for the successful achievement of limited objectives within a broader plan. In this, from our standpoint, the word 'strategy' is misrepresented. Such a device is in fact a tactic whereas, as Australian theorist Graeme Donald Snooks argues, a strategy is a plan 'designed to achieve broad objectives' (Snooks, 1998, p. 7). The principles outlined in this book and anticipated by corporate entities follows that strategy is designed to achieve broad objectives and goals. We might reinforce this with the identification by Johnson and Scholes that a corporate strategy is concerned with the overall purpose and scope of an organization and how value will be added to the different parts (Johnson and Scholes, 2001, p. 10). Further, we argue that a plan is not a strategy unless it is in competitive alignment. In other words, a plan may have a long view but it does not become a strategy until such time as it competes with alternative plans for the same ground – the same finite resources, among them land, labour and capital. Thus a corporate communication strategy is concerned with communicating the overall purpose and scope of the value of the different parts of the corporation. Within a corporate strategy lie business strategies which focus on how to compete in different markets. At another level lie operational strategies where the component parts of an organization deliver corporate and business strategies by effectively employing resources, people and processes.

## STRATEGY OFFERS LONG-TERM DIRECTION AND SCOPE

For corporations operating in global and local markets there is inherent value in the conceptualization and operationalization of effective, enterprise-wide, corporate strategic communication. Strategic communication is different to everyday communication.

Strategic communication advances specific interests. It creates favourable conditions. With the right tools at their disposal communicators transform corporate communication from asymmetrical information flows into symmetrical relationships with broad stakeholder engagements. Successful corporate strategic communication is symmetrical between a corporation and the stakeholders. Information flows and the application of feedback are vital to success. It is important to clarify here that corporations, through their management structures, as we have discovered, place shareholders above all other stakeholders. It does not follow, however, that corporations and their managers avoid or are intrinsically antagonistic towards other stakeholders. As we shall see, the array of stakeholders impacting upon goals and aims requires corporations to invoke more diffuse and more complex communication strategies than ever before.

When Toyota Motor Corporation, a publicly listed Japanese automotive company, conceptualized a luxury car, it sent a management team to live in America for two years to determine what Americans wanted in such a vehicle. The result was the Lexus (Luxury EXport United States). Corporations do well when they understand their stakeholders and when they allow stakeholders to understand them.

Global industry transformation is being brought about by the tensions between deregulation, structural change, excess capacity, mergers and acquisitions, environmental concerns, protectionism, changing customer expectations and technological discontinuities. Successful strategic communication is the key to balancing these tensions.

Towards the end of the twentieth century American businessman Jack Welch turned America's General Electric into the world's most powerful corporation. But he rarely talked about the past. Welch preferred to talk about and focus on the present and the future – to look to the long-term direction and scope of General Electric (Slater, 1999, p. 10). Yet the past plays a vital role in the future of every corporation. Paradoxically, Welch argued that he could not change the past so there was little point dwelling upon it nor reliving old experiences. But it is the experiences of the corporation that make it what it is. And it is the ability to learn from those experiences and events that go towards allowing a corporation to live a long and prosperous life.

How long do corporations live? How many have made it to the end of the 300-year-long boom that began with the collapse of the South Sea bubble in 1720? In 2012 the BBC asked the question 'can a company live forever'? Kim Gittleson of BBC News, New York put the question. It was prompted by the untimely deaths of global corporates Saab, a Swedish automotive corporation, and Lehman Brothers, an American financial company. Gittleson quoted research from Yale's Richard Foster that indicated the average lifespan of a US corporation listed on Standard & Poor's 500 Index had been reduced from sixty-seven years in the early part of the twentieth century to fifteen years at the beginning of the twenty-first. There is a correlation between corporate longevity and human longevity. Japan, for example, boasts companies which have been around for more than one hundred years. The Japanese word *shinise* means 'companies that live for a long time'. But companies are not always corporations. Small, family-run companies frequently live through generations and are underpinned by social rather than profit motives. The world's oldest extant limited liability corporation is Stora Enso, a Finnish paper manufacturer. It began life as a copper miner in 1288.

Corporations do not share publicly the secrets of their communication strategies just as they do not share the core competences that provide them with a competitive advantage. Yet they have enormous expectations that their stakeholder 'publics' will take at face value the rhetorical tokens they employ and thus continue to invest widely in their goods and services.

If corporations are to recognize, communicate and build stakeholder relationships beyond ritual investor stakeholder boundaries they must grasp the significance of the way in which communication strategies are engineered, constructed and delivered. If a corporation remains reliant on singular ritual investor stakeholder performance it will fail. Societies which allow corporate entities to practice within their boundaries do so on the assumption the corporate entities will act for the benefit of society. Governments, as traditional legislators of corporate activity, sometimes fail to act substantially on behalf of the societies they purport to protect. Societies themselves, at the outset of the twenty-first century, have thus intervened in monitoring and negotiating corporate activity within their boundaries. While strategy can and does exist at all levels of personal and professional life – personal career strategy, business unit strategy, corporate strategy – it is important that a communication strategy is undivided, that is, that it takes a position at or near the top of the hierarchy and that it is distilled throughout each level of a corporate entity. If a corporate communication strategy is *top-down* it has the potential to enervate each part of a business. It is not enough for a corporate chief executive or managing director to be a good communicator; successful grand strategy is built on effective and sustainable enterprise-wide strategic communication.

Corporations must provide a framework for the construction of strategic communication by way of understanding how theories, models and stakeholders fit together in a socioeconomic context. In some industrial and service sectors strategic corporate communication is not well identified and corporate goals and aims are perceived to be incompatible with western socioeconomic norms. There is inherent value for local and global corporations in the conceptualization and operationalization of effective, enterprise-wide, strategic corporate communication. Value is realized when there is a transformation of asymmetrical information flows into symmetrical relationships with broad stakeholder engagement. Successful corporate strategic communication is symmetrical between the corporation and stakeholders.

## WHO OWNS PUBLICLY LISTED CORPORATIONS?

As we have seen above, investors, particularly large investors, are of greatest importance to corporations. These large investors include other corporations, pension funds and governments. Very little information is made public about large corporate investors. The annual report of a publicly listed company may provide the names of its top twenty shareholders. Many shareholders are nominee holding companies. This means they hold shares in corporations on behalf of other corporations. Individuals also hold shares as nominees for a variety of reasons. British company Rio Tinto plc, one of the world's largest resource and energy corporations, offers individuals a nominee service. The service allows individuals to anonymously hold, purchase and sell shares in Rio Tinto. Shares are held electronically in an 'uncertificated' form – without a certificate of authenticity. The Rio Tinto nominee service is operated by Computershare Investor Services, itself a multinational corporation. Individuals who participate in the scheme are the beneficial owners of the shares but the shares are held by the nominee company. We will see in Chapter 3 that there is some difficulty associated with any analysis of corporate annual reports and the object of obtaining information about nominee shareholders.

BP, or British Petroleum, one of the world's largest oil and gas corporations, offers advice to ordinary shareholders who use a nominee company. It defines a nominee shareholder as a person or company who holds shares in a company on behalf of someone else. The nominee's name appears on the share registry. In place of a share certificate a statement is issued from a nominee holder – a bank or broker showing the number of BP shares in the account. BP communicates with investors directly by way of an electronic website. It makes an investor plea that states: 'The BP Proposition is to deliver growth in sustainable free cash flow in support of growing distributions to shareholders. We are focused on value over volume' (BP, 2014, p. 2). In its 2014 annual report BP began by stating: 'We aim to create long-term value for shareholders by helping to meet growing demand for energy in a safe and responsible way. We strive to be a world-class operator, a responsible corporate citizen and a good employer' (BP, 2014, p. 2). As BP indicated in the report, it was incumbent upon the company to reveal its major shareholders, governed as it was by the *Companies Act 2006*, the UK *Financial Conduct Authority's Disclosure and Transparency Rules* (DTR) and the US *Securities Exchange Act 1934*. Thus in 2014 a little over 29 per cent of its shares were held by Guaranty Nominees Limited, a nominee of JP Morgan Chase Bank NA and 6.25 per cent by BlackRock Inc. Preference shares were held by the National Farmers Union Mutual Insurance Society (13.07 per cent), M&G Investment Management (7.3 per cent) and Duncan Lawrie Ltd (5.04 per cent) (BP, 2014).

Individuals and entities invest financially in publicly listed corporations. They also invest in privately owned corporations. We are interested in the analysis of both forms of corporation but as we shall see it is sometimes difficult to obtain information about private entities. Frequently private or closed corporations are owned by non-government organizations (NGOs). Their value is not traded on a stock exchange but their global worth is evident. Privately held corporations include Bosch, KPMG, PwC, Aldi, Rolex, Bechtel, S C Johnson and Mars. It is difficult to estimate the revenue, employment and sales of these corporations. It is important for us to distinguish between private companies in the west, which are those companies that do not trade on a listed stock exchange, and private companies that may exist or have existed in non-western countries and which were not state-owned. Many of the corporations emerging and establishing in China are underpinned by state investments. Unlike Russia, which maintains a *command economy* and thus supports state-owned corporations such as Gazprom,[1] China runs what is called a *state capitalism economy* in which corporations are financed by government but are allowed to operate independently.

When we attempt to analyse the communication structures of private corporations we are confronted by a major hurdle: private ownership is not held to the same reporting requirements as those publicly listed. There are fewer obligations to communicate activity. While this does not imply secrecy or illegal activity, the nature of private ownership confers a degree of opacity that is difficult to penetrate. Public corporations are required by law to divulge and reveal financial and other data. No such requirement is imposed upon private entities. This raises an interesting aside – why then, if such scrutiny is imposed upon them, do the world's major corporations continue to be widely publicly traded? Scottish economist Adam Smith (1776) argued that private enterprise would remain more important than public corporate activity because individuals were better at managing their own

---

[1] Gazprom is the largest joint stock company in Russia. It claims to have more than 500,000 shareholders with 50 per cent of the company owned by the government.

finances than managing those of others. Part of the answer to the continued success of publicly listed entities emerged in the 1980s when governments, particularly in the west, or 'common law' countries, began 'de-nationalizing' – selling state-owned assets to corporations underpinned by the argument that corporations would be more interested in keeping the assets profitable. It was also a way for governments to create income.

## CORPORATIONS IN SOCIETY: AN AUSTRALIAN CASE STUDY

Corporations are the lifeblood of democracies. Countries with popularly elected governments have the largest and most profitable corporations within their borders. We generally know very little about corporations, even large publicly listed ones. What we do know is that they create an illusion of needs and desires. Some of these needs have become embedded. We find it hard to do without a dishwasher, a washing machine, a refrigerator. Everything that is made by corporations – all products, all services – is designed to be sold for profit. There is nothing wrong with making a profit. In fact it's a good thing. But in the quest for larger and larger profits corporations create illusions of needs and wants that become more surreal. We can't do without fridges and toasters but even these products were once thought of as superfluous to basic needs. Today we find it difficult to live without a tablet computer or a smartphone.

Corporations use a variety of tools to get us to take notice of their offerings. Before the invention of television, radio was the favoured medium for advertising and before that newspapers and magazines. Advertising as we know it is an invention that parallels the history of corporations. When we think about corporate advertising we generally focus on big television campaigns – the advertising that accompanies reality programmes such as *Masterchef*. Television programmes such as *Masterchef* and *The Voice* are built around the advertising of products and services created by corporations. We generally don't make a strong connection between corporations and specific products and services until we come up against them in some way – needing a refund, making a claim against them – then we discover their size and power.

Corporations create an illusion of being attached to us by sending us advertising messages in ways that resonate with us, ways that have us believe we are buying products and services with a direct connection to us. If there is no direct connection, corporations go about building one so that we feel comfortable with their products and services. In Australia in the twentieth century motor vehicle corporations Holden and Ford (both owned by US companies General Motors and Ford) created campaigns that pitted buyers against each other. You were either a 'Ford man' or a 'Holden man'. It was a clever strategy because both corporations were able to line up potential buyers for generations. They knew from decade to decade how many cars they could sell to one specific person. Today, motor vehicle retailers have trouble retaining their long-term buyers. A Holden girl might never buy a Ford, but her head might be turned by a Toyota Yaris.

It may be a little easier for retail corporations and service providers. Once you have a bank account, for example, you tend to stay with that bank. You return regularly to your music and DVD supplier because of a perceived level of convenience and price. Large retail chains – in-store and online – provide an array of goods so one has a 'shopping experience'. And large goods retailers such as car sellers are beginning to use the same strategic communication. When you have your car serviced you will get a text message and an email from the service department thanking you for servicing your vehicle and asking if you enjoyed the 'experience'. A vehicle service, like shopping for a pair of shoes, is now an experience. Corporations set the tone for your shopping experiences. They own the shopping malls and the shops and they fill them with products and services they want you to buy. They create a strategy that includes direct and indirect advertising. Direct advertising includes all the brochures and leaflets you get in your mailbox – (your house mailbox, not your computer mailbox, though that, too, is often filled with direct advertising matter). Large publicly listed corporations make profits from selling goods and services. Some of them you need to live – food, clothing, heat and shelter – but a lot of products and services we might call discretionary goods. Discretionary goods are those you tend to buy without giving them too much rational thought. In other words, you buy them because you don't think, not because you think too much.

Consider competing brochures that arrive in your mailbox. There are two of them. One is 84 pages and the other is 134 pages. The brochures advertise toys. Only toys. And neither is from Toys R Us. The brochures are advertising products that corporate entities want you to buy. You hold to a belief that Kmart and Big W are shops that sell cheap affordable products. They have no connection to large publicly listed corporations. In fact Kmart is a part of one of the largest corporations in Australia – Wesfarmers. Wesfarmers also owns Target, Bunnings and Coles. Wesfarmers is the largest private employer in Australia with more than 200,000 employees. It also owns Bi-Lo, Liquorland, Vintage Cellars, 1st Choice Liquor, Officeworks, Pharmacy Direct, Lumley Insurance and Harris Technology.[2] When Wesfarmers pops an 84-page catalogue of toys in your mailbox, it is deadly serious about getting you to use some of your discretionary funds to buy a Leap Frog talking lap pup named Violet for $25; a Spiderman Mega Blaster web shooter with glove for $25; or a Monster High C A cupid doll, also for $25. If you don't see anything among the 84 pages that takes your fancy, you can spend time browsing the 134-page Giant Toy Spectacular catalogue popped into your box by Big W. Big W is one of the largest discount department stores in Australia. It has 168 locations and is owned by Woolworths which is the largest retailer in Australia. Woolworths competes with Wesfarmers for your discretionary dollar in all the same places because it owns Safeway, Food For Less, BWS, Dan Murphy's, Dick Smith, Tandy and Masters Home Improvement stores.[3] Woolworths also owns 75 per cent of ALH Group, a hotel and poker machine company which makes Woolworths the largest owner of gambling machines in Australia. Big W wants you to buy a Disney Princess Rapunzel Baby for $24, a Dr Dreadful Zombie Lab for $24 or a Mr Quetzalcoatlus Extreme Interaction Figure for $24. Twenty-four dollars is not the most you can spend. At Big W you can part with $998 if you take home an Action Raised Cubby, and from Kmart you can leave behind $229 when you take home an Xbox or PlayStation3. The brochures from both corporations are seriously glossy and seriously well designed to make all the toys look their best. A Beach Barbie for $5 at Big W or a Spiderman face mask for $9 are the lowest priced items but there are not many of them. Most of the toys start at $20. Corporations like to make a connection with us that is product- and services-based. If goods and services can be purchased easily so that we have a 'shopping experience' we will continue to buy

---

[2] In 2016 Wesfarmers invested A$705 million (£340 million) acquiring Homebase, a British hardware and garden retailer. Its strategy was to reposition Homebase as Bunnings.

[3] In 2016 Woolworths announced it would cease its joint venture hardware operation with US-based Lowes.

them. The strategy behind corporations that sell us goods and services is to get us to spend our time in the same places so that we do not spend our money in other places. Hence we have the invention of the shopping mall. We can spend days in shopping malls and we never need to know what the weather is like outside because the temperature in the mall remains constant. Large shopping malls in the United States, the United Kingdom, Asia, Europe and Australia are owned by corporations. Fifty per cent of the population of the United Kingdom visit a shopping mall every fortnight (Mall Secrets, 2014). Intu Properties is the largest mall owner in the United Kingdom, followed by Hammerson. Westfield is the largest shopping centre owner in Australia. In the United States malls are owned by Simon Property Group (the world's largest mall owner), followed by General Growth Properties (*Estate Investor* 2010). In France, Klépierre SA is a dominant player while in much of Europe, Multi, a subsidiary of US-based Blackstone, is a major owner.

Corporations build reputations on being profitable and making goods and services. The products and services they make are the public faces of the corporation. Woolworths stakes its reputation on its catchphrase 'The Fresh Food People'. Coles began its life in the early twentieth century with a cost-conscious slogan 'Nothing Over 2/6' which moved on to 'Save Every Day' which in turn became 'Down Down, Prices Are Down' and more recently 'There's No Freshness Like Coles' which is in direct competition with Woolworths. (Coles claims 35 per cent of the grocery and liquor market to Woolworth's 40 per cent.) In the corporate world the product and service is the face of the corporation. It is rare for a corporation to identify with its employees and management. Some corporate chief executives become known, most often when they do something wrong. Unlike politicians who stake their claim on public recognition, corporate chief executives can walk down the street on Saturday morning without attracting attention. Even if they are recognized it is hard to put a name to the face. Some seek celebrity status to assist their businesses. As country rock outfit McAlister+Kemp sing, 'There's a lot of people we remember, but not what we remember them for'.

## THINKING ABOUT THE HISTORY OF STRATEGIC CORPORATE COMMUNICATION

Corporate communication has always been strategic. It is axiomatic. Corporations exist for the benefit, through increasing share prices, of shareholders. We can look back over three hundred years of corporate activity and imagine from this point in the early twenty-first century through the twentieth and nineteenth centuries to a starting point to activity that began with the financing of global trade out of England, France and the Netherlands. The instruments of globalization that emerged three hundred years ago provided the institutional framework for the establishment of contemporary strategic communication. The strategies and tactics of corporate entities as *agents* may differ technologically from those employed in the eighteenth century but socially and politically they remain the same. They have developed directly from the strategies and tactics of corporate entities such as the Dutch East India Company, the South Sea Company and the Mississippi Company. The same strategies and tactics were used to promote the subprime mortgage market in the United States in the early twenty-first century. The structures set in place in the eighteenth century along with those underpinning early twenty-first century activity assisted in the construction of an image of the corporation in society. We will examine further in the following chapter the historical circumstances that brought us to the present state of corporate activity.

## CONCLUSION

This introductory chapter has examined corporations as they exist in society. It has provided a definition of what it is to be a corporation and to function in a societal framework and it has provided a definition of strategic corporate communication. It presented examples of corporate communication and set out the differences between publicly listed corporations and the more difficult-to-evaluate private corporations.

Corporations are artificial creations in law. They have many stakeholders. Corporate value is measured by market capitalization, or sometimes sales revenue or income. Corporations are defined by where they fit in societies and how they see themselves located in those societies. Corporate value is derived from a knowledge base or, more commonly, core competences.

Strategic corporate communication has long-term direction and scope. It is part of a corporate grand strategy and it is dynamic and functional. It must use tactics and resources to achieve a competitive advantage. Corporate strategic communication influences stakeholders and public opinion.

Strategic communication will be effective when theories, models and stakeholder engagement fits seamlessly in society.

 **DISCUSSION QUESTIONS**

1  What is a publicly listed corporation?
2  Who owns publicly listed corporations?
3  Why are corporations important to societal goals and objectives?
4  Are corporations compatible with democracy?
5  How important is strategic communication to the goals and objectives of corporations?

# 1

# A BRIEF HISTORY OF CORPORATE COMMUNICATION

This chapter presents an overview of corporate communication history in the west from the earliest recorded communication strategy that in 1710 transformed the Sword Blade Company into the global financial South Sea Corporation. It pinpoints a number of historically important corporate communications culminating in the communication strategies of global entities such as Bank of America at the time of the Global Financial Crisis (GFC). From the patterns that formed during the past three hundred years it offers a glimpse beyond the GFC to the future of corporate strategic communication.

There are two strands to corporate history. One concerns the history of individual companies and how they frame an image of their interests and activities. Another word for this is hagiography, though many companies employ professional writers and look to accuracy in the representation of what they may have achieved over time. Others find their voice through a narrative that attempts to define them. In Chapter 6 we will look more closely at the ideas behind narrating corporate history and at narrative theory as it reflects asymmetrical communication. In this it is impossible for a corporate entity to write its corporate history from any other than its own dominant position. Despite all the bad things that befall corporations they look to underpin their histories with positives. This is a natural extension of human behaviour. We attend funerals for the dead and speak positively about their lives. Corporate websites are like funeral eulogies – they elevate the good and bury the evil. The second strand of corporate history reflects on the chronology of the totality of the entities. It seeks to map the highs and lows, the successes and failures of corporations over time. We are interested in where corporations began in the western world, how some of them survived or died and how they contributed to the development and growth of societies. If we link them to society we can explain to some extent the nature of human involvement with corporate entities. This raises the question of investment. Why do people invest in corporations when they know so little about their actual activities? Corporate history is inevitably tied in with economic history, financial history, government history and sociopolitical history. Economic and financial history might also include such things as the history of money and investment. While we are interested peripherally in the finances of a corporate entity, this book is focused upon corporate communication and its strategic deployment. We will thus limit our observations to some of the events and activities to which corporate entities have been aligned.

Corporations, like societies for the past three hundred years, have experienced wild fluctuations in their health and well-being both collectively and individually. At some points in time individual corporations have been responsible for enormous growth in social structures while at others they have contributed substantially to the collapse or near collapse of nations and countries. There have also been moments when collective corporate action has contributed to the safety and security of the world.

Points of departure for the beginning of corporate history are many and varied depending upon standpoint. One nation may view its corporate history differently to another, or one may see its corporate activities as being beneficial and benign while others hold a binary view. Today more than at any other time in history, corporate activity is scrutinized and analysed to the point of tedium. It is one thing to assume corporations go about doing bad and therefore must remain under constant surveillance. It is another entirely to take an ideological position and to attack corporate activity in a wholesale fashion because it is out of ideological alignment. There are a number of corporate global activities that once were fashionable but are now labelled evil; whaling, mining and forestry spring easily to mind.

We have chosen as our starting point the corporate activities of an English company known as the Sword Blade. Again, there were a variety from which to choose and there were also various times at which we could have assembled. We chose Sword Blade for its connection to an event that shaped corporate and social history and continued to do so for the following three hundred years.

## WHY THREE HUNDRED YEARS IS IMPORTANT AS A FRAMEWORK FOR CORPORATE HISTORY

We live in a dynamic world in which we experience changes in markets and institutions. Changes might be incremental or they may be abrupt. What we do know is that corporations and the societies in which they are located are dynamic and therefore situational. Like Graeme Snooks following John Maynard Keynes, we agree the 'flux of reality is too complex to be represented by a set of simultaneous equations' (Snooks, 1998, p. 3). In his prescient work on technology and industry, David Landes (1969) remarks on the rapid technological change that brought about the industrial revolution in Europe and England, arguing that the scope and effectiveness of private enterprise was one of two contributing factors to its diffusion and subsequent success. The second was the high value placed on 'the rational manipulation of the human and material environment' (Landes, 1969, p. 15). Landes was willing to go further, arguing the role of private enterprise and trade subsumed the earlier economic control maintained by a system of medieval estates, thus creating whole new societies with new cultural and economic priorities. These new societies – underpinned by private capital – knew no bounds. There was no precedent and no counterpart – no mirror in which to reflect the recast magic, marvel and miracles of the new industrial societies of Europe and England. Given such an enthusiastic environment it is no wonder kings and queens also fell in love with private capital. War and trade became enmeshed. Private property became institutionalized. The old system of lord and serf had worked well for hundreds of years but with the advent of private ownership of the means of production there was a new requirement for consistency – a smoothing out of the inconsistencies of personal relationships through the invention of a system of new laws and rules that favoured private capital. Equally, there was the need to balance the enthusiasms of invention with the rationalities of reason that had taken hold in the west. It may have been one thing to have acquired pots of money from which almost anything could be conceptualized and operationalized but it was entirely another to go off willy-nilly and end up broke. The importance of a rational approach to investment and capital in the form of private enterprise was self-fulfilling; the prospect of a loss of capital focused the minds of private sector operators to the point where various European states, by the end of the seventeenth century, could see that the freer their economies were, the greater the innovation and comparative advantages in trade.

As it is today and has always been, corporate or private activity was bound inexorably to political power. So it was not unreasonable that the greatest minds of the time would turn their attention to the linkages between corporate activity and the state. One such mind belonged to John Locke. While Locke's life and work were products of the seventeenth century, his influence became obvious in the eighteenth – his argument for limitations on government and an expansion of free enterprise echo still in the mahogany halls of corporate America and conservative political parties across the west. His ideas that rulers had responsibilities to the communities they ruled, that government should be subordinate to law and that moral restraints should be placed on power were not new. They followed John Hooker who in turn had drawn from medievalists such as Thomas Aquinas.

The substance of Locke's argument, like Thomas Hobbes's before him, lay in the role society ought to play in the protection of property and the protection of additional private rights that may not have existed in nature. In this Locke was doing no more than observing the changes being wrought around him in England and in Europe in the late seventeenth century and having a bet on the outcome. What he assisted in creating, however, was an enduring ideology of the rights of private ownership of property and, given the earlier agrarian economy of Europe and England, the means of production which were expanding rapidly from cottage industries into corporate global trade.

Some of what Locke envisioned – civil power for public good defined by laws with penalties, regulating and preserving property, and community empowerment – we shall investigate in detail in Chapter 8 when we engage with corporate social responsibility, particularly the contemporary idea of *social licence to operate*. We might also consider, given the substantive content of this book is concerned with communication, the notion that earlier medieval society developed institutions based on regular prospects of physical danger and insecure communication. Such were the times that conquest and quick reward were the order of the day. Societies struggled for self-sufficiency but if that failed they fell to conquest to replenish stocks of food and goods. They looked to subordinate individuals and to control settlements with local policing. Framed as a bigger picture, rulers raised standing armies, roamed widely across the European and Asiatic land masses, conquered or were conquered. Cartographic discovery coupled with the desire for greater reward impelled the more powerful nations into previously undiscovered (from the perspective of the west) lands, some resplendent with treasure, others less so. A popular contemporary television series, *Vikings*, presents the image of conquest, commerce, conquest.

## SWORD BLADE AND THE SOUTH SEA BUBBLE

The prospect of rich rewards has always been an inducement for individuals to part with their money. Today we are regularly sucked in just as our forebears were three hundred years ago. Consider the case of the South Sea Company – a joint stock venture established in England. For the privilege of obtaining an operational charter in the early eighteenth century a corporation made a loan to the government. The Sword Blade Company, precursor to the South Sea Company, paid £50,000, a staggering sum at the time. The Sword Blade partnership comprised George Caswell, Elias Turner and Jacob Sawbridge.

In 1710 George Caswell made direct overtures to the chancellor, Robert Harley, in what can be considered to be one of the first acts of corporate relations in modernity in the English-speaking world. Caswell was attempting (successfully it turned out) to persuade a government of the value of an action in its relationship to a proposed public company. Sword Blade had begun life in 1691 as Hollow Sword Blade Company, manufacturing hollow-ground rapiers. Its founder, Stephen Evance, had seen an opportunity arise when in 1691 a war between England and France disrupted the trade in swords from France. Evance obtained a charter and got a few French artisans to relocate to England upon which he began manufacture.

A joint stock company was effectively what we now know as a corporate entity. Today we use the words *incorporated* and *limited liability* when we speak of company stock ownership but the basis was the same. The Sword Blade Company was legally allowed to issue shares and to own land. But by 1702 the company's owner had extended himself beyond his original remit – he had insinuated himself into the court to become an excise commissioner, and then later, jeweller to the king. The death of the king in 1702 changed the game and seeing no avenue available, Evance killed himself, leaving the company in the hands of one of his more able swordsmiths.

It is an interesting aside that the swordsmith, Herman Mohll, continued manufacture, then in 1832 the company changed its name to Mole. In 1922 it was bought by Wilkinson Sword. It is now owned by Energizer Holdings and its main product is razor blades. But it had a number of different owners and histories after the 1970s. Even more interesting is the fact that Wilkinson Sword continued to make swords, manufacturing the ceremonial blade for the golden jubilee of Queen Elizabeth in 2012. It may seem a little complicated but it appeared that Mohll, continuing to manufacture swords under his own name, freed up the Sword Blade charter for potential purchase. Subsequently the Sword Blade Company was indeed sold. It was relocated as what we would today call a shelf company to a location in London owned by a lawyer named John Blunt. Under Blunt it began buying land in Ireland, large tracts of land that had formed part of the English settlement and were now forfeit. In a further sleight of hand that was to benefit the owners of Sword Blade, Blunt lobbied the government to effect a change to legislation that had granted Irish land to army personnel after England's violent takeover of Ireland. Blunt's lobbying was successful: the government reversed the grant legislation in favour of the land being sold. Sword Blade snapped up the land but to pay for it, Blunt and his cronies issued shares in Sword Blade. The issue, however, was not directly to the public – Sword Blade sold the shares to the army in exchange for its own debt from buying the land back from the grantees. The deal gave Sword Blade directors a taste for ever increasing profits: short-term profits with their basis in exchange rather than manufacture. Sword Blade was starting to look very much like a bank – a situation that was not appreciated by the existing Bank of England which itself had a charter to issue shares and raise funds. Sword Blade extended its reach by offering mortgages to others interested in buying Irish land. It even issued its own notes and took cash deposits. The upshot was that the Bank of England used some interesting tactics in its strategy to keep its monopoly, which it succeeded in doing.

The bank was not prepared for the attacks that were to be made on it to open up competition. It had for some time been the government bank and it was then a privately owned company. It had negotiated to become the monopoly lender to the government and it did not wish to be subjected to competing interests. In 1710 Robert Harley was made chancellor. The government was fighting two wars and its debts were mounting. The Bank of England was not providing the service Harley desired. At once he set about discrediting the bank while boosting the alternative: a company named Sword Blade. The Bank of England had used a device called a lottery to raise funds for the government but by 1710 its successes were less than spectacular. Meanwhile, Harley had needed to find £300,000 to pay the army fighting in Europe. It was provided by, among others, George Caswell of Sword Blade as a loan.[1] Harley by his actions was not a man who had what we might now call a moral compass. His next move was to award a new lottery to Sword Blade which was acting as a de facto bank. Unlike the Bank of England's lottery, Sword Blade's initial lottery was a spectacular success and was followed by a similar success. The government was now in debt for around £9 million. There was no International Monetary Fund (IMF) to bail it out and default would have made it the target of further attacks from without and within. We will see below that in the three hundred years since, similar situations have been faced by governments with external and internal debt problems. In 2015 Greece owed the IMF €1.5 billion. Difficult situations confronted other countries in the early 1700s. France held enormous public debt driven by the folly of war, while the Netherlands had experienced the first financial bubble and subsequent financial collapse some years earlier (Ferguson, 2008). But Harley was nothing if not inventive. In 1711, after chairing a committee whose objective was to break the Bank of England monopoly, he arranged for his brother Edward along with John Blunt to invent a debt consolidation scheme. Part of the package was the granting of a monopoly on trade with South America – hence the South Sea label. In 1711 a charter was granted to the South Sea Company. As historian John Carswell (1993) noted it was pretty obvious that the creators of the corporate entity knew there was no money to invest in trading and that there was probably no real trade to be had. Shares in the entity known as South Sea Company were pumped up and publicized, traded and held in what might now be referred to as a public–private partnership between a government and a corporation.

For all of its drama and its capacity to hoodwink some of the kingdom's finest minds, including Isaac Newton and Jonathan Swift, the bursting of the South Sea bubble was less of an event than its contemporary, the bursting of the Mississippi Company bubble in France, or the earlier spectacular crash of the Dutch flower market. The South Sea Company crash inadvertently created legislation so that England might be proofed against any similar future crash. Many other joint stock companies had been established in the wake of the South Sea success, some with bizarre schemes that precipitated the bursting of the bubble.

When the bubble burst a great number of investors lost their money and many of the joint stock companies went broke but the South Sea Company managed to stay afloat despite its shares rising from £100 to £1,000 then dropping back to near par value. It had been involved in the slave trade and in whaling but its main interest remained in managing government debt. It was dissolved in 1853. The South Sea Company and its directors had provided England and international investors with a world of new experiences and it had cemented a new and innovative linkage between corporations and governments that remains steadfast.

---

[1] Another lender was Hoare's Bank, a private bank at the time and now the oldest bank in the United Kingdom. It was founded in 1672 by Richard Hoare and it remains in family ownership and was managed until recently by the eleventh generation of Richard Hoare's direct descendants.

| 1866 | Overend, Gurney & Co |
|------|----------------------|
| 1920 | Florida land bubble |
| 1929 | NY stock market bubble |
| 1970 | Poseidon bubble |
| 1991 | Nordbanken |
| 2000 | Dot com bubble |
| 2001 | Enron |
| 2002 | Worldcom |
| 2007 | US real estate bubble |
| 2008 | Lehman Brothers |
| 2008 | Northern Rock |
| 2014 | Banco Espirito Santo |

**Table 1.1**   Some of the more interesting corporate bubbles

## YOU'D THINK WE WOULD HAVE LEARNED

Despite the vastness of the financial devastation caused by the South Sea bubble and the Mississippi Company bubble it appears human nature was such that it could not resist the temptation to invest in stupid schemes or at the very least, over-invest. In the early nineteenth century Spain over-reached to the point where its investments and control of South American economies were lost. While there have been debt bubbles that have disrupted countries, including the models of global industry, Japan and South Korea, we are more interested in the role played by corporations or listed companies and how, given regulations that exist to stop such things happening, they might cause financial bubbles.

## NOT ALL DOOM AND GLOOM HOWEVER

A history of corporate activity is not one-sided. It ought not to dwell too long on the negative aspects of corporations that have been evil or have done evil. There are far more corporations which have done good and far more that have thrived and prospered. What usually happens in a society, however, is that corporations that do good tend to act within the legislation prescribed by the government of the country in which they are located. Proscriptive legislation on the other hand tends to be enacted when a corporation has done evil. It is usually designed to stop or at least reduce future activities that are not good for society. Many corporations have individual histories that have involved some pretty shady activities at one time or other. Others have wreaked havoc on the physical environment. But there are far greater numbers throughout the west that have long untarnished histories. Let's look at a few of those and then conclude with some who started out in dodgy business only to become dignified and acceptable at later dates.

Since their invention corporations collectively as markets have been more financially powerful than governments and central banks. Within sharemarkets lie corporations that make things and corporations that finance things. They list on stock exchanges and investors invest without concern for the activities of the corporations they invest in. They look for more important things such as yield and capital growth. For the western world the corporations that make things are far less favoured today than they were last century. Primary industries such as mining and oil extraction are *locative* industries – they are where they are. Corporate owners must go to them. Secondary industries such as manufacturing have become global. Along with their tertiary industry counterparts such as services they are the drivers of globalization. Manufacturing goods such as clothing and textiles that might once have been located in the country where the corporation lived are now made in China. This means for example a British corporation which has its basis in textile manufacture might have its headquarters in England but its manufacturing is done in factories in China or other parts of Asia. Clothing manufacturers frequently source their raw material globally – wool from New Zealand or cotton from Egypt – have it processed in another country then ship the processed matter to China for manufacture. The item of clothing is then shipped back to England to a distribution centre before being shipped to retail outlets around the world. The unit costs of manufacture in China are low enough for the corporation to do all that shipping and still make a profit.

Tertiary sector activities – things that don't require being dug up or made – are the darlings of the stock market. Corporations that invent technologies and use cyberspace to distribute their services do not have the burden of infrastructure that is imposed upon miners and manufacturers. These corporations include banks, fund managers, insurers, lawyers, tourism, entertainment, hospitality and advertising agencies.

The largest advertising agency in the world, WPP, is a company listed on the London Stock Exchange (LSE) with revenue in 2014 of £11.5 billion. WWP began life in 1971 as Wire & Plastic Products to manufacture wire shopping baskets, hence the initialism WPP. In 1985 it moved into advertising and today it owns powerful advertising and public relations subsidiaries Grey, Ogilvy & Mather, Young & Rubicam, JWT, Hill & Knowlton, Burson-Marsteller, Group M, Cohn & Wolfe and Brand Union.

The five largest agencies are all listed corporations and they are located in London, New York, Paris and Tokyo. Omnicon is listed on the New York Stock Exchange (NYSE) with revenues of $US14.5 billion. Omnicon owns BBDO, DDB, TBWA Fleishman-Hillard, Ketchum and Porter Novelli, among others. It began life in 1986 with the merger of BBDO, Doyle Dane Bernbach and Needham Harper. Its public relations subsidiary Ketchum is retained by the government of Russia. Another subsidiary Gplus works with the world's largest energy company, Gazprom, a Russian corporation.

Publicis, a French agency established in 1926, had revenues of €6.6 billion in 2012. Publicis owns Saatchi & Saatchi and Leo Burnett. It is traded on the Paris Stock Exchange. It is known as a Société Anonyme (SA) which means it is a corporation that once had anonymous shareholders who collected dividends by surrendering coupons attached to share certificates. Today, depending upon the country, a Société Anonyme company is a public limited company in common law jurisdictions. These include France, Switzerland and Belgium. It is equivalent to the Dutch NV (Naamioze vennootschap), German AG (Aktiengesellschaft), Swedish AB (Aktiebolag), United Kingdom plc (public limited company) and Japanese KK (Kabushiki Kaisha). Interpublic is based in New York and listed on the NYSE with revenues of $US7 billion. Interpublic was founded in 1960 as McCann-Erickson. It has three networks: McCann Worldgroup, Lowe & Partners and FCB. It owns a large number of other companies that work across public relations, marketing and healthcare. Dentsu is the fifth of the large agencies. It is a public KK corporation and was founded in 1901. In 2010 (latest figures) it had revenue of ¥1.6 trillion. It was originally founded as Japan Advertising and Telegraphic Services. In 2011 it formed an alliance with Facebook to develop Facebook pages, advertisements and marketing strategies. Dentsu owns an array of companies which it bundles into four groups: foreign markets, national advertising markets, new markets and advertising-related markets. As we can see Dentsu has been in existence for more than one hundred years, Publicis for almost ninety years and WPP in advertising for more than thirty years. Advertising is clearly a profitable mid- to long-term business.

## MAPPING HISTORY

If we were to attempt to map the course of history of corporations what would we find? Are there some sectors in which corporate activity is maintained over the long term, for more than one hundred years for example? Or is long-term profitability not related to economic sectors at all but to the capacity of the corporation to change with the way societies themselves change? Do we seek to invest in or to support corporations that we trust? If we trust them, do we have an expectation that they will be around for the long haul?

Relationships with governments appear to be a key factor in the longevity of corporate activity and thus banks are the sector which has done best in the long term.

Some banks that are familiar to us today were established three hundred years ago. There was a flurry of activity in the nineteenth century and many of those names are still in existence. Some countries followed the English (1694) and Scottish (1695) leads and created national banks in the eighteenth century. They included Spain (1782) and Ireland (1783). The nineteenth century saw national banks, or central banks, established in France (1800), India (1808), Brazil (1808), Finland (1811), the Netherlands (1814), Denmark (1818), Sweden (1820), Greece (1841), New Zealand (1861), Canada (1864), Italy (1865), Germany (1870), Australia (1893) and Egypt (1898). Other non-national banks were also established across this period of time. Most notably, those we recognize today were Barclays (1690), Lloyds (1765), La Roche (1787), Lombard (1796), JPMorgan Chase (1799), Schroders (1804), N M Rothschild (1811), Citibank (1812), Wells Fargo (1852), UBS (1854), Credit Suisse (1856), Santander (1857), HSBC (1865) and Goldman Sachs (1869).

## WHY BANKS ARE HISTORICALLY IMPORTANT TO CORPORATIONS AND GOVERNMENTS

In 2014 Australia received a report on its financial system:

> Since the GFC, a persistent theme of international political and regulatory discourse has been the breakdown in financial firms' behaviour in failing to balance risk with reward appropriately and in treating their customers unfairly. Without a culture supporting appropriate risk taking and the fair treatment of consumers, financial firms will continue to fall short of community expectations. This may lead to [...] the undermining of confidence and trust in the financial system.
>
> (Financial System Inquiry, 2014, p. 7)

Banks are corporations. But they are also tied to the health and well-being of governments and to societies. It has always been so. As we have seen, the Bank of England and the South Sea Company vied to become the lender of choice for the English government in the early eighteenth century. The Bank of England clearly came out on top of that struggle as it is still the lender of choice to the British government. But what of banks as corporations and where does the idea of a central bank fit into a society?

A central bank, sometimes known as a reserve bank or monetary authority, manages the money supply of a country. Its function is to control money supply but it will usually take the additional responsibility of overseeing the commercial banks of that country. The first central banks were established in the Netherlands and Sweden. The Swedish Riksbanken was controlled by the Swedish government to whom it lent money. England went a step further and incorporated the Bank of England and gave it possession of government money. It was also allowed to issue banknotes. Today, central banks finance governments but they also control the value of the currency, create and distribute banknotes and act as a lender of last resort to commercial banks in crisis. Throughout the past three hundred years there have been many instances of central banks 'bailing out' commercial banks when they become illiquid. Some countries were relatively late in establishing central banks – the Federal Reserve Act of 1913 created the Federal Reserve in the United States; Australia's Reserve Bank was established in 1920; Mexico's in 1925; Canada's in 1934; and New Zealand's in 1934. The People's Bank of China became a central bank in the early 1980s. With the advent of the European Union (EU) there was a need to control money across what became known as the Eurozone. The European Central Bank (ECB) was established in 1998 with the Treaty of Amsterdam. Shareholders in the ECB are the central banks of the twenty-eight member states of the EU. The additional job of the ECB is to keep prices stable. The ECB is in fact a corporation with shareholders and capital. Between 2010 and 2015 five Eurozone countries sought assistance for 'rescue funds' to repay debt or to bail out their own domestic markets. This became known as the European debt crisis which had ramifications for all EU countries and those outside the EU as trading partners, which was pretty much every country in the world.

There was not much difference between some of the actions of the Eurozone states that asked for help and the actions of John Blunt's South Sea Company and John Law's Mississippi Company when it came to poor judgment and bad investments. In Spain and Ireland unsustainable property bubbles left those countries in dire straits. Portugal and Cyprus also sustained injuries while Greece's problems continued from 2010 until well into 2015 when it threatened to pull out of the Eurozone if its demands for long-term funding could not be met. The irony of Greece's argument was not lost on other Euro countries, particularly Germany and France which in the past had provided deep support. The IMF and the ECB were prepared to extend funding but the reforms to the Greek monetary system and institution that they proposed were not acceptable to the Greek government (BBC, 2015a). Rather than acquiesce to the demands of the IMF and ECB Greece was willing to leave the Eurozone and the EU. Greece's belligerence had a dire effect on its sharemarket. Confidence in the market – the Athens General Index – dropped almost 20 per cent over four trading sessions, a situation that reflected a lack of confidence in the Greek economy. As we might expect such a dire position had far-reaching social consequences. We can see clearly from this that there is a direct connection between corporate activity and social well-being.

The Federal Reserve system is the central banking system in the world's largest economy, the United States. In the one hundred years since its establishment the Fed, as it is known colloquially, has altered in structure. Since the 2009 GFC the Fed has been responsible for regulating commercial American banks, whereas its original monetary policy mandate was less onerous: keep prices stable, maintain employment and balance long-term interest rates. An additional task, but one which is not directly allocated, is the maintenance of the US currency as the benchmark for global currencies. The 'greenback', as US dollars are known, replaced the original benchmark, the gold standard. The Fed is peculiar among global central banks in that it represents the interests of the government but also the interests of public and private banks. In the United States, private banks have always been a crucial part of industrial development. Also peculiar to the US system is that its monetary policy decisions are made independently of the executive and legislative arms of government. The freedom and elasticity of the US economy prior to the establishment of the Fed meant that there were frequent market panics and banks, with grim regularity, went bust. It was established in 1913 but that did not stop one of the biggest panic attacks and runs on banks in 1929 which led inexorably to what we now call the Great Depression. Unlike the Eurozone in which all country central banks are members of the ECB, not all US banks are members of the Fed. National banks are required to be members but state chartered banks can only join if they meet specific requirements, thus only a third of commercial banks are members.

## SUBPRIME MORTGAGE CRISIS EQUALS SOUTH SEA CRISIS

Despite all of its checks and balances, its regulations and stipulations, the Federal Reserve was unable to impede the flow of the GFC or to quell the economic and financial devastation wrought by the subprime mortgage crisis. The subprime mortgage crisis as it became known was a nationwide banking debacle that coincided with a recession in the US economy. As it had been in England in 1720 when the South Sea bubble inflated land prices to more than 40 per cent of their real value, so the lending regimes of many American banks and pseudo banks caused the same problem in 2005. Predatory lending, speculation, risky mortgage products and overbuilding were factors that contributed to the US housing bust. The blame was laid squarely with subprime lenders. These lenders provided financial support at higher interest rates to people who may not normally have been viewed as good credit risks. Prime borrowers were those who had good credit ratings and who were very likely to pay back what they owed. Countries other than America were also culpable – banks in Australia at the turn of the century were lending to anyone who had a pulse and some who didn't. The effect was felt less in Australia and indeed in England and Europe because there was less exposure to the vast numbers who were approved as subprime candidates in the United States. Before 2008 the rest of the world had not heard of the American government-sponsored enterprises (GSEs) Fannie Mae and Freddie Mac. But like KFC and McDonald's their names were about to become synonymous with something far less appetizing. These two publicly listed corporations were blamed in part for the GFC.

A subprime mortgage is money lent to an individual or collective whose credit is not as good as it could be. People with poor credit histories in which they may have long-term debts on their credit cards or car loans are not known to be prime repayers, hence the term subprime. Historically banks and other lending societies were reticent about lending to subprime candidates. If they did so, the interest rate charged was higher than normal because the lenders' risk was higher. This seems like an unusual situation – the prospect of getting money back from a subprime candidate at a low interest rate is risky but the higher the interest rate, it would seem the greater the probability that the borrower would default on the loan, which is what happened in the United States sometime between 2007 and 2009. As in England three hundred years earlier, the inflated price of housing meant borrowers were borrowing more to pay for a house that was not worth what it was being sold for. Housing bubbles are like balloons and as such they burst like balloons.

Subprime mortgages had historically been managed because they were not available in large numbers. The catalyst for the bust in 2008 was the large increase in subprimes from around 8 per cent to more than 20 per cent of the mortgage market (Simkovic, 2011). As Michael Simkovic points out, US mortgage policy security has always been focused on competition and it has always been misplaced. A competitive policy, he says, has been floated three times – in the 1880s, 1920s and the first decade of the twenty-first century – with the same result: a 'destructive financial and economic crisis' (Simkovic, 2011, p. 214). Simkovic blames mortgage securitization – the purchase of loans from mortgage origina-tors by organizations who then on-sell the packaged product to investors. This is a complex business and one whose detail is outside the scope of this book but it is important because the advertising and public relations pitches associated with such packaging and selling lie at the heart of corporation strategic communication. The clue to the failure of securitiza-tion lay in the fact that it was harder to see where the money was coming from. Earlier, loans were analysed more prudently because there was an interface between the lender and the borrower. If a bank or mortgage broker did not like the look of the security on offer or the capacity of the borrower to repay, the loan would not be forthcoming. The anonym-ity of securitizations within GSEs meant they might have looked good on paper but were anything but in reality.

Martin Wolfe argues the subprime crisis in the United States should have come as no surprise (Wolfe, 2008, p. 193). He says countries that run large current account deficits spend more than they earn (Greece in 2015 continued the process). If corporate invest-ment in the production of tradable goods and services is also high then there is less chance of a crisis. In the case of the US market there was more spending on consumption and less on tradable goods and services. A credit-led spending spree followed. Credit was cheap on large and small items – credit cards for household items and mortgage loans for houses and motor vehicles.

## FANNIE MAE AND FREDDIE MAC

In the United States, as in the rest of the western world, the beginning of the twenty-first century saw a large increase in competition to lend money at high interest rates. Much like three hundred years earlier, unscrupulous lenders, including investment banks and commercial banks, competed with each other, as GSEs joined the fray, to make as much money as they could. Increased competition, as we have seen, leads inexorably to increased risk which itself leads to an increase in the frequency of crises.

Fannie Mae is a colloquialism for Federal National Mortgage Association (FNMA) which began life in the United States in 1938 during the Great Depression. It is a publicly listed GSE and as such its remit is to create products known as mortgage-backed securities or securitized mortgages. Securitized means underwritten by the federal government. The original object was to make way for middle- to lower-income earners so they could buy and own their own houses. Fannie Mae lent money to banks so they could finance risky mortgages. In the west, historically, lower-income earners rent while higher-income earners own. By bundling and paying for the mortgages the government attempted to free up investment; lenders could use the money again to make more loans. In 2014 Fannie Mae had income of $14.2 billion and assets worth $3.248 trillion (Federal National Mortgage Association, 2015). Earlier, in 1970, the government changed the direction for Fannie Mae, allowing it to buy conventional mortgages, and it was listed on the NYSE. At the same time the government created the Federal Home Loan Mortgage Corporation (FHLMC) – Freddie Mac – to be in direct competition with Fannie Mae. It was, in retrospect, an unusual act given the United States was from its origins sceptical of government and keen for a robust private sector. It appeared that Fannie Mae suffered from political pressure at various times in its life. The Clinton administration in 1999 pressed the GSEs to increase loans to low-income earners in poorer inner cities. The *New York Times* reported that Fannie Mae was 'taking on significantly more risk, which may not pose any difficulties during flush economic times. But the government-subsidized corporation may run into trouble in an economic downturn, prompting a government rescue similar to that of the savings and loan industry in the 1980s' (New York Times, 1999).

Throughout the western world the era of low-doc, no-doc loans was taking hold. This meant mortgages and loans were made with little or no documentation to assist in analysing whether or not a borrower was capable of repayments. Strategic communication from the GSEs and publicly listed corporations was in line with government policy. The Department of Housing and Urban Development reported in its 2002 activities pitch that the market was demonstrating the 'ability to obtain a thirty year fixed rate mortgage with a low down payment [and to provide] the continuous availability of mortgage credit under a wide range of economic conditions' (United States Department of Housing and Urban Development, 2002). Sadly, as we now know, the range of conditions was not wide enough to absorb the dramatic risk.

Corporations regularly expose themselves to risk. Sometimes the risk pays off; sometimes the corporation suffers. There has been in the modern world a belief that governments will underpin corporate entities no matter how great their exposure to risk because they provide the well-being societies overseen by governments expect and demand. This was indeed the case for the US government during the GFC. Not only did it bail out its sponsored corporations, Fannie Mae and Freddie Mac, but it also bailed some of the world's largest banks. We need to keep in mind that it also let some go under – a bit like there being not enough lifeboats for all the passengers on the *Titanic*. The question though is why the US government let some sink while it supported others through the GFC.

As late as 2008 Fannie and Freddie owned more (including guarantees upon) than half the mortgage market which was around $12 trillion. Bonds issued by Fannie and Freddie were owned widely by giant superannuation (retirement) funds and by governments, including the Chinese government. The government was so concerned about the burst bubble that it created the Emergency Economic Stabilization Act 2008 which allowed it (the Treasury) to buy risky debts from the lending corporations. Debts included mortgages, school loans and vehicle loans. Again, the communication strategy was to show that there would be regained liquidity and thus confidence in the banking system. In its rush to divert the crisis the Treasury printed more money and sold Treasury bonds. By the middle of the year the government had taken control of one of the world's largest insurers, AIG, with a loan guarantee of $85 billion. The mantra of 'too big to fail' had well and truly been deployed.

## BANK LIQUIDITY IN THE UNITED KINGDOM

The UK government was also under enormous pressure to provide a rescue package to banks which had found their way into but not out of the GFC. In October 2008 the government provided £500 billion for the various banks that were in too deep. It was as if John Blunt and British financial history had been swept away on the tide. The bailout was the consequence of a rapidly dropping sharemarket and both perceived and real bank instability. The Bank of England provided £200 billion in special loans and the government underwrote a further £250 billion on eligible lending. The measures began being referred to as 'austerity', the same or similar measures that the EU attempted to impose upon Greece in 2015. Yet ironically, the Greek community opposed such measures arguing they had been austere for far too long already.

The difference in the UK bailout was that its government bought actual shares in the banks while in the United States the government bought the actual problem products. Some UK banks presented their own underpinnings and survived handsomely without government support. HSBC worldwide put more than £750 million into its UK operations; Barclays recapitalized through private investors and Standard Chartered did likewise. Lloyds and Royal Bank of Scotland were the major banks to receive support. The UK model was indeed the benchmark from which other countries measured their successes. As the UK model radiated outward absorbing other countries who undertook similar actions, the world's stock markets hit bottom and confidence came slowly back to the market.

It had been an expensive global exercise and one which should have put financial and other corporations on notice that such risky business would not in the future be communicated as acceptable. But as Chris Berg noted as late as 2014, after the publication of Australia's interim report of that country's financial system inquiry, the question of how big was too big to fail has not been answered. It remained a major problem, Berg suggested, because when corporations did fail there was an expectation that taxpayers would bail them out (Berg, 2014). The final report of the Australian inquiry noted that the GFC 'prompted policy makers and regulators around the world to reconsider their approach(es) to maintaining financial stability. Some countries at the epicentre of the crisis have since expanded their prudential perimeters and adopted more formal and centralized institutional arrangements' (Financial System Inquiry, 2014, p. 233). In the following chapters we will examine in detail some of the corporations mentioned here.

## CONCLUSION

Corporations as we know them have existed for more than three hundred years. There have been some spectacular successes and there have been some equally spectacular failures. Communication has played a major role in the successes and lack of communication has contributed to the failures.

Financial systems and banking underpin corporate activity. But they are not immune from fluctuations in fortune. Corporations and the societies in which they live are dynamic and situational so their strategic communication must also be dynamic and situational.

Corporations have historically followed the democratic notion of the protection of private property. Joint stock companies were formed so that directors could issue shares and the company could own land.

Corporate bubbles have burst at various times throughout the last three hundred years.

Governments prescribe legislation in which corporations must operate and most do so to the benefit of societies.

 **DISCUSSION QUESTIONS**

1 What does history teach us about the contemporary corporation and its communication?
2 Did the 2008 Global Financial Crisis teach corporations how to communicate better?

# 2

# REVERSE ENGINEERING CORPORATE STRATEGIC COMMUNICATION

This chapter provides a detailed prescription for analysing corporate strategic communication. It presents a *reverse engineering* strategy similar in shape to that which is used by manufacturers to discover competitor secrets. It presents a step-by-step guide to the reverse engineering of corporate strategic communication that underpins the following chapters. Reverse engineering is an analytical tool focused on the various tactics required to understand corporate strategic communication.

When a manufacturer is confronted with a competing product, the manufacturer obtains the product, takes it apart and examines in detail how it was made. This is known as reverse engineering. The same can be achieved when a corporation is confronted with a competitor with a communication advantage. Reverse engineering works by examining the components of the strategy, in the same way a product is broken down into its component parts, including examination of public documents, analysis of media matter and engagement with stakeholders through surveys, focus groups and other informational reception channels.

An example of the reverse engineering process might be in the agricultural sector of a country that is competing for global markets – the United Kingdom, France, the United States, Australia or New Zealand, for example. Low levels of interest, lack of goal compatibility, low levels of involvement and a dangerous lack of problem recognition are the attributes of most agricultural sector stakeholders.[1] A variety of elements contribute to a sectoral communication strategy for agriculture including annual reports of publicly listed companies and co-operatives within the sector. Reverse engineering gathers the reports and investigates the published detail – text and images. It constructs a matrix which serves to identify elements within the sector. The same process can be used for individual corporations operating within a sector, for example the corporate entities within the global dairy industry, which in turn is part of the global agricultural sector. French, Italian, New Zealand and Australian dairy companies seek global markets, global supply and expansion into the emerging Chinese dairy market. Analysis of the published matter of companies such as Parmalat, Fonterra and Danone ought to provide evidence of the success or otherwise of their communication strategies. The reverse engineering process is then continued into media coverage of the corporation or the sector and public pronouncements by the corporations such as speeches by the chief executives. Media coverage is analysed using a similar matrix. An additional component can then be added – engagement with stakeholders – so that the complete process is triangulated, providing a strong underpinning for the assessment of the strategy.

---

[1] Stakeholder attributes are discussed in detail in Chapter 4.

So, let's get started. We need to think about what it is we want to know about a corporate entity and why we want to know it. We can then work out where and how we might go about finding our information. Our first thought about reverse engineering was that it was old school – it was about trying to make a better car by taking someone else's apart and then building your own with a better fuel pump or a faster tyre. It was originally all about old industrial products. But it is now part of the technology competitiveness of some of the world's largest computer companies, including semiconductor makers. It is part of the bioscience field and plays a large role in the development of better pharmaceuticals. It is the lifeblood of *uber upstarts* (more on them in Chapter 10).

When we reverse engineer a process we need to be mindful of a number of legal implications. We must not attempt to breach intellectual property rights or copyright. Generally speaking, the reverse engineering of published matter does not breach copyright or infringe intellectual property rights as it is interpretive. While copyright exists over published matter the interpretation of its content is an acceptable objective.

In reverse engineering the strategic communication of a corporate entity, we are interested less in the discovery of a new and better way to communicate and more in the possibility of enhancing existing communication. It is a *deductive goal* covering existing matter aimed at competitor analysis. Reverse engineering can only be of value when it is applied using pre-existing metrics and known objectives and when it is triangulated as part of a model that aims to locate corporate communication within a society. It would be pointless to reverse engineer the various elements of a corporate entity if there were no benchmark against which to frame the deductive processes.

## WHY REVERSE ENGINEERING NEEDS A BASIC ARCHITECTURE

In Chapter 6 we will find the details of the taxonomies that we require to set up an analysis of corporate communication. We might find it useful here to start with a definition and to see how taxonomies are important to the reverse engineering process. Chikofsky and Cross (1990) describe reverse engineering as a major link in the life cycle of software technology, although terminology is a sticking point for further development. They identify both technology discourse and market discourse as impediments to further liberalization. It is similar for us in the field of corporate communication. A corporate entity may, for example, employ particular terms to its core competencies. Our interpretation of those terms must be close to the technical relevance with which they were originally employed otherwise our analysis and evaluation will be skewed. Chikofsky and Cross defined reverse engineering as 'the practice of deciphering designs from finished products' (Chikofsky and Cross, 1990, p. 13). Its application, they suggest, is to 'improve your own product as well as to analyze a competitor's products or those of an adversary in a military or national security situation (Chikofsky and Cross, 1990, p. 13). The idea that corporations are in competitive conflict with each other is not new – they battle for increased market share. While Chikofsky and Cross use the image of a life cycle for software technology development to identify the frame in which reverse engineering might take place, we can think of a period of history of a corporation as the same as a life cycle. But we are not resource rich – we are unlikely to take the whole of the life of the corporation and reverse engineer every piece of communication it has made throughout its history. We can take a chunk or a slice out of it and analyse that as if it were a life cycle. We may choose for example to analyse all the media coverage of Northern Rock immediately prior to and immediately after its financial collapse in 2014 and, say, for six months either side. We may then analyse published matter – speeches by its chief executive, press releases issued either side of the collapse – to determine if any change in focus occurred. As an aside, we could do the same for the South Sea Company; we could analyse the written matter from the time, especially that written by known personalities involved in the scheme – Daniel Defoe and Jonathon Swift, for example. We might do the same in analysing Northern Rock – we could look at what journalist and finance expert Martin Wolfe may have written. Chikofsky and Cross present two other terms that are relevant to us: *subject system* and *abstraction levels* (Chikofsky and Cross, 1990, p. 14). In reverse engineering of software technology the subject system is the starting point. It is the end point which is then propelled backwards. In corporation communication there is not always a line in the sand that can be identified as the end point as it is a continuous process. In reverse engineering a corporate communication strategy we must therefore define the end point of our action before we can begin to work backwards. It may be that we identify the subject system as a campaign – a specific or discreet communication within the overarching and ongoing communication of the corporate entity. Abstractions in the life cycle of computer technology are much the same as levels of abstraction in corporate communication. Much more abstract action is taken at the beginning of a campaign than at the end. Abstractions are linked directly to the frame in which a corporation presents its communication. A logo or the colours a company uses to display its products and service are early examples. Corporate colour must always be exactly the same. It must be a Pantone Matching System (PMS) colour and usually requires a corresponding breakdown of the exact percentages for conversion to standard four-colour (cyan, magenta, yellow, black) printing. So, there is no 'abstraction' associated with a corporate colour one it has been implemented which is why we are less interested in the fundamental regulations applied by companies and more interested in the *interpretations applied to their vocabularies*.

One of the key objectives of reverse engineering a corporation's communication lies within the corporation itself. It is more usually referred to as a communication audit – an event much like a stocktake at the end of a financial year. Corporations employ consultants to audit their existing communication and to evaluate their success against given metrics. Such an exercise is valuable but it does not get to the guts of what a corporation's communication is achieving nor the probability of what it is capable of achieving. It is worth restating that reverse engineering is all about *expanding our apprehension of the corporate communication concepts and operations as they exist*.

## REVERSE ENGINEERING AND THE WTO

As Samuelson and Scotchmer (2002) point out, reverse engineering has been so widely used in so many sectors that legally there has never been a challenge to its use nor have the courts thought it necessary to 'explain the rationale for this doctrine' (Samuelson and Scotchmer, 2002, p. 6). No rights exist to protect organizations from reverse engineering. Patent law in most countries does not constrain the process although, as Samuelson and Scotchmer suggest, in theory a patent is a detailed explanation of how a product works – it is publicly available. There is no need to reverse engineer patented products. Corporations do not, however, patent their strategic communication.

While there is a social calculus of reverse engineering in the traditional sector of manufacturing a similar situation is less evident in the sectors of technology and services. Within the WTO there is an agreement between member countries that focuses on intellectual property (IP) and intellectual property rights (IPR). It is known as the Agreement on Trade Related Aspects of Intellectual Property Rights (TRIPS) and it is of most interest to corporations whose revenues are defined by their international trade agreements. The WTO is a dispute resolution mechanism – it is there to resolve trade disputes between its member countries; it is not therefore very interested in the social calculus of IP and IPR.

While engineering design is the conceptualization and operationalization of components or systems, reverse engineering is the reconceptualization of the principles of the component or system by analysing structures of operation. Its diffuse application, to the extent that we have here invented a new model of reverse engineering for communication purposes, means it has been difficult for regulators such as the WTO to frame it. It has made numerous attempts to involve itself in the legitimate transfer of technology and the transfer of information between member states. As we might guess very few corporations are really interested in handing over their core competences or their *trade secrets* for the advancement of nation states or other corporations within them. Stoll, Busche and Arend (2009) make the point that the act of marketing a product or service legitimizes the process of discovery. Analysis of a product's manufacturing or a pharmaceutical formula by competitors is a natural process. And there is no prohibition on reverse engineering under WTO rules including Article 39.2. The focus of Article 39.2 of TRIPS is the protection applied to information that might be considered secret and that has commercial value precisely because it is secret. It must also be demonstrated that particular processes have been put in place to keep such information secret. Undisclosed information and trade secrets benefit from protection under the TRIPS agreement which by its nature does not impact upon the reverse engineering of corporate strategic communication.

## REVERSE ENGINEERING THE GUTS OUT OF IT

Let's look at the process of reverse engineering a corporate strategic communication campaign. Let's also determine the best ways to go about the process and how we might obtain the collateral we need to get the job done. Let's also focus on the corporations that are most important to us – there is little return to be had from analysing a corporation that is not directly related to our own interests. Keep in mind that we do not have unlimited resources or finances for this exercise – competitors want to find out what's going on but they do not yet value it highly. They may value reverse engineering of a service more highly which means they will invest more in it financially. Let's say we work for a large multinational company with interests in a particular sector of the economy. It might be primary, secondary or tertiary. These are the three traditional economic sectors. Within these our corporation might be directly invested in agriculture or fishing (primary), aerospace or beer (secondary), banking or health (tertiary). There are many more subcategories within these three sectors and, for the most part, corporations do not stick to one or the other. Corporate activity goes where there is profit. So there is a good chance our corporation will seek *comparative advantage* through the implementation of a vertical hierarchy. These are also known as downstream and upstream linkages or channels; a corporation which is involved in and best known for retailing seafood, for example, might also own boats. It might catch the fish it sells. It might process the fish before it sells it. This is known as controlling the value chain. If we work for a competitor who wants to know how the fishmonger controls so much of the global market for seafood we can analyse the various components of its communication.

## Fishing for information

The fishing industry in Japan is one of that country's biggest exports and one of its most important domestic primary activities. Two of Japan's largest fishing companies are Maruha Nichiro and Nippon Suisan Kaisha which employ between them more than 20,000 people. Nippon Suisan Kaisha is a publicly listed company founded in 1911 which in 2012 had revenue of ¥566 billion. Nippon trades as Nissui and among its assets are US-based Gorton's, a frozen seafood company. Maruha Nichiro is also a publicly listed company with revenue of ¥8.6 billion and subsidiaries in the United States, Europe, Australia and New Zealand. Its primary activities are fishing and fish processing so it crosses two economic sectors: primary and secondary. It also produces canned food and frozen food. It is the largest seafood corporation in Japan and, valued at $8 billion, the largest in the world. In 2014 the company was forced to recall more than 6 million frozen seafood items after the product had poisoned 3000 consumers. The incident was blamed on an employee of a subsidiary company, Aqlifoods. The incident led to the resignation of Maruha Nichiro president, Toshio Kushiro, and caused a subsequent restructuring of the company. It cost the company ¥3.5 billion.

Let's assume we work for the second largest company, Nissui. We want to know a number of things about our competitor since the poisoning – has it recovered its position in the market, has it changed its way of communicating with its stakeholders, what is it planning for the future, how did it deal with the poisoning issue and what effect did the restructure have on the ways in which it communicates its corporate reputation, image and brand? We will deal with the specifics of reputation, image and brand in Chapter 8. For now we will focus on the question of what we can discover and what we can analyse. Primary access to Maruha Nichiro is its global website. Corporations provide an enormous amount of information on these sites but not all of it is valuable. Much of it is the output of corporate public relations departments that like to present bubbly but ultimately meaningless phrases. A number of these phrases have made their way into the Maruha Nichiro site. In what it describes as its 'top message' president Shigeru Ito speaks of the need to monitor the risks associated with changes in a 'global society'. This is a significant statement but it is distilled by the addition of the subsequent sentence that such an environment means 'we must always think for tomorrow while fighting to survive today'. In an allusion to the earlier poisoning, Mr Ito suggests further that the group's basic mission is to provide wholesome, safe and healthy food needed by society. Within three sentences he had invoked the word 'society' twice. As we know, corporations cannot exist without a robust society but it is unusual for a corporate executive to mention the relationship of the corporation to a society in such stark terms (Maruha Nichiro, 2015).

The element of safety and health is underpinned in the next level of the site under group vision. The group philosophy is distilled into one sentence which is predominantly the same as the president's message: 'The Maruha Nichiro Group aims to contribute to the betterment of people's daily lives, through providing wholesome, safe, and healthy food with sincerity and integrity' (Maruha Nichiro, 2015). Without researching previous corporate site information we might assume the word 'safe' has been included since the poisoning episode. Would we be inclined to introduce such a word to our own competitor site? The group vision continues the theme:

> [Maruha Nichiro] aims to become an excellent company of the 21st century making global contributions in the food industry, while still conducting business in a manner that is environmentally friendly; aims to become a provider of satisfaction for the ever-changing needs of our customers, as a value-generating corporation; aims to progress into new global businesses and markets, developing strategies for sustainable sourcing and enhancing technological innovation capabilities.
>
> (Maruha Nichiro, 2015)

Much of this is valueless corporate rhetoric. We can find very little to analyse that will assist us with our reverse engineering. The section entitled corporate data is equally underwhelming. It provides the names of the business operations, its location, its capital (¥20 billion) and companies within its group. When we click to the history section we get a better sense of value although it is circumscribed by the fact that the last entry is dated 2008. There are some important points along its historical path, most notable among them are its incorporation as a KK in 1924; the loss of its overseas assets and operations in 1945; and restrictions brought about in 1977 by the adoption around the world of the 200-mile coastal exclusion zone. The section headed 'Group Companies' is slightly more valuable. It provides, under different subheadings, names, addresses, locations and websites for its global operations. Some of the sites have spun their own delightful but valueless webs of words. Peter Pan Seafoods, Seattle USA for example states: 'For as long as fishermen have dipped nets into the sea, the oceans have yielded their bounty to the world.' Peter Pan has a section entitled 'Press' but within lies one item – Ocean Watch which provides a one-page overview of the 2014 salmon season in Alaska. There is nothing to identify the publisher of Ocean Watch (Peter Pan Seafoods, 2014). It would be hazardous to use it as part of our reverse engineering. Group companies are located in the United States, New Zealand, Bangladesh, Namibia, Peru, Micronesia, the Netherlands, Spain, China, Malaysia, Indonesia, Australia, Thailand and Korea. We can see from the list that all processed foods come from Thailand and China, with one offshoot in Korea. Fisheries and aquaculture are spread around while processing and trading is dominated by the United States, the Netherlands and China. Kingfisher Holdings, a processed food company in Thailand, claims to be 'a company with vision'. Yet in 2015 the company was forced to respond to a claim that it was using slave labour on its boats – the fish that ended up in US supermarkets had been caught by labourers imprisoned on boats at sea. The Associated Press (AP) story drew interesting conclusions. Not only were slave labourers used to catch fish and other sea creatures but the haul ended up in the aisles of Walmart and Safeway, as calamari at fine restaurants, as 'imitation crab in a California sushi roll' and in being 'fed to the family cat out of a can of Meow Mix' (McDowell, Mason and Mendoza, 2015). The AP investigators named Kingfisher. In response Kingfisher published a statement outlining its code of conduct under three separate subheadings:

1  business determination;
2  human rights; and
3  protecting and preserving the environment.

Kingfisher wrote: (1) 'In pursuing our vision to be a world-class supplier of premium quality foods, the Group is determined to operate our business with transparency and accountability, under the rule of law and in accordance with the highest ethical standards. We aim to protect the environment and promote human rights and sustainable development, and meet our responsibilities to employees, business partners and community.' (2) 'The Group reinforces human rights must be promoted and respected. These rights include the right to basic living conditions, equal access to essential resources, freedom from unlawful detentions, as well as freedom of thoughts, expressions, associations, belief and religions. Moreover, these rights include the treatment of children and youths in accordance with universal principles. The Group will only do business with those partners who operate their business in accordance with the principles of human rights and the rule of law. The Group will monitor its operations by properly following up in order to prevent any violations of human rights.' (3) 'To achieve its goal, the Group, along with related organizations and supplier networks, will develop conservation concepts into its manufacturing and servicing processes. The Group will minimize waste and will not use endangered species for business purposes. The Group will not purchase materials from any source that violates human and animal rights or that trades in illegal products.' (Kingfisher, 2015)

As we can deduce much of the matter included in the code of conduct was directed towards the AP story. But it was difficult to find the specifics of the code on the website. Under the subheading 'CSR' was a message from the managing director published in 2006. It contained statements and further 'CSR activities that include promotion of the knowledge of CSR; preservation of religious beliefs, provision of cooking classes for sustainable careers and a contribution to conservation' (Kingfisher, 2016).

The Kingfisher website included the information that Kingfisher began life in 1972 as an Australian, Thai and Hong Kong joint venture which built a tuna canning factory and named it SafCol. In 1989 the company changed its name to Kingfisher and in 1990 it stated 'one of the biggest seafood enterprises in the world, Maruha Corporation joined Kingfisher as a shareholder' (Kingfisher, 2016). It is an interesting turn of phrase – Maruha joining Kingfisher rather than Kingfisher becoming a subsidiary of Maruhu. The Maruha Nichiro Group was in fact the mother company for various companies around the world that vertically integrated the seafood business. The companies included Seafood Connection, Peter Pan Seafoods, Trans Ocean Products and Kingfisher. In 2013 a trade journal, *Undercurrent News*, wrote that Maruha Nichiro was looking for the right partners to grow its business and in this it already owned 'several large operations outside Japan including pollock and cod processor Westward Seafoods and salmon processor Peter Pan Seafoods in the US as well as shrimp and tuna processor Kingfisher Holdings in Thailand' (*Undercurrent News*, 2013).

The corporation makes no mention of its relationship to Kingfisher and the AP story. Maruha Nichiro was mentioned in earlier media coverage. In 2008 *Newsweek* published a long article on slave labour in the computer industry, concluding with a shot over the bows of the fishing industry. Reporter George Wehrfritz wrote that the supply trail was particularly difficult to determine. He made reference to a company known as Sirichai Fisheries which was alleged to have breached the human rights of its ship's crew. 'There's a good chance you or your pet have eaten fish caught by Sirichai and similar operations though in the fishing industry the supply trail is particularly murky. One of Sirichai's main buyers is Kingfisher, which supplies leading western brands and is controlled by Maruha Nichiro Holdings, Japan's leading seafood retailed' (Wehrfritz, 2008).

## TACTICS FOR DISCOVERING WHAT WE NEED TO REVERSE ENGINEER

Now we ought to think about what we might need so that we can go about the reverse engineering process. Our starting point is a good search engine. As we have seen above, we can gather a lot of relevant matter online. When we have exhausted our online search we might like to find additional matter in hard copy but in today's world of communication, everything we need should be available in electronic format. Corporations provide an electronic version of their annual reports online which can be either downloaded or copied for reference. Many countries have a requirement that corporations publish hard copy annual reports but unless you are a shareholder you are likely to encounter difficulty in obtaining a hard copy. Corporate public relations departments will direct you to their online sites.

The objective of reverse engineering a corporate brochure such as this is to determine its target stakeholders. To whom is it pitched? What is its message? Why is it designed and written the way it is? If we use Maruha Nichiro as an example we can see there are two sites presented by the company: one for its major Japanese stakeholders and another English version for its western world partners. We are particularly interested in extracting information from the representative corporate sites but we are equally interested in obtaining information from other sources that we can vector towards the corporate site. Before we begin analysing the data and information we create a list of what is available. We also create a file into which we can download the matter. To create our list we might enter terms and words specific to your discovery objective. The first words would therefore be the name of the company – Maruha Nichiro. If we choose to use Google as our search device (Google itself is a multinational publicly listed corporation with revenue in 2016 of $US66 billion and more than 55,000 employees) we have options of looking for web matter, images and news – the three relevant areas for our investigation and analysis. The first website is the corporate site of the company. This was followed by subdivisions of matter that appeared on the corporate site including top message, fishery operations, a Wikipedia reference, a Tokyo stock quote, a LinkedIn connection and promotions of the company by its affiliates in Europe and America such as Trans-Europe Seafood Sales (TESS).

The next section, images, provides hundreds of pictures of related products, personnel, logos of associated companies and advertising. When we click on the news subsection we find a number of articles published in the trade journal, *Undercurrent News*; others published by newspapers *Asahi Shimbun*, *New York Times* and *Japan Times*; others by agencies such as Bloomberg and Reuters. We might anticipate the matter published by news media used unfavourable angles while the trade journals looked for positive 'spin' – trade journals survive on advertising from the corporations that they report on.

Within the search engine database there were more than 288,000 entries for our chosen corporation under web matter and almost 4000 under news. Our reverse engineering process must extract matter which is most relevant. We do not have the luxury of analysing all items thrown up. The next step is to make decisions about what to analyse and what to set aside. A simple two-column list will suffice to extract salient matter (see Table 2). Keep in mind that we are interested in analysing what the company publishes about its self as well as cross-referencing that with what others say about the company.

When we have our list – and it does not need to be exhaustive at this stage – we might overview what it is we are looking at. We will think about our analysis in a more complex fashion in Chapter 6 when we develop our understanding of narrative theory and how we

| Salient | Less Salient |
|---|---|
| Company site | Wikipedia site |
| *FIS* Suppliers site | LinkedIn site |
| Westward Seafood site | *Undercurrents* story |
| TESS site | *Asahi Shimbun* story |
| *New York Times* story | *Japan Times* story |
| Bloomberg story | Facebook site |

**Table 2.1**  Reverse engineering a corporate brochure

can apply it. For now let's look at the corporate profile of Maruha Nichiro. There are two versions of the site, a Japanese version and an English translation version. The Japanese site is far superior – as you would expect it to be. Western corporations create translated versions of their websites in other languages whereby there is a loss of fidelity and a loss of resonance. In the case of Maruha Nichiro, the Japanese language site includes superior images and text while the English version evinces a number of typographical and grammatical errors. If we explore the site itself we find embedded in it a document entitled 'Corporate Profile' which is a series of pdf (portable document format) files all unlinked. It is necessary to download each individually rather than as a whole document. When we look at the documents we observe a number of elements: images, colours, text and layout. The human eye has a default way of looking at printed matter – western literature reads from the top left to the bottom right of a page. This process is embedded in us from early childhood. Japanese, however, is read from right to left so we can see immediately that we are dealing with two different ways of visual acceptance and access to written text. But before we see text on a page we look at and interpret images. This is why the traditional vertical newspaper layout subscribed to the positioning of a picture above the headline and the headline above the body copy. In the Maruha Nichiro corporate profile there are many colourful images but little in the way of detailed text. It represents itself more as an advertising brochure than as a corporate information site. There is a fondness for graphs. These appear on most pages in different formats – a Venn diagram that includes the words and phrases 'global procurement', 'customer's needs', 'group's integrity', superior product development' and 'our core identity is fish'. Under the heading 'Global perspective and capability of product development' there is a picture of cattle grazing in a field. It maps its world domination under the heading 'Marine products centres' and shows the type of fish caught and the global locations of activity. It represents its history with a simple Gantt chart labelling corporate and operational events on a timescale. The images support the written text. Much of the story is absorbed with facts and figures while smaller sections are crowded with rhetorical flourishes. Under the heading 'Passing on the Bounty of the Seas to the World' the subheading reads 'bringing the bounty of the seas to dining tables worldwide, delivering the true delight of great food'. Under the subheading frozen food business unit is the curious sentence: 'This unit provides retail frozen foods, including cooked foods that create hit products featuring gourmet and trendy recipes, as well as frozen vegetables that are managed centrally all the way from the farm'[2] (www.maruha-nichiro.co.jp/english).

---

[2] Contrast this with Box, discussed in Chapter 10.

## LOOKING AT THE EXTERNALS

When we have gathered and subdivided the published matter presented by the corporation we can begin to overlay it with external artefacts. These might be news reports, feature stories appearing in trade journals as we have seen above, blogs with direct relevance to the corporation, social media responses to its activities and stock exchange information. We can gather most of this information from the World Wide Web. We might choose additionally to seek out face-to-face information from groups and individuals as stakeholders in the corporation. There may be supporters groups or activist groups opposed to the actions of the corporations. One of the news media that reports most often on Maruha Nichiro is *Undercurrent News*. Information about *Undercurrent News* can be found on the web. It was founded in 2012 by two journalists, Tom Seaman and Eva Tallaksen. *Undercurrent News* is based in the UK and has a 'mission', to 'bring quality business news and information for the seafood industry using all the dimensions digital technologies can add'. It claims to 'pride ourselves on being wholly independent, telling the news like we see it, with no corporate agenda'. In its advertising it compares its advertising coverage to its stakeholders with three other seafood-focused journals: *FIS.com*, *IntraFish.com* and *SeafoodSource.com*. It claims more than 88,000 visitors to its site each month and to have more than 10,000 newsletter subscribers. As we know, online newsletter subscribers are one of the most valuable sources of communication with stakeholders. There is no evidence that Maruha Nichiro has a newsletter subscription base.

*Undercurrent News* claims readership demographics by subsections of the fishing industry – 19 per cent aquaculture; 15 per cent fishing; 13 per cent wholesale; through to 6 per cent research. Its largest readership is 41 per cent in North America, and 37 per cent throughout Europe, the Middle East and Africa combined. It claims 19 per cent readership in the Asia-Pacific region. The *Undercurrent News* site publishes testimonies from readers. Colin MacDonald, chairman of Clearwater Seafoods wrote: 'I read undercurrentnews daily as it brings me up to the minute global news on the fishing industry … sorting rumour and speculation from facts. It is a great aid in developing strategy and marketing initiatives.' (www.undercurrentnews.com).

What is most interesting about this testimony is the idea that a news journal is a valuable strategic tool in itself. Colin MacDonald's company, Clearwater Seafood, is itself a public company listed on the Canadian stock exchange. Under a subheading on its website entitled 'Corporate Social Responsibility', Clearwater refers to its employees as being 'communities'. It uses the word four times in four paragraphs. We will return to the notion of communities and corporate social responsibility in Chapter 8.

Clearwater, with a global workforce of 13,000 – far fewer than Maruha Nichiro – works in the same global industry and as such appears to grasp the significance of online communication and trading. Its website can be viewed in English, Japanese, Spanish and French. It is based in Nova Scotia so the French Canadian connection is evident. It has a large base in Argentina which accounts for its Spanish translation. And to place itself in competition with the largest seafood corporation, it represents itself in Japanese. Its corporate communication strategy is competitive and as such is something we will revisit below.

Meanwhile let's return to our brief overview of external agencies such as *Undercurrent News*. As noted, it makes readership comparisons with three other sites – *FIS.com*, *IntraFish. com* and *SeafoodSource.com*. *FIS.com* is the website of Fish Information and Services, naming itself the 'standard for global seafood industry information on the internet'. It claims to publish in Japanese, English and Spanish and to have more than 133,000 companies in its database. It claims 333,000 site visits a month and 24,000 newsletter subscriptions.

IntraFish is an organization which owns a number of publications and provides online market information to the seafood sector. It claims its journal *Seafood International Digital* is the leading global publication for seafood marketing professionals, providing current, actionable content that will 'help you boost your seafood sales'. IntraFish Media, the parent company, began life as a telefacsimile newsletter for the Norwegian salmon market in 1994. *Intrafish.com* was started in 2012 and is published from the United States and Europe. It claims a circulation of almost 22,000 and close to 80,000 views a month. IntraFish is owned by NHST Media Group which claims its strategy is to be 'a leading news provider both in Norway and globally within the select segments where we operate'.

*SeafoodSource.com*, the third competitor named by *Undercurrent News*, claims 40,000 subscribers, publishes a directory of more than 2000 companies in the sector, has 47 per cent of its readership in North America and 38 per cent in Europe. It claims to be part of a global seafood portfolio that includes exhibitions in North America and Asia. The journal appears to be part of a large portfolio of media including conferences and publications owned by Diversified Business Communications, a company based in the United States. Its corporate brochure under print and digital states: 'we engage with our audience by delivering cutting-edge content, interactive dialogue, marketing opportunities and education platforms'. It adds that 'we make it easy for our customers to stay connected to their community, continue to build their relationships, further their exposure and access the most current information about their industry from anywhere at any time'. The company claims to service sixteen industries in fourteen countries including architecture, education, fitness, food, healthcare, and oil and gas. All four publications have social media sites:

- *SeafoodSource.com* claims 10,500 followers, follows 5244 accounts and has tweeted 9773 times. It claims to be 'your source for news and opinion on the global #seafood industry'.
- *IntraFish.com* has 7344 followers, follows 2626 accounts and has tweeted more than 12,000 times. It claims to be the 'leading provider of news and information to the seafood industry around the world and around the clock'.
- *FIS.com* claims 4277 followers, follows 661 accounts and has tweeted 6108 times (as of July 2015). It claims to be 'the best portal for the commercial fishing, seafood and aquaculture industries worldwide'.
- *Undercurrent News* has 3823 followers, follows 1955 accounts and has tweeted 5251 times. It claims to 'bring you all the best and latest in international seafood business news'.

## SETTING OUT THE MATTER SO THE ANALYTICAL TOOL CAN BE DEPLOYED

We are now in a position to gather more diffuse information about the corporation through the reporting of these four journals. We might also gather all the tweets with direct relevance to Maruha Nichiro. Let's start with the tweets. We might use our own Twitter account to discover what the journals have been tweeting about Maruha Nichiro. First we will need to 'follow' the journals' Twitter accounts. We can then examine each tweet to see if it contains relevant words or phrases, such as 'Maruha Nichiro' or 'Kingfisher'. *FIS.com* tweets included a bracketed piece of geographical information – where the story originates. It also tweets in Spanish. *Undercurrent News* and *IntraFish.com* include links to the stories they are tweeting. *SeafoodSource.com* includes a sign-off tag, #seafood news, in most of its tweets. This sign-off, however, is ambiguous. Tweets with the tag #seafood also get mixed up in the feed – restaurant news, dinosaurs and today's dinner are some of the matter which is irrelevant to our analysis. When we have all the relevant tweets we will be ready to do our analysis.

We can now gather matter from the journals. To do this we might open each one in a browser window on our computer and use the searchable facility within. If we type 'Maruha Nichiro' into the *IntraFish.com* site, we receive 266 hits for stories that include the name of the corporation. To get the full story we would then need to sign up to the *IntraFish.com* newsletter.

*Undercurrent News* requires a sign-in to receive its stories but it is a free service. There is no indication of the number of stories it has published using the corporate name.

*FIS.com* offers more than 12,800 results with full access to the stories that does not include a requirement to sign in to the newsletter – at least, not after accessing a small number of stories.

*Seafoodsource.com* provides access to fifty stories with no requirement to sign up to its newsletter.

Now we need to determine which, if any, of these accessible pieces are relevant to our reverse engineering and, if they are, what we need to do to assist the process of creating typologies that will fit with our overall aim of understanding Maruha Nichiro's corporate strategic communication. We might find additional matter that overlays appropriately with our corporate matter and our external agency matter. But for now we are content with what we have. Our next step is to gain an understanding of the theories that drive corporate communication and how corporate image and branding connect to reputation. The connection between corporate reputation and the importance of good media follows the discoveries we have made in this chapter.

## CONCLUSION

Reverse engineering the strategic communication of a corporate entity enhances existing communication and allows the discovery of new and better ways to communicate. It is the reconceptualization of the principles of a communication system through analysing structures of operation. Reverse engineering is a valuable tool because it is applied using pre-existing metrics and known objectives. It is triangulated as part of a model that aims to locate corporate communication within society.

Reverse engineering needs a defined start point and end point of the communication being investigated. The subject system is the start point but it is difficult to identify the end point unless it is a discreet campaign being evaluated. There are many abstractions at the beginning of a communication campaign, fewer at the end.

Reverse engineering expands apprehension of the concepts and operations of corporate communication. Corporate entities are not protected against reverse engineering of their products or their communication.

DISCUSSION QUESTIONS

1 How might we define the concept of reverse engineering in a corporate communication sense?
2 Does reverse engineering a corporate communication breach copyright, patent or other legislative boundaries?

 CASE STUDY: FireEye

### Building a framework to tell your story

*Vitor Souza – Vice President Global Communications*

When I joined FireEye as the Vice President of Global Communications, no one had heard of us. This small start-up based in California's Silicon Valley was doing some really outstanding things to fight the bad guys who were trying to hack into networks and steal information, but our brand name recognition was nil. Normally, that wouldn't be such a big deal – plenty of companies flourish within their small spheres all the time with no need for anyone outside that industry to know who they are. But we were about to go public with an initial public offering (IPO). Before that IPO, we needed people to know our name. We had to increase brand awareness and my communications team was tasked with making sure that happened.

We weren't satisfied with just name recognition, though. From the start, we wanted a narrative approach to our communications programme. We wanted to tell our story and we wanted to do it in a way that differentiated us from other security vendors. It was important that people not only knew the name FireEye, but that they recognized that we do things differently from our competition. By setting ourselves apart we could develop new stakeholders while strengthening our brand.

The narrative approach we took was very similar to writing a book: we created a story, we developed the characters to tell their stories, and we decided how and where to tell those tales. The path we took was very carefully laid out in a particular order; every good story has a flow to it, with details revealed at just the right time to enhance stakeholder understanding. If we got too far ahead of ourselves and told things out of order, we'd lose our stakeholders. We actually made that mistake and had to backtrack to get our stakeholder back in sync with us.

It's a key lesson of the communications world – tell your story in a coherent, methodical way and make sure your stakeholder gets it. Listen to the feedback. If they don't understand, back up and find a new way to hook them and get them on board with you again.

### The FireEye Book: Chapter 1

### The Foundation

We started with a story-mining session with key stakeholders. Together with the company's thought leaders, including our founder, CEO, CMO and other influencers, we mapped out the three most important things we wanted to tell the market at

*(Continued)*

that time. Keep in mind, we were just about to go public, so it was crucial that people became familiar with both our name and our niche in the market.

We agreed on three *pillars* on which to base our story: *Growth*, *Innovation* and *Ecosystem*. Each of these pillars formed the basis of our communication plan. Let me expand on each of them, so you can see how we used them to build our story.

*Growth*: We have some fierce competition in the cyber security industry. It's tough to compete against household names like Cisco and McAfee, but that is what we were doing. Rather than having our name lumped in with them, we needed to establish our own identity and to differentiate ourselves. We didn't want the market comparing us to them or benchmarking our growth against theirs. We were growing quickly but efficiently, while they were already established companies. That became the basis of our growth story.

*Innovation*: While all security vendors are attempting to do the same thing – stop cyber breaches – the FireEye product line is unique. Today's highly sophisticated cyber attacks can easily get past traditional defences that have long been thought to be effective; things like firewalls and antivirus protection just aren't enough anymore. The FireEye Threat Prevention Platform provides real-time, dynamic threat protection against different stages of an attack. Our products work differently from traditional cyber defences and innovation is a key part of the FireEye strategy in the marketplace.

*Ecosystem*: Nothing happens in a silo. We knew it was important to work with others in our industry and outside it, to fuel our growth and our customer base. We identified partners including other security vendors, associations, universities and government to better position the company within the public eye.

### The FireEye Book: Chapter 2

### The characters

With our pillars identified, we thought about who might be the best person to tell our story within each of those pillars. That meant we needed a storyteller – or a narrator, a character in our book. For our first pillar, *Growth*, we knew Dave DeWalt was the perfect narrator. As our CEO, no one was more focused on growing the company than Dave. He's had years of experience building innovative tech companies, and his track record provided the credibility needed to tell our growth story and convince the market that FireEye was on solid, capable and comfortable terrain while in his hands.

Our founder, Ashar Aziz, was the natural choice to tell our *Innovation* story. Several years before he started FireEye, Ashar looked at malware as both a technology challenge and a business opportunity. His foresight – seeing the kind of malware that existed back in 2004 and imagining how it could morph over time – led him to create our company to protect against it.

We cast Steve Pataki, our Senior Vice President of Worldwide Channels and Alliances, to tell our *Ecosystem* story. Why? Quite simply, he had more connections than anyone else. A natural salesman, Steve understands how to work together to benefit both parties. In a role that required reaching out and forming alliances, he was the obvious spokesperson.

One important note, here: we decided not to focus the same attention on all three pillars simultaneously. In the early days, we paid much more attention to the *Growth* and *Innovation* pillars, and not so much on *Ecosystem*. Our focus changed based on where the FireEye story was at any given time. Sometimes one aspect required more attention than others and we adjusted as needed given market conditions and feedback.

### The FireEye Book: Chapter 3

### Telling our story

We had the stories and the characters in place; now we needed to decide where to tell our tale. We lined up interviews with major business outlets, including *The Wall Street Journal, Barron's* and the *Financial Times*. We timed speaking engagements around when those articles would appear so we could amplify the message. Each time we had an interview or a speaking opportunity, we involved the character that could best reach that stakeholder. We put our CEO in front of Bloomberg for the business stakeholder, while our founder spoke with *CSO* magazine to reach the technical stakeholders.

Through it all we made sure that the right character told the right story. It wouldn't have made sense for Dave to talk about our products; he was our corporate growth guy and his charisma was perfect for convincing stakeholders we were on the right track for success. Ashar's tone is very different – his engineering background meant he needed to talk about our products and the innovation behind them, not our commitment to partners. We made sure every time our story was told, the right person was telling it.

### The FireEye Book: Chapter 4

### Timing is everything

With the IPO looming, we knew we needed to make sure the market was receptive. We put far more attention on the company's growth just before we went public to ensure the market saw us as viable and robust. For instance, every time Dave DeWalt spoke, he hit the same message: he intended to focus on growth instead of profitability, and hire as many people as it took to drive that expansion. It was up to him to make sure that people understood our business model and why we were growing so quickly, so the market felt comfortable buying our stock.

And they did. Our stock was offered to the public for the first time on 20 September 2013. We priced roughly 15 million shares at $20 each that Friday, and by the end of the first day, shares were trading at $36.00. We'd told the story of FireEye convincingly, and our stakeholder was hooked.

### The FireEye Book: Chapter 5

### Lessons learned

There is plenty to be learned about how the communications plan for FireEye positioned us for success in the marketplace. Starting with our storyline and developing our cast of characters, we carefully wrote the script for our company. We had to tell the story in order, though, and we learned that the hard way.

For example, we got very excited to tell the market about a new product – the Multi-Vector Virtual Execution, or MVX, engine. At the heart of our *Innovation* pillar, this tool lets our customers identify and confirm a cyber breach while blocking it from going

*(Continued)*

any further. As you can imagine, we are very proud of this technology and couldn't wait to tell the market about our shiny new tool that could stop an advanced attack. But we were so excited about our shiny new tool that we forgot to tell the market it needed our shiny new tool. In other words, we told the story out of order.

Once we realized that, we regrouped. We refined the message and shared it with everyone who would listen. We explained how cyber attacks don't happen overnight. They take careful planning and months of execution, with malware lingering in a network for an average of 205 days before it's detected – which means it's had ample time to carry out its mission of stealing data or passwords, spamming an inbox or crashing a system.

The MVX could change all of that by identifying and stopping an attack. And once we made sure people understood the problem, they were ready to hear about the solution we had to offer them. Then, and only then, did our stakeholders respond to just how revolutionary this technology was. And they embraced our shiny new tool with open arms.

Our lesson was clear: we needed to listen to the market and change our story accordingly. We didn't change the main pillars or the cast of characters. That all stayed the same; only the narrative needed to change. This story was real-time and dynamic, and it had to evolve based on the feedback we were getting. We changed the narrative to fit our story.

### The FireEye Book: Chapter 6

### Conclusion

The FireEye story continues today and our communications framework allows us to continue to tell it dynamically. The structure we built – based on the pillars of *Growth, Innovation* and *Ecosystem* – allowed us to tell our story coherently while still letting us tie it all together.

My FireEye experience has taught me many things. At the top of that list are these lessons:

- Innovate, but make sure the market understands why they need your product
- Grow, but help the market see growth as a positive
- Listen to the feedback you get, and adjust accordingly
- See your mistakes as an opportunity to get it right next time
- Change the pages to fit your story.

Our story is still being written. I hope our script helps you write yours.

### About FireEye

A standout within the world of cyber security, FireEye leads the industry in detecting and preventing network threats to enterprises and governments across the globe. FireEye has over 3700 customers across 67 countries, including 675 of the Forbes Global 2000.

The FireEye Global Communications team fits under the Corporate Marketing Officer's domain. Corporate Communications lead all the marketing communications activities including: PR & AR, Internal Communications, Social Media, Channel Communications, Government/Public Affairs Communications and Product Communications.

# A NEW THEORY FOR CORPORATE STRATEGIC COMMUNICATION

This chapter provides an analysis of the theories that drive corporate communication. It looks at how corporate reputation, image and brand connect and how all three are underpinned by effective corporate strategic communication. It argues that most old school corporate strategic communications are imbued with rhetoric and act in a one-way asymmetrical sense without considering the requirements of the location of the corporate entity in society. Part of the explanation for the global clash between gas exploration/ supply corporations and community activist groups lies in the corporate argument that they have obtained a *legislative* licence to operate. Had they developed wider stakeholder relationships the requirement for a *social* licence to operate may have never surfaced. This chapter proposes a new theory for corporate strategic communication.

## THEORY DRIVES CORPORATE STRATEGIC COMMUNICATION PRACTICE

Corporate strategic communication is not the same as organizational communication. Contemporary organizational communication theory has its bases in the works of Frederick Taylor and Max Weber, among others, which focused upon the internal aspects of how organizations were structured relative to their communication flows. Taylor worked on the idea that efficiency could be achieved through technology while Weber asserted that social science might play an overarching role in making workers happier and thus more productive. Essentially, organizational communication theories focused on labour and productivity.

A theory that embodies corporate strategic communication must take a combined view – external and internal. It must answer questions of perception as well as questions of application. Thus we are confronted by the opportunity to invent a theory that at once takes into account conceptual and operational aspects of communication within and without the corporate entity. Sometimes there is confusion between concepts. We are not referring here to the idea of a corporate culture. A finance director for a large multinational cosmetics company remarked that during interviews for accountancy positions within the firm he was always asked one question by all candidates: what is the culture of the company? He says this is an impossible question to answer because company culture is not something that is set out and mandated within the theories or models that can be attributed to corporations (author interview 2016).

The tendency of most books and articles about corporate communication is to avoid a determination of theory and to concentrate on the practical explanations of what corporations engage in. Some include the word 'theory' in their titles (for example, Cornelissen,

2014) but use it interchangeably with other words such as 'definition' and 'scope'. We have defined corporate strategic communication in the Introduction and we will provide a broader grasp of scope in the following chapters. But before we can advance our praxis we need to create a *general social and economic theory of corporate strategic communication*. It must be socially bound because we are most interested in the corporation as part of the structure of society. It must be economically supportive because national economies are underpinned by corporate activity. We have chosen to follow Graeme Snooks in framing a theory of corporate strategic communication. But before we frame our theory we need to present a brief overview of what theory actually is. A former director of communication for the United Nations, Shashi Tharoor, had a favourite and oft repeated story about a Frenchman and an American, both Security Council diplomats, who were in conversation. They were speaking about a security problem to which the American responded by saying, 'I know how we can solve it, we can do this and this and this'. The Frenchman replied enthusiastically, 'Yes, yes, that will work in practice. But will it work in theory?' Tharoor's image of the American practitioner and the French theorist has its roots in the relationships those countries have shared for the past three hundred years. Nothing appears to have changed. America is a 'can-do' country, evinced contemporarily by Barack Obama's political campaign communication slogan 'Yes We Can'. France, on the other hand, has always assumed a left-of-centre theoretical discourse before action can be taken. This is an extreme view of course. Not all American social or economic activity is action first. It has yet to create a national health scheme although it has been on the political agenda for many years. And French action through NATO is action first, theory later.

So what is theory? And is it important? Tharoor's American diplomat thinks not – action is the byword of success. The *Oxford English Dictionary* (*OED*) describes theory as (1) the knowledge or exposition of the general principles or methods of an art or science, especially as distinguished from the practice of it; (2) a system of ideas or statements explaining something, especially one based on general principles independent of the things to be explained; a hypothesis that has been confirmed or established by observation or experiment and is accepted as accounting for known facts; (3) a mental scheme of something to be done, or of a way of doing something; a systematic statement of rules or principles to be followed; and (4) the formulation of abstract knowledge or speculative thought; systematic conception of something. A theorist it concludes is one who is an expert in the theory (as opposed to the practice) of a subject. Most academics teaching in universities are theorists. This is not an indictment rather it is a reality; academic work is axiomatically theoretical. Theoretical is therefore something that is of the nature of or consisting in theory rather than practice; existing only in theory; ideal; hypothetical. It is from this point that we can begin to build our general social and economic theory of corporate strategic communication. In later chapters we will apply what we have built. We will then be in a position to determine if the exposition of the general principles we have framed can be confirmed by both observation and experiment. We will then see if it can be accepted as accounting for known facts.

## A THEORY OF CORPORATE STRATEGIC COMMUNICATION

The 2014 cinema film, *The Theory of Everything*, is a biographical story of the life of theoretical physicist Stephen Hawking. It is a romantic drama that intertwines Hawking's life and work. In real life Hawking set forth a theory of cosmology by combining the general theory of relativity with quantum mechanics. A number of earlier films and television series had been made using the theorist to underpin their drama and comedy. One such television series was *The Big Bang Theory* which captured the imagination of its audience by representing some nerdy young scientist who had no social or romantic skills. One of the characters, Howard Wolowitz (played by Simon Helberg), did not have a Ph.D. He had a masters from MIT and with this he was able to overcome the derogation heaped on him by Sheldon Cooper (played by Jim Parsons) because Howard's engineering degree allowed him to actually make things that got sent into space while his friend Sheldon (a theoretical physicist researching quantum mechanics and string theory) played with nothing more than abstract concepts.

Communication has been argued as art and science, as a combination of both, as one or the other. But it is not for us to evaluate it as fitting into either space. Corporations act in a scientific way. They employ data in quantitative measure to determine their objectives and outcomes. They measure their success against profit – a quantitative value. Societies measure their success qualitatively. Communication values can be measured as either quantitative or qualitative. Or a mix of both.

The general social and economic theory of corporate strategic communication we have conceptualized is self-sustaining – it generates strategic demand. Following Snooks' dynamic-strategy model, it anticipates fluctuations across different timescales of socio-economic activity: short run, medium run and long run. It anticipates human behaviour within a competitive global environment and an orthodox static economic environment. At the same time it must apprehend the external forces which impact upon the core competences of its operational activities. While it creates a discourse around the distribution of goods and services it must also anticipate a non-static environment – one with potential financial, economic or social turning points. The significance of the parallel in the theory – the impact of exogenous and endogenous variables – allows the corporate entity flexibility when a turning point changes rational thought to irrational, or irrational to rational.

General principles of the corporate strategic communication theory are that:

1 it may be either two-way symmetrical or two-way asymmetrical;
2 it seeks to communicate demand maximization;
3 it seeks to differentiate competitive and comparative advantages;
4 it seeks to maximize expectations, either long run or short run;
5 the scale of investment in the strategy will be determined by the expected outcomes;
6 corporate strategic communication will act as an advancer in any speculative activity undertaken by a corporate entity; and
7 speculative activity must be underpinned by dynamic confidence in the relevant socioeconomic system.

As Snooks outlined in his theory of longrun dynamics, competing societal groups are 'strategic groups not class groups' (Snooks, 1998, p. 18). This is crucial for corporate entities to grasp if they are to communicate strategically with stakeholders and others. Snooks identifies three groups which he says 'cut across Marx's class groups' (Snooks, 1998, p. 18):

1 strategists (profit-seekers);
2 non-strategists (employees and dependents); and
3 anti-strategists (rent-seekers).

He does not differentiate anti-strategists as either conservative or radical, a point that we will return to below when we discuss activist groups in their opposition to corporate activity.

A theory of corporate strategic communication requires an understanding of the principles of investment. Corporations exist because individuals and collectives provide them with the capital to do what they set out to do. The object is not benefactory; it is the pursuit of yield against investment. Snooks argues there is no dynamic theory to explain why investors invest; there is 'no endogenous driving force' (Snooks, 1998, p. 45). Part of the explanation of why investors invest is tied inexorably to corporate strategic communication. Human nature is such that consumption has been turned into a form, surrounded as it is by design and advertising, that approaches art. The other part is the attractiveness of the perception of great wealth that has been generated by the invention of global technology. Corporations emerge and invent technology-based products and services that become overnight sensations. Google (USA), Tencent (China), Facebook (USA), Baidu (China), LinkedIn (USA), Box (USA) and Yandex (Russia) are among the most valuable Internet and digital media companies in the world. They make computing and communications companies such as Apple, Samsung and Microsoft look like they emerged from Jurassic Park. The profit from computer corporations comes from products that still need to be built; they need components that are assembled and distributed. They are time-consuming. Keep in mind that the Internet and digital tech companies would not exist if the computer companies did not make boxes from which they could launch. But investment does not consider such rationalities. Investors seek to maximize profits in the short term. Global market shocks, natural disasters and man-made disasters all account for a shorter investor attention span and partly account for the extraordinary rise in popularity of Internet stocks. The other part of the calculus of the question of investment lies with the sophistication of corporate communication.

## CORPORATE RIB: TO LIVE WITH OR LIVE WITHOUT

Corporations communicate strategically, as we have noted above, so that they gain a competitive advantage. A triangulation of reputation, image and brand (RIB) is meant to provide a competitive edge. While this triangulation is laudable it does not explain the disposition of some investors to seek short-term gain while others go with the longer term and sink their capital into readily identifiable, perceptibly longer term corporate products and services. A bank will attempt to capture your savings and loans by highlighting its long-term existence and reputation. A car maker will use image to get you to drive away (on-road costs included) in its latest all-wheel-drive hatch, while a shoemaker or watchmaker will get you to wear their latest designs based solely (no pun intended) upon the brand (think Jimmy Choo). The communicative strategy of the corporation overarches all three tactics. We argue that the framing of reputation, image and branding is a tactic within a corporate strategy rather than independent models or instruments. This argument is underpinned by the fact that elements of all three come in to play as agents of strategy at some time or other in the life cycle of corporate communication but only as tactical instruments, not as stand-alone entities. Nonetheless we will look more closely at all three independently and attempt to identify the artefacts of a corporate communication with which they fit.

## Reputation

The *OED* defines reputation as (1) the condition or fact of being highly regarded or esteemed; distinction, respect, fame; (2) the general opinion or estimate of a person's character, behaviour etc; the relative esteem in which a person or thing is held; (3) the honour, credit or good name of a person or thing; and (4) the fame, credit, or notoriety of being, doing or possessing something. All four of these definitions can be applied to corporate entities. The *OED* is silent on the meaning relative to a corporation. We often hear companies or businesses spoken of as being reputable. The *OED* definition of reputable is having a good reputation, of good repute, honoured, respectable. So a good reputation might lead to a corporation being spoken of in positive terms as reputable. Can a corporation adopt a meaning that has traditionally been aligned with individuals? Public relations firms and business consultants like to attempt to conflate corporate and reputation. McKinsey, a consulting firm, argues that economic crises such as the GFC create the need for corporations to look to their reputations more so than when economies are in equilibrium (Bonini, Court and Marchi, 2009). The reputational challenge, they suggest, is more serious than usual with 'the perception that some companies in certain sectors [...] have violated their social contract with consumers, shareholders, regulators, and taxpayers' (Bonini, Court and Marchi, 2009). A consequence of reduced reputation, they suggest, was the need for action rather than 'spin' to rebuild. *Business dictionary.com* suggests corporate reputation is the 'collective assessments of a corporation's past actions and the ability of the company to deliver improving business results to multiple stockholders over time'. It does not indicate over what timescale such delivery might take place, though we suspect it may be the short run. The *Financial Times Lexicon* defines corporate reputation as 'the observer's collective judgements of a corporation based on assessments of financial, social and environmental impacts attributed to the corporation over time'. Reputation also adheres to corporate products and services that are meant to behave consistently over time – food, for example. We have an expectation that when we buy a 'home product' container of cayenne pepper from Carrefour (France), Tesco (UK), Lidl (Germany), Coles (Australia), Spar (the Netherlands) or Aeon (Japan), we will get the same product each time we buy it. It will not differ in taste, colour or quality. The reputation of the retailer pivots around consistency in quality and price. We may not feel the same about fresh food from these retailers. Consistency may vary from month to month. The retailers will advocate on behalf of their fresh products with advertising that points out seasonal differences, sourcing differences (different countries at different times of the year) and time it takes to get the products to market. Fruit may not look the same each time you go to buy it. Or it may not feel the same. Fish may not have brightness of eye. We differentiate home-labelled products so that we can get a sense of reputation rather than brand.

A corporation can accumulate value through reputation. Reputable activities are consistent with continued support from investors and customers.

## Image

Image has a number of meanings with particular reference to humans or things in representative form. In corporate terms image is the embodiment of a quality or characteristic perceived by its publics. It is interlinked with the idea of a favourable reputation. Reputation is achieved through the internalization of action; image is cultivated through the externalization of reputation. When we think of *image* we imagine. Corporations use specific colours and text in advertising and communication that are designed to have us imagine products and services in specific ways and to consistently seek out those imaginations every time we consume or invest. McDonald's Golden Arches logo is probably one of the most ubiquitous images in the corporate world. It shines above motorways and byways throughout towns and cities across the world. It has been described as a cultural icon and it has been in place since the early 1960s. The current iteration was designed in Germany in 2003 along with the catchline '*Ich liebe es*' which soon became '*I'm lovin' it*' in English-speaking countries.

### Brand

A corporate brand is an identifier that has value. It was once believed that the Coca-Cola logo was the most highly valued in the world. There are a number of competing models of brand value. They value the Coca-Cola brand at around $US70 billion, Apple between $US33 billion and $US180 billion, McDonald's $US35 billion and Nike $US15 billion. The word 'brand' comes from an alternative use, whereby a mark of some description was made to identify something, especially cattle, which generally have a similar appearance. The *OED* describes brand in this sense as being synonymous with impressing indelibly on memory, which is in keeping with our corporate image identifier. A 'brand image' it defines as being the 'assumed impression of a product in the minds of potential consumers'.

## COLLATERAL THAT SUPPORTS THE CORPORATE RIB

Corporations invest directly and indirectly in the sustainability of reputation, image and brand. Direct investment includes a hierarchy of published and broadcast matter with the glossy annual report at the top. Direct investment is controlled while indirect investment might be called uncontrolled collateral. It is therefore understandable that corporations tend to invest more in controlled collateral simply because they control the message and they control the medium. Indirect investment is most often the how, why and when a company appears in the media.

Controlled collateral is everything a corporation publishes, broadcasts or otherwise disseminates using internal and external mechanisms. Controlled collateral is *rhetorical*; a corporation is not in the business of creating damaging narratives. All communicative matter emanating from the corporation is framed in accordance with a core narrative. We will look more closely at some examples below. Uncontrolled collateral is dependent upon exogenous stakeholders such as news media, governments, activists and competitors. These stakeholders act in either a *braking capacity* or an *empowerment capacity* – the taxonomies of which we will also discuss in detail in Chapter 5. A braking capacity is a metaphor that is the same as a car when it brakes. Exogenous stakeholders can put the brakes on a corporate activity in a number of ways – news media publish and broadcast stories with negative angles; governments create proscriptive legislation; activists blockade sites and competitors disseminate false information. None of these is new. As we have seen above all four elements attempted to put the brakes on the South Sea Company as it expanded under the pressure of its own hot air bubble. Contemporaneously all four attempted to put the brakes on Greece in mid 2015 as it expanded its spending bubble, with the addition of a fifth column in the shape of the EU.

## THE ANNUAL REPORT

A corporate annual report sits at the apex of corporate strategic communication. It is the prime artefact in a corporate communication strategy and as such its tactical representation and content drives the corporate narrative. It is all too often underestimated. If a corporation lives in a legislative environment with mandatory reporting structures then the annual report is the instrument of delivery. In these circumstances it is sometimes perceived to be just that, a vehicle that fulfils a corporate legislative requirement that a corporation behaves in an ordinary fashion. When a corporation grasps the significance of the annual report as the narrative driver, its existence is extraordinary.

An annual report is a progress report to stakeholders but it is also:

1  a controlled public relations tactic;
2  a category of organizational media;
3  a process as much as a publication (a comprehensive review);
4  an information tool to advise community and business of activities and results;
5  a record of highlights and challenges; and
6  required by law of public companies.

It can be a simple statement of financial details and corporate executives or it can be a glossy magazine-style publication either in hard copy or online. Most corporations today publish smaller runs in hard copy and direct stakeholders and stakeseekers to their online presence.

A glossy magazine style of report is a corporation's most expensive written contract with its stakeholders. It provides requisite information, affirms investor loyalty, attracts new investors, enhances the corporate reputation and forms the basis of other relationships, general corporate information and the marketing platform. It requires the serious input of two key corporate people: the chief communication director and the chief financial director. The financial director provides the content and the communication director provides the tone.

The annual report includes sections devoted to:

1  key result areas;
2  key performance indicators;
3  strategic direction; and
4  divisional/operational lines.

Its overall tone ought to be one of corporate vigour although this is sometimes overreached and reports turn into rhetorical mudheaps. The annual report ought to begin with a chairman's or chief executive's report which could be used to present a strong leadership image or to attack government legislation. A close reading of an annual report will reveal a number of issues; it may reveal a poorer than anticipated financial year or an embarrassing internal issue. Fortunately for most corporations stakeholders other than those who hold shares rarely read the detail of the annual report.

An annual report should have embedded within it the goals and objectives of the corporation. It should present a balanced objective picture and avoid misleading or false information, even by implication. It should reflect stakeholder opinion.

While the annual report is considered an advocacy artefact the complexity of its financial statements is problematical. If the statement by the annual report's auditors (following the financial information) represents full disclosure of the accuracy of the financial details (auditors cannot, or should not, participate in misrepresentation), they cannot be considered advocates. If stakeholders have an interest in accurate information regarding a corporation and its activities, they must consider the halves of an annual report. The first half – let's call it the narrative section – is an engagement in advocacy to persuade and influence rather than a representation of full disclosure. The second half, the financial statement, is the representation of full disclosure of corporate investment, income and profit. Published financials are audited and signed off by registered company accountants. Sometimes these accountants fail to take their fiduciary duty seriously. The pursuit of a deeper explanation of this lies outside the framework of this book. We should point out, however, that corporate financial auditors are generally not responsible for detecting fraud from their audit of a company's accounts. PricewaterhouseCoopers (PwC), a consulting company, notes that corporate fraud is a persistent fact of business life across all industries. It argues fraud and poor governance are 'serious risks for all organizations [and] dishonest behaviour [...] undermines profits, operating efficiencies and reliability [and] can seriously damage an organization's reputation' (www.pwc.com.au).

As we will see when we come to Chapter 7, social influence and rhetorical practices are powerful *narrative disruptors* that sometimes hold sway over the actions of corporate reporting. This raises the question of populism and populist culture and whether they are actively embedded in an annual report. If an annual report is a public document, which we will assume it is because it is publicly available, does the rhetoric of its narrative (its text and images) support an argument for wider populist meaning? In other words, should a corporation be using its annual report to seek to appeal to stakeholders across universal grounds or is it a reflection of the corporation as a financial entity only? The pressure on a corporation to make appeals on universal grounds is substantial. If a year's activities do not stack up that way then there is every possibility that the annual report may misrepresent what really went on. We are interested here in learning to read the annual report and to use it as our first point of reference in our reverse engineering. We will then move on to examine briefly some uncontrolled collateral.

## Analysing the annual report

Let's now turn to how we might analyse an annual report and see what questions we need to answer.

- Are corporate goals and objectives embedded in our chosen annual report?
- Does the annual report, as a tactic, have a good 'fit' with the strategies?
- Is the annual report a balanced, objective presentation; does it avoid misleading implications?
- How does the annual report affect stakeholder opinion?
- If stakeholder publics have an interest in accurate information regarding the investments they are invited to make can we consider the first half of the annual report to be

an engagement in advocacy to change public opinion rather than a representation of full disclosure?

- If the annual report is a public document does the rhetoric embedded in its text and images contribute to diffuse populist meaning or understanding?

Annual reports form the basis of the relationship between a public company and its stakeholders. Many other organizations choose to report issues and activities annually, without legal obligation, as part of their *corporate social responsibility*. An annual report is a progress report and as such it is a process as much as it is a publication because it provides a comprehensive review of issues and activities. It is different to other written tactics because it is not information about what is happening in the present or what is going to happen in the future. It is a summary of what has already happened. It might include projections by senior management of what it thinks may happen in the future, given certain business, social and political conditions, but the body of the report is historical. It provides a historic record of the highlights and challenges that faced the organization during the preceding year (Stanton, 2007). The annual report is the benchmark communicative instrument of the corporation but it is equally the core artefact for our discovery through reverse engineering.

The accuracy of the annual report is paramount, for public companies especially, because they are scrutinized by more than one stakeholder group. Annual reports are subdivided into sections to convey specific information. Subdivisions include:

- key result areas
- key performance indicators
- strategic direction
- divisional operational lines
- management presentation
- corporate direction and performance
- a Chairman's report.

The subdivisions on financial performance require no understanding of prose. They are usually arithmetical. The prose subdivision of the report appears towards the front. It includes information on the organization's:

- corporate social responsibility
- environmental responsibility
- corporate governance
- promotion of equal opportunity
- present and future sustainability.

Corporate goals and objectives are embedded in the prose. When reading an annual report, a stakeholder will identify and link the reading to known strategies. Successful prose is achieved if the writer assumes they are the stakeholder most interested in the material.

The section on corporate social responsibility should begin with a description of what it is to be socially responsible. It must avoid jargon but present the material so that it has veracity. The question to ask at this point is what is corporate social responsibility? Once that has been defined as the first part of the section, the middle section should reflect what socially responsible objectives the corporation has achieved and what it is intending to achieve.

The next section about environmental responsibility tends to illuminate conflict rather than demonstrate the embedding of objectives. For this section to be effective and to have resonance with stakeholders it must demonstrate that the environmental issues are part of the corporation rather than exogenous to it.

A section on corporate governance requires images that represent the language of *leadership*, whereas environmental responsibility and social responsibility both require the language of *inclusion*. The language of leadership in a corporate governance section might also invoke inclusion.

In theory we ought to be able to examine any annual report and find within it the same or similar information. It may be presented in slightly different forms to what we have outlined above. Let's look at a couple for comparison.

## Toyota Motor Corporation

The question for any corporation concerns what to include and what to omit from an annual report. We might assume that the larger and more diverse the company, the more information is omitted. Given the diffuse nature of the World Wide Web, corporate information can be published in almost unlimited quantities. But stakeholders, especially potential investors and existing investors, do not have all day to spend trawling around the web digging into layers and layers of stuff that might not be relevant to them. We can apply specific attributes of publics to shareholders (we will discuss these attributes in detail in the following chapter); high goal compatibility with the corporation; actively seek information; and high involvement (Zaltman and Duncan, 1977). Despite its somewhat culturally unusual tagline – 'aiming to achieve sustainable growth and to bring smiles' (Toyota, 2014) – the design and content of the Toyota annual report for 2014 provided a classic example of what a shareholder might expect to receive from the company in which the shareholder was planning to continue to invest.

The report included a message from the president; an overview of the four business units of the company; a section on history and the future of the company; a message from the executive vice president responsible for accounting including consolidated performance highlights; a review of operations, management and corporate information; financial information; and investor information. The report represented leadership and inclusion. The text of the message from the president, Akio Toyoda, demonstrated inclusion in the first sentence: 'First I would like to extend my sincere gratitude for your continued support and understanding.' It was here, at the start, that the message was clear and unambiguous. Mr Toyoda revealed immediately that since the GFC the company had had its ups and downs but the 'strengths of its management practices and culture' had seen it through the tough times and the company was now 'in a position to take a definitive step forward toward sustainable growth'. Throughout the report the word 'culture' appeared eight times. 'Sustainable' appeared thirty times.

Mr Toyoda spoke, too, of an unprecedented milestone – the sale of 10 million vehicles worldwide. He pointed to the future as the ability of the company to grow 'in the face of adversity'. The word 'adversity' appeared three times. Mr Toyoda spoke of the company's pursuit of 'bold innovation and [...] aggressive forward-looking investments'. 'Innovation' appeared throughout the report thirty-two times while investment(s) appeared thirty-four times. Other equally emotive and relevant words that appeared in Mr Toyoda's message were sprinkled liberally throughout the Report: 'environment(al)' (61), 'technologies' (52), 'growth' (44) and 'resources' (21). Words we might have expected to see in larger quantities were 'communities' (12) and 'ownership' (4). 'Profit' or 'profitability' appeared forty-one times while stakeholders appeared four times and strategy six. Of most relevance to us, which we will pursue in further reports, the word 'society' appeared a total of forty-two times. In order of appearance, the words we might use as our baseline and those we may look for in our forthcoming analysis of a variety of annual report narratives were:

| | |
|---|---|
| Environment | 61 |
| Global | 53 |
| Technologies | 52 |
| Growth | 44 |
| Society | 42 |
| Future | 42 |
| Profit | 41 |
| Investment | 34 |
| Competitive(ness) | 34 |
| Innovation | 32 |
| Sustainable | 30 |
| Brand | 28 |
| Resources | 21 |
| Communities | 12 |
| Image | 10 |
| Expectations | 9 |
| Culture | 8 |
| Strategy | 6 |
| Ownership | 4 |
| Adversity | 3 |
| Reputation | 0 |
| Leadership | 0 |

**Figure 3.1**  Key words in the analysis of the Toyota annual report narrative

Given the nature of the core business of Toyota – the manufacture of vehicles and engines – it is not surprising the most used word is 'environment'. It appeared sixty-one times in sixty-eight pages. 'Global', 'technologies' and 'growth' were also anticipated given Toyota's worldwide markets. For our purposes it was 'society' at number five in the list with forty-two mentions that is of equal interest.

One section of the report aligned the company more distinctly with society and humans than the actual words employed. The section was entitled 'Toyota's DNA Will Endure for the Next 100 Years'. In this section it reflected upon its 75-year history and created a platform to launch its next 100 years. It alluded to an alignment with society and humans by invoking the idea that the company has DNA. Deoxyribonucleic acid is a molecule that contains biological information or hereditary matter in humans and other organisms. We can assume Toyota was attempting to create a powerful metaphor with 'drawing on our corporate DNA, we will continue to innovate and ensure that tomorrow's Toyota is even better than today's'. As such it may also align with Zaltman and Zaltman's (2008) idea of deep metaphors. Deep metaphors, Zaltman and Zaltman argue, are frames of reference that live deep within us and orient our lives. They are universal and subconscious but there are not many of them. This is why they are crucial to brand awareness and image development for a corporation. Brand loyalty, argue Zaltman and Zaltman, is developed in a consumer by product consistency and emotional resonance (Zaltman and Zaltman, 2008). In its special feature section with its links to human biology Toyota attempted to draw on the deep metaphor of connection (Olson Zaltman, 2015) and its associated identification of inclusion by suggesting the company is the same as humans – it has DNA and it will therefore behave in a rational and conscious manner within the society in which it lives.[1] It is worth quoting the first few sentences of the special feature section for the interpretation we might make of the deep metaphor and how it relates to our consciousness when we think about buying a car:

> With the goal of making ever-better cars, the Toyota Global Vision is an articulation of the kind of company we want to be. It is based on shared values and a spirit of monozukuri (conscientious manufacturing) passed down since our foundation and embodied in the core values of Sakichi Toyoda, the Guiding Principles at Toyota, and the Toyota Way. We use the image of a tree to illustrate our vision: the roots are our shared values; the ongoing upward growth of its branches represents our efforts to expand business; the fruit represents making ever-better cars and enriching lives and local communities; and the trunk is our stable base of business. As the trunk of the tree grows bigger and stronger, it is able to support more branches—the creation of ever-better cars. This is the trajectory that puts Toyota on the path toward sustainable growth. Of all the components of our vision, building ever-better cars takes priority. We want to deliver products and services that surprise and excite our customers. We want to be a company that puts smiles on faces—and keeps them there.
>
> (Toyota, 2014)

Toyota not only connected to us as humans by suggesting there was such a thing as corporate DNA but added an additional vector – the image of the company as a living organism such as a tree. The Special Feature ran to thirteen pages concluding with similar sentiments:

> Toyota has embarked on a path of embracing new values and achieving sustainable growth over the next 10 years and 100 years. In making tomorrow's Toyota even better than today's, we are focusing on the following three areas. The first is initiatives for the future that focus on pursuing innovation. We aim to embrace new values centered on

---

[1] It is also relevant to Durkheim's term *organic solidarity* as a societal reference point (Durkheim, 1964).

*the future and people. This is a departure from our previous approach, which centered on cars. Toyota hopes that its products and services will change people's lives for the better. The second is to cultivate an adventurous spirit as we enter new fields. Leaving our comfort zone, we aim to create new industries and businesses by taking in the best ideas and knowledge around the world. The third is to ensure that Toyota plays an ever more essential role in society through its efforts to find solutions to social problems. We aim to build a win-win relationship between Toyota and society, and to deepen this relationship as we create shared values together.*

(Toyota, 2014)

Toyota's annual report, along with that published by Shell, which we will examine below, are the bases of our analysis of the most important communication instruments within the corporate sphere. They are the first and most important engagement a corporation can make with the public sphere, which we will discuss in detail in Chapters 7 and 10.

## Royal Dutch Shell

The prospect of the Shell 2014 annual report (Royal Dutch Shell, 2014) was different to Toyota. Its opening image was of an employee whereas Toyota chose to adorn its outside front cover with a product. While Toyota generated content across sixty-eight pages, Shell did so in no less than two hundred pages. Shell's first ninety-nine pages were absorbed with strategy and corporate governance issues; the remaining hundred explained its financial position, provided shareholder information and disclosed US Securities Exchange information.

As with the Toyota report, the chairman's message from Jorma Ollila set the scene for the Shell annual report. The one-page statement – entitled 'Strategic Report' and including three subheadings: 'Robust Strategy', 'Climate Change' and 'Innovation and Innovators' – contained the words and phrases 'invest', 'innovation', 'technology', 'economic environment', 'long-term view', 'shareholders, competitive', 'renewable energy', 'future demand', 'climate change', 'sectors of society', 'forward-thinking' and 'global stage'. The tone of the chairman's message was different to that of Toyota. It was less leadership-oriented and more combative; less inclusive, more defensive. There was no attempt to lock into a deep metaphor nor to engage shareholders with anything more than the strategic position of the company as it existed at that point in time. The uncertainty of the market for energy was the prime focus of the message. It adopted a negative posture, citing slowing global growth, a decline in crude oil prices and the need for government support for carbon pricing as markers that were making the economic environment unattractive. The Chairman's Message was followed immediately by the eponymously entitled chief executive officer's review. CEO Ben van Beurden used a more positive tone, almost as a counterpoint to the chairman. Words and phrases included 'key priorities', 'financial performance', 'enhanced capital efficiency', 'strong project delivery', 'prudent investment strategy', 'competitive performance', 'commitment to shareholder returns', 'improved operational performance', 'organic capital investment', 'economically-sound investments', 'future growth opportunities', 'energy efficiency', 'pursuit of efficiency' and 'secure our leadership role'. It is more difficult to extract specific words from the Shell report because they were mostly run together as clichés – 'come a long way', 'position of strength', 'work to be done', 'remain cautious', 'curb spending', 'tackle climate change', 'making tough choices', 'stepping up our drive'. This creates a difficulty in finding single words that we could use as a baseline for our analysis.

Following the CEO was a 'Business Overview' which began with a few paragraphs of history and company activities. It included some tables and graphs and defined its reporting activities as 'upstream', 'downstream' and 'corporate'. Due to the risk-based nature of the business of energy production Shell then provided four pages of information on 'Risk Factors'. Risks, the company argued, should be considered by investors. The company set out the risks in an interesting fashion. It was not inclusive but it represented a connection between the company and its shareholders.

A one-page 'Strategy and Outlook' section followed 'Risk'. Words used to describe this section included 'leader', 'responsible', 'balance', 'growth', 'competitive', 'investment', 'safety', 'environmental', 'social', 'technology', 'excellence', 'distinctive', 'longer-term', 'efficiency', 'customers', 'commitment', 'core', 'expertise', 'strengths', 'future'. This was a far more positive tone but it included a reductive caveat: 'The statements are [...] based on management's current expectations and certain material assumptions and accordingly involved risk and uncertainties.' An enormous amount of detail was included under this section heading: twenty-eight pages of data and text. There were no pictures.

Environment and Society were included under one heading which extended to five and a half pages, again, without pictures. Subheadings included 'Safety', 'Climate Change', 'Spills', 'Hydraulic Fracturing', 'Oil Sands', 'Exploration in Alaska', 'Water', 'Biofuels', 'Environmental Costs' and lastly, 'Neighbouring Communities and Human Rights'. The section began by stating:

> Our success in business depends on our ability to meet a range of environmental and social challenges. We must show we can operate safely and manage the effect our activities can have on neighbouring communities and society as a whole. If we fail to do this, we may incur liabilities or sanctions, lose business opportunities, harm our reputation or our licence to operate may be impacted.
>
> (Royal Dutch Shell, 2014)

There was nothing to indicate whether the licence was legislative or social. We will discuss this further in Chapter 8.

The tone of the text in this section was explanatory rather than inclusive. It was asymmetrical in its provision of information about hydraulic fracturing, oil sands extraction and spills. The information was broad-based and included explanations about the toxicity of the chemicals used in some activities. But the information was guarded. It was interwoven with statements about the legislative rules under which the company operated. It spoke to the need for,

> clear rules and expectations for how we engage with and respect communities that may be impacted by our operations' where 'major projects and facilities are required to have a social performance plan and an effective community feedback mechanism. This helps the business to understand the social context in which we plan to operate, identifies potential negative effects on the community and manages impacts. In addition, we have specific requirements intended to minimize our impact on indigenous peoples' traditional lifestyles and on handling involuntary resettlement.
>
> (Royal Dutch Shell, 2014)

A final part of the strategic section of the report was under the heading 'Our People' with subheadings 'Employee Overview', 'Employee Communication and Involvement', 'Diversity and Inclusion' and 'Employee Share Plan'. In this it referred to symmetrical work practices that involved dialogue between management and staff that included personal emails from the CEO, webcasts, online publications and team meetings. Under the sub-heading 'Diversity and Inclusion' it stated:

> We have a culture that embraces diversity and fosters inclusion. By embedding these principles in our operations, we have a better understanding of the needs of our varied customers, partners and stakeholders throughout the world and can benefit from a wider talent pool.
>
> (Royal Dutch Shell, 2014)

The strategy section was signed off by company secretary Michiel Brandjes. Then followed forty pages of information on governance including graphs outlining executive salaries. The final section on financials ran to eighty pages which would be a reasonable number of pages for one of the world's largest public companies. This section included tables and graphs but, again, no images or pictures.

We can see that the Shell report and the Toyota report differed in design. But both communicated information to stakeholders. It was not so much the design difference that held them apart, rather it was the tone of the presentation and the use of language that identified to whom they were pitching their reports. We will examine more closely below the way information presentation is communicated so that it is attractive to different stakeholders. For now we might state that the language used to attract energy investors was substantially different from the language used to attract automotive investors even though both corporations were faced with similar societal embedding – both are working with what might be considered redundant raw material: fossil fuel.

## MEDIA – TRADITIONAL AND NEW: TWEETING THE DETAILS

Corporations rely for their existence on a variety of stakeholders, most notably investors, but they also pin their reputations, images and brands on the exposure and treatment they receive in and from the media. Media has come to be synonymous with news and current affairs ('newscaff') in a variety of forms including published, broadcast and online. Some forms have moved tangentially, becoming social media and entertainment media. We are interested in how we might analyse media content to add value to our reverse engineering of corporate entities. We might note that neither Toyota nor Shell acknowledged the media in their annual reports – neither coverage of their activities nor their existence as corporate stakeholders, yet the media have the capacity to actively and consciously report subjectively on corporate activity across the globe. Corporations become agitated, for example, when a social media site such as Facebook engages in discourse on their activities. It does not take long for such discourse to 'go viral' – to spread across the world and to effectively put into the public sphere information that a corporation may not have wanted to become public. Traditional media sites such as radio and newspapers use social media as primary sources. Aggregation sites online gather news and bundle it for redistribution, a practice which allows all media to know instantaneously what is going on around the world. If Shell begins drilling for gas using hydraulic fracturing the site will be photographed with a cell phone by anyone nearby. The images will be uploaded to a social media site. They will then appear on the web pages of local newspapers, flow upstream to metropolitan newspaper sites and radio stations, and within hours appear on national television newscaff bulletins around the world in a hundred different languages. Such is the power and immediacy of social media that corporations frequently find themselves acting defensively where a moment before there was no signifier.

One of the more powerful social media sites is Twitter. Twitter was invented by an American, Jack Dorsey, in 2006. Considering its short lifespan it has made remarkable inroads into the space previously occupied by conventional media. Along with its fellow travellers, Facebook and LinkedIn, Twitter has become globally popular; it accounts for almost 2 billion search queries a day, has more than 500 million users worldwide and 1000 employees. Twitter has a variety of applications including the useful idea of creating a tag, known incorrectly as a hashtag (#), to generate conversations among like-minded individuals. Tags such as #agchat in which 'Tweeps' join an online conversation about agriculture or #healthchat where the discussions around health issues are beginning to replace talkback radio. An online Tweet chat is similar to talkback radio in that individuals can see what is being discussed but it has the advantage that contributors can tweet their own ideas and opinions at any time. Reality television and current affairs programmes seek to make a connection with their stakeholders by asking them to tweet to the hashtag of the programme. It is an interesting tactic designed to keep stakeholders engaged. While it is an interesting idea with a lot of potential to engage stakeholders in a new and dynamic setting, it advertently or not, creates a side issue. Because radio and television edit or censor the tweet, there is a tendency for those tweeting to 'ramp up' their tweets so that they will be chosen to appear on screen while a show is on air. This creates a competitive challenge among Tweeps which may not represent the actual value of Twitter as a source of information and news. But it is an interesting sideshow and it is equally interesting that allegedly serious and sophisticated media such as the BBC and CNN choose to employ such a populist tactic.

Corporations use Twitter for two reasons. First, they can get short messages to customers very quickly. If for example we 'follow' a Scottish fishing tackle shop, we will receive tweets from that store telling us about all sorts of things such as weather, where the fish are biting and when there are specials on tackle and gear. We may also follow a couple of fishing shows or some fishing guides in Canada and Scotland. We may also follow a few individuals who like to fish. We may even combine an interest in fishing with an interest in media and follow like-minded individuals such as Robson Green. Twitter is an ideal forum for creating and engaging with widespread opinions and ideas. For the uninitiated it may appear to be less friendly than wandering down to the corner store and coming away with an easy to read copy of *The Times*. In a sense it is more difficult because it requires a user to have access to technologies – mobile telephones or other portable devices – but once that hurdle is vaulted there is no limit to its uses.

The second reason corporations like Twitter is because it offers them instant access to what people are thinking about them. If a stream of tweets appears to rubbish a product or service, a corporation or business can set about correcting the problem before it gets out of hand. This only works if corporations know how to respond to this type of communication and there is no clear evidence that global corporations have taken it up substantially. Some businesses use it to drive 'traffic' to their websites while others do so to boost brand recognition. Fewer appear to use it to avert crises, though this is the most important test of the value of the medium.

Governments and politicians use Twitter for a variety of reasons, most frequently to applaud their own deeds or to attack the deeds of their opponents. There was evidence that Barack Obama, in campaigning for a second presidential term in the United States in 2012, employed Twitter to his advantage by using it to attack his opponent, Mitt Romney. The attacks were not direct but substantial enough to put doubt into the minds of the voters.

The media use Twitter effectively to drive followers to their own and their employers' sites where they can find expanded versions of the matter at hand.

Individuals, too, find Twitter to be of value. Individuals advocating an issue or event can use Twitter to 'crowdsource' solutions or to appeal to anonymous individuals to attend demonstrations or town hall-type meetings. Crowdsourcing is a problem-solving tactic where problems or issues are broadcast to unknown receivers to which they submit solutions and ideas. The broadcast nature of crowdsourcing was applied through traditional media such as radio and television and was therefore limited to how it was manipulated and disseminated by those in control of the medium's mechanics. Crowdsourcing on Twitter is a narrowcast model. But it is far more effective than the broadcast model because it targets its specific stakeholders who either follow the narrowcaster or follow a narrowcaster's hashtag. Crowdsourcing has been around for a long time. When the publishers of the OED were looking to acquire word meanings, they asked for volunteers to provide examples of how words might be used. They got more than 6 million submissions throughout the 70-year life of the project.[2] A crowdsourced favourite.

## CONCLUSION

A social and economic theory of corporate strategic communication is self-sustaining because it generates strategic demand. It anticipates fluctuations across different timescales of socioeconomic activity and it anticipates human behaviour within a competitive global environment and an orthodox static economic environment. It conceptualizes external forces which impact upon core competences of its operational activities. It anticipates a non-static environment – one with potential financial, economic or social turning points. It allows flexibility when a turning point changes rational thought to irrational, or irrational to rational.

The new theory may be either two-way symmetrical or two-way asymmetrical; communicate demand maximization; differentiate competitive and comparative advantages; maximize expectations; provide scale for investment determined by expected outcomes; and act as an advancer in any speculative activity which itself must be underpinned by dynamic confidence in a relevant socioeconomic system.

For corporate communication to be relevant and to gain a competitive advantage it must include reputation, image and brand.

Corporations invest in reputation, image and brand directly and indirectly. Direct investment is controlled while indirect investment is uncontrolled. Corporations tend to invest in controlled collateral because they control the message and they control the medium. Indirect investment is most often the how, why and when a company appears in the media.

---

[2] For a fine description of the OED process it is worth reading S. Winchester (1998). *The Surgeon of Crowthorne*, Viking.

## DISCUSSION QUESTIONS

1 How important is it for corporations to think about strategic communication theory?
2 What should corporations do to maximize their investments in corporate communication theory?

## CASE STUDY: The Absolut Company

### A tradition of innovation

*Elin Wibell, Senior Manager Corporate Communications*

Our vision within The Absolut Company is to drive our progression by being (eco-) conscious, egalitarian, entrepreneurial, collaborative and transparent. Our corporate communication strategy is to proactively lead our corporate culture, identity and corporate social responsibility through engaging communication and actions.

The corporate communication strategy is outlined by the corporate communication department. It is aligned with the leadership team and implemented throughout the organization. It aims to reinforce the corporate culture and spread our values both internally and externally starting from within. The brand teams have specific communication strategies for their brands.

### Our Corporate Social Responsibility Policy

The CSR vision: *Pernod Ricard contributes to a sustainable world through responsibility and conviviality.*

The CSR mission: *Pernod Ricard aims to act and to be recognized as the leader of responsibility in the alcohol industry through the company's commitment to promoting responsible drinking, protecting the planet, developing communities, engaging partners and empowering employees, all with an entrepreneurial spirit.*

Pernod Ricard believes there is no sustainable economic performance without social responsibility. Our CSR policy is a key strategic component, which is fully embedded in the Group's business; rooted in the Group's culture; and involves all employees.

### Responsible Drinking

Pernod Ricard has been strongly committed to responsible alcohol consumption since the 1970s. As ambassadors for our brands we have a big responsibility – one that we take seriously. We have partnered with global and local organizations on wide-ranging initiatives that aim to curb excessive and inappropriate alcohol consumption. Preventing alcohol consumption by minors and educating consumers about the dangers of drinking and driving are two of our biggest focuses. But we know that our 19,000 Pernod Ricard employees from eighty countries are our biggest stakeholder advocates. Each year we bring them together for our *ResponsibAll Day* event to share knowledge about encouraging responsible alcohol consumption.

## Partnerships and The Absolut Company

Since 2006 The Absolut Company has been a strong partner in a Swedish initiative called Prata Om Alcohol (POA) – Talk About Alcohol. This internationally recognized school programme teaches young people how to say no to alcohol and how to resist peer pressure. POA has reached an incredible 450,000 students and 10,000 teachers, and 75 per cent of Swedish secondary schools now use the programme. It has been so popular, in fact, that it has been adapted for use in driving schools, and has spread internationally to Denmark, Faroe Islands, Finland, Estonia and Lithuania.

Our preventative work with young people is a cornerstone of our outreach. And so our partnership with Fryshuset, one of the world's largest youth centres, was quite natural. The centre focuses on social inclusion and self-esteem. We are strong supporters of their no-alcohol dance party *The Wave*, and their *Event Evolution* programme that educates young people about organizing drug-free events.

We also support our home city of Stockholm. We are partners with a local organization called Nattskiftet (Night Shift), which brings together city officials, local police and the popular nightclub Trädgården to help people feel safer in Sweden's capital city at night. The organization has a group of trained volunteers who offer their company to bar-goers on their way home.

## Tools for Smart Drinking

The global market in which we operate is full of different regulations – both legislative and cultural – when it comes to alcohol consumption. That's why our strong code of ethics ensures that all of our marketing supports moderation and safety. We also strive to be helpful and informative, giving consumers of drinking age tips and tricks for drinking in moderation – and staying safe.

In 2014, Pernod Ricard launched the *Wise Drinking* app – a fun and interactive tool for nights out. It helps people track the number of drinks they've consumed, warns them if they've had a bit too much, and helps them call a friend at the end of the night for a ride home. The app is available in thirty languages, and is adapted to local regulations regarding alcohol consumption.

## Our Recognize the Moment Programme

absolut.com offers easy-to-use tips and tools to help people make better decisions when it comes to alcohol consumption. The programme is linked to the extensive cocktail database at absolutdrinks.com and our app Drinkspiration, where there are alcohol-free suggestions for those who want to abstain but still want to enjoy a tasty cocktail. We have also developed tools that help younger people make healthy choices when faced with peer pressure to drink. Our mobile application *Buddy Check* helps friends stay together during a night out. The app combines GPS functionality with timed buddy checks. Friends can message each other on the app. 'Geofencing' technology lets them know if anyone gets too far away from the group. It's a tool that makes it more fun and safer to stick together throughout the night.

*(Continued)*

*The Environment*: One source, one community, one superb vodka crafter in the village of Åhus. Every single drop of Absolut Vodka comes from One Source. Absolut Vodka is made from winter wheat from the rich fields of southern Sweden, pristine water from our local deep well and continuous distillation for the perfect character. Absolut Vodka is then blended, bottled and sealed in the village of Åhus to guarantee impeccable Swedish quality. Our passion for quality goes hand in hand with our commitment to our community. Most of our suppliers and partners are based in and around Åhus in southern Sweden. Because of our long-standing relationships we work together to improve our impact on our community. We call it continuous improvement. And our aim is high with a long-term vision of creating one sustainable, circular source. To get there it all comes down to the actions of passionate people who want to make a difference for the better.

## Our Stakeholders

*Absolut Farmers*: The fertile fields in southern Sweden are ideal for growing wheat with yields more than twice as high as the global average. With this efficiency, less land is required for the production of vodka. We use hardy winter wheat, sown during the fall, requiring less crop protection. We work with local farmers to reduce usage of fertilizers and evaluate this every year. All of our purchases of crops are made this way, with care for our precious soil and groundwater. We also contribute to *Project Skylark*, introducing non-cultivated patches among the farmland. This creates a healthy habitat for wildlife, such as the skylark and other birds, insects and plants.

*Absolut Partners*: Our bottles are manufactured at our nearest glassworks in Limmared in southern Sweden, which limits the need for transportation. The purity of our vodka is reflected in the bottle's clear glass. Our clear bottle is made from 40 per cent recycled glass, which reduces energy consumption in the otherwise energy-intensive glass manufacturing process. Glass is recyclable again and again, and glass scrap from production is, of course, used to make new Absolut bottles.

Our aim is to create beautiful and durable packaging, and we use eco-design methods to achieve this. We choose colours and production techniques that minimize energy use in the glass design process, avoiding repeated or extended treatments in the furnace. We also limit the number of details on each bottle that can prevent recycling, ensuring our glass bottles can be recycled. Production waste such as cardboard and plastic packaging is also recycled. Our strong Swedish heritage makes this a natural part of our culture, as Sweden is among the top countries in the world for recycling.

*Absolut Distillers*: We are proud that production at our facilities is climate-neutral. Thanks to extensive recycling of heat, change to district heating and renewable hydro-power, we have reduced energy consumption by 45 per cent and carbon emissions by 80 per cent per litre of vodka over the last ten years. Globally, we have the lowest energy consumption per unit among large distilleries. We offset the limited emissions we have not yet eliminated by supporting a reforestation project, where small-scale farmers in Mexico plant new trees with their crops. This is a long-term project that has been certified according to Plan Vivo, a framework that helps communities manage their natural resources more sustainably.

Our production process creates by-products that some see as waste, but what we see are resources. The stillage left over from wheat fermentation is sold as fodder for 40,000 cows and 250,000 pigs – every day. Some of the $CO_2$ emissions from fermentation are sold to other industries which use them for things like producing carbonated beverages. Re-using and recycling is about attitude – we even separate food scraps at our staff canteen to be used for biogas!

Innovative improvements are just one part of our environmental communication. Our day-to-day work is equally important. We keep track of all our resource consumption, emissions, waste and shipping, and find creative ways to improve our environmental performance. This daily check is known as *management systems* and our operations are certified to meet the ISO 14001 (Environmental Management Systems) and ISO 50001 (Energy Management Systems) standards.

Over the last decade, we have consistently reduced our water use per litre of vodka, and we are always looking for ways to recycle even more water in the production process. Every year we contribute 25,000m$^3$ of production water to a nearby pond which is used by local farmers for crop irrigation, saving precious groundwater.

*Absolut Carriers*: Our distillery and bottling plants, main suppliers and partners are all located in southern Sweden. We work closely together to reduce our $CO_2$ emissions from local transport by 50 per cent by 2020 and we are well on our way. In 2013 a quarter of the fuel used by our wheat suppliers for transport had to be biofuel. And in 2014 we built a biodiesel station at our distillery for the trucks that transport wheat stillage to local cows and pigs. About 40 per cent of stillage transport uses biofuel that is produced locally and our goal is to switch all vehicles over in the next few years.

*Absolut Community*: Only one of our delivery trucks at a time is allowed to be in the village of Åhus, reducing traffic-related disturbances and noise pollution. There is a parking area outside the village where other trucks can wait their turn. From the port of Åhus, 75 per cent of all Absolut Vodka bottles are shipped directly to other ports around the world. In 2007 we showed our commitment to cleaner water by joining the Clean Shipping Index, which puts pressure on ship owners to report on and reduce their emissions and chemical use.

### Stakeholders and Stakeholder Attributes

Our corporate communication at The Absolut Company engages both internal and external communication. Important stakeholders for us are TAC employees and alumni; consumers who want to know more about the company behind the brands; media; collectors; and opinion-makers. These stakeholders often want to know if the company behind the brands is a responsible company and what it stands for. They are curious and concerned about corporate citizenship.

More recently we have decided to use social media channels to communicate with our corporate stakeholders. To be transparent. To tell our stories; what we stand for and what we do. Our consumers for our brands are high users of social media so it is a natural habitat. A recent example of a communication project we launched is a project we call Creative Space. Creative Space is made out of four shipping containers that we have transformed into a hub for innovation around sustainability. We arranged a three day hackathon to find ways to minimize waste, focusing on briefs such as reduce, recycle, refill and re-use.

*(Continued)*

The main purpose of the space was to improve ourselves when it comes to sustainability. It was to find a better solution for packaging but also to highlight the issue and drive progress. We came out with a winning idea – a refill solution in eco-design which helped optimize transport, plus many other ideas and important collaborations for the future.

### About Absolut

The Absolut Company is based in Sweden and is responsible for global strategic marketing and origination of Absolut Vodka, Malibu, Kahlúa, Wyborowa, Luksusowa and Our/Vodka. The Absolut Company is a family of five hundred co-workers from around the world and a brand-owner company within the Pernod Ricard Group. Pernod Ricard was created in 1975 with a tradition of entrepreneurship and innovation. The Absolut Company (TAC) has found a natural place among Pernod Ricard's stable of brands, and has contributed to the Group as a world leader in premium spirits.

In addition to Absolut Vodka, the world's fifth largest international spirits brand, TAC also added the global management of Malibu and Kahlúa in 2009 and the Polish vodkas Wyborowa and Luksusowa in 2010. The focus on innovation has generated several product developments as well as our new brand Our/Vodka. The head office in Sweden's capital city of Stockholm employs two hundred people, who handle all strategic brand management and innovation for the brands. TAC also employs staff in Canada and the United States.

Just as it always has been, all Absolut Vodka is produced in Åhus, southern Sweden, where the company has three hundred employees. With 99 per cent of all Absolut Vodka sold abroad, it is Sweden's single largest export food product.

# STAKEHOLDERS: THEIR IDENTIFICATION AND RELEVANCE

This chapter explains the significance of *stakeholders, stakeholder engagement* and *stakeholder management* as core elements within corporate strategic communication. It provides an analysis of all conceivable stakeholders and teases out their relative relationships with corporate entities and with themselves. It examines different stakeholders in different contexts. For example, regulators are crucial and can make a corporation's life very tough. Communication and dialogue are crucial. But this raises issues for corporations internally; the communicators versus the lawyers; and the business units versus the lawyers. All have different agendas, pulling corporations in different directions. Internal and external stakeholders impact on a corporation's goals and objectives and activists operate in both spaces. They include shareholders, unions, suppliers and distributors. Once a stakeholder is defined in these wider terms the relative importance of effective corporate strategic communication becomes clearer. The strategic nature of activity ought to be embraced within the long-term scope and direction or it will serve only to act as a problem-solving mechanism.

## DEFINING STAKEHOLDER

As we have seen in Chapter 3, stakeholders can be divided into three groups for the purposes of evaluation against corporate activity. They are:

1  strategists (profit-seekers);
2  non-strategists (employees and dependents); and
3  anti-strategists (rent-seekers).

There are a number of questions surrounding corporations and their stakeholders. Who are they? Are some more important than others? Is there a hierarchy of stakeholders and, if so, do they receive different treatment depending upon where they sit in the hierarchy? Are shareholders paramount? Can a corporation which makes things afford to neglect its unionized labour? Are unions more powerful in some countries and not others? If so, do corporations have different communication strategies for unions in different countries? Are customers high on the list? Or does advertising form a separate communication strategy for customers – one that will attract them without the need to think about them as stakeholders? At issue is the question of whether a corporation conceptualizes different communication strategies for differing stakeholders. To answer this question we need to know how corporations identify stakeholders.

We have seen from the reports of Toyota and Shell that there is a different vocabulary for the two companies and that they pitch their narratives in different ways to different stakeholders. 'Stakeholder' in corporate terms is a recent addition to the lexicon. It is defined broadly as one who has an interest or concern in something, especially a business. A 'stakeholder economy', according to the *OED*, is one which provides all members of society with a stake in its success. Historically, aside from its meaning as a stout stick or post, it meant a sum of money wagered on a race or a prize for winning a race. A stakeholder was an independent party who held the money wagered by the parties to the bet.

Before the end of the millennium Clarke and Clegg (1998) had identified a paradigm shift in management theory and practice which required a new way of thinking about stakeholders. The old paradigm included the objectives of profit, growth and control; the new objective was a sustainable enterprise. The old orientation of the firm, they argued, was strategic planning and rational strategy; the new orientation – strategic thinking, innovation and core competence (Clarke and Clegg, 1998, p. 6). It was a more complex and demanding corporate environment, one in which success, Clarke and Clegg argued, required companies to 'build better relationships with everyone they do business with' (Clarke and Clegg, 1998, p. 6). Clarke and Clegg identified some obvious stakeholders. Investors they said needed a better relationship but they also identified customers, employees, suppliers, creditors and something called 'the wider community'. There was no indication if this was a hierarchy of stakeholders. Clarke and Clegg then got to the guts of what it meant to operate in the so-called new paradigm. If companies were to do well they needed to think about the 'stakeholder approach' as it had a direct influence upon supply chain management, quality and marketing. Reciprocity and partnership were based on more open communication, a situation which forced out and attempted to destroy the old practices of 'upholding different messages and values for different audiences' (Clarke and Clegg, 1998, p. 7). (For a more detailed analysis of the shareholder versus stakeholder orientation of corporate management see Wall and Greiling, 2011).

Corporate activity has lead inexorably to globalization. We cannot have one without the other. Globalization has expanded considerably the range and variety of individuals and groups seeking stakeholder status. Jagdish Bhagwati argues the early anti-globalizers sought recognition as stakeholders in the globalization process to the extent that they wanted a voice, a vote or a veto of activities they considered inappropriate (Bhagwati, 2004, p. 28). Two strands, he argued, attempted to present their credentials as stakeholders: stake-wielders and stake-asserters. The stake-wielders provided the street-theatre – the demonstrations, violent and non-violent – while the stake-asserters preferred to seek a stake by way of *reasoned discourse* through publication of policy papers and briefing notes. Bhagwati contrasted the activities of NGOs seeking stakeholder recognition by governments and it is important to grasp their significance because they influence government policy relative to corporate activity. We will look more closely at this in Chapter 8 – where we will analyse the social licence to operate. This is a layer above the legislative licence to operate, above a government's approval. It is society approving of corporate activity and it has enormous ramifications for corporations that fail to acknowledge its existence much like the warnings provided by Clarke and Clegg among others at the beginning of the century. As Bhagwati acknowledges, the economic aspects of globalization are less in question that the social aspects. Thus a benign economic globalization may promote a more malignant social world in which poverty is accentuated, unionization of labour is eroded, indigenous cultures are destroyed and the environment is damaged. One of the more meaningful issues of the day – climate change – is concerned with environmental damage through the continued and expanding use of fossil fuels for energy. As we have seen above, many of the world's largest and most profitable corporations have their basis in the continued use of fossil fuels so there is a conflict between them and those who wish to shut down all extractive industries such as coal and oil – those who are now stakeholders in the macro-socioeconomic world.

In Greece at the beginning of the twenty-first century stakeholders opposed to that country remaining in the EU staged street theatre protests – some violent, some passive – to indicate their dislike for a conservative government and then later for a socialist government controlled as they were perceived to be by external agencies: the central bank and local banks to whom they owed many millions of euros. In this example the prospect for rational discourse through continued engagement in communication between stakeholders was limited by the positions taken by the opponents of the policies being put forward – the stakeholders were Bhagwati's stake-wielders and they had the most to lose.

## WHO ARE THE CORPORATE STAKEHOLDERS?

Identification of stakeholders assists in the task of reverse engineering a corporate communication strategy. Before we can work out what they want and where they fit we need to know who they are. Let's make a quick list. We will think about a hierarchy later. We will also attempt to define some of the words and terms in greater detail in Chapter 6 when we discuss narrative theory. Investor, for example, is ambiguous. The construction of a stakeholder map will also aid the reverse engineering process.

| Stakeholder | Engagement |
|---|---|
| Shareholders | Buy, hold and sell shares in public companies |
| Governments | Set policy frames in which corporations operate |
| Regulators | Monitor and control the policy frames set up by governments |
| Employees | Work and are paid wages by corporations |
| Managements | Set direction of corporations, paid salaries and bonuses |
| Boards of directors | Set policies of corporations within government frameworks |
| Suppliers | Deliver goods and services to corporations |
| Distributors | Deliver goods and services from corporations |
| Unions | Invest in the interests of a corporation's employees |
| Creditors | Banks and other institutions or individuals who provide capital |
| Business partners | Companies that work directly with corporations |
| Media | Investigate and report corporate activity |
| NGOs | Monitor and report corporate activity |
| Government agencies | Monitor and report corporate activity |
| Not for profits | Organizations with a social rather than economic objective |
| Redemptive agencies | Seek social justice for individuals from corporations |
| Financial analysts | Specialists who analyse and report on corporate activity |
| Stockbrokers | Agents who analyse and advise on corporate share investments |
| Loyalty rewards | Offers of additional products and services for loyalty |

**Table 4.1**  A stakeholder map supports reverse engineering

This is not an exhaustive list but it will serve to identify the main actors and a few peripherals. It does not include groups or individuals who may refer to themselves as community-oriented or community-focused. We will return to them in Chapter 8.

## Shareholders

Individuals or collectives who hold scrip in a public company are referred to as shareholders. They own a legal part of a public or private company or business. The shares represent part ownership of the company. Shareholders have legal rights such as voting for board members, the receipt of dividends and first choice to buy when new shares are issued.

Shareholders range between 'mom and pop' holders of small parcels that provide them with small amounts of income to corporate holding companies that invest billions to underpin the value of a corporation. Shareholders in public companies have the advantage of not being liable for the debt accrued but they have a disadvantage in the fact that a drop in company value equals a drop in the value of their shares.

Shareholders are eligible to attend company annual general meetings. This avenue has been taken up by activists who buy shares in companies with the specific objective of attending and disrupting the proceedings. Public corporations provide shareholders with information including the annual report.

## Governments

Governments are serious stakeholders for public companies as they set the operational framework for all corporate activity. Governments are responsible for granting corporations access to resources and for granting legislative licences to operate. A corporation cannot operate without government permissions. A mining company might be given permission to explore; an oil company to drill offshore; a manufacturer to set up a factory; a service company to operate a technology; or a bank might be given a licence to act as a bank.

The degree to which governments act in stakeholder roles varies from country to country and by type of government. A traditionally conservative or liberal government usually plays a less interventionist role in corporate activity while a socialist or progressive government might be more controlling of what goes on under its jurisdiction and be more concerned with *socializing* company profits. A change in a government may cause a corporation to change countries. The structure of globalization means governments have become far more active as stakeholders when they wish to retain or reject corporate activity.

## Regulators

Regulators are government agencies that keep watch over corporate activity. We will look more closely at them in Chapter 9. Throughout the twentieth century, corporations behaved in ways that were not always in the best interests of the societies and environments in which they operated. As governments perceived the increase in awareness of civil society and its requirements for greater corporate social responsibility, they began to focus upon the actions of corporations. Legislation that enabled corporations and corporate activity shifted from prescriptive to proscriptive. Prescribed legislation might have been the act of setting out where and how a corporation could do something. Proscribing the same action meant limiting or prohibiting it. Regulators are generally put in place as a proscriptive measure. In Australia, for example, there are three statutory corporate regulators: the Australian Securities and Investment Commission (ASIC), the Australian Competition and Consumer Commission (ACCC) and the Australian Prudential Regulation Authority (APRA). Similar regulators exist in all western countries. The increase in regulation in Australia occurred in the late 1990s when a report to government (the Wallis Inquiry) identified technological innovation, a more competitive business environment and changing customer needs as areas where corporate activity was outstripping government responses.

## Customers

Customers are the stakeholders who buy the products and services created by corporations and other businesses. Most of the world's traded manufactured goods are today the product of corporate entities. As such, customers ought to be high on the list of stakeholders – near the top with shareholders. In the professional era a customer is also said to be a client or buyer. But customers are not the same as consumers; customers buy products and services while consumers use them. A mother shopping for new clothes for her daughter is a customer; the daughter is the consumer. Someone who invests in a new car is a buyer, while another who invests in business-to-business services such as printing or web services might be called a client.

Customers can be further categorized as internal and external. A corporation such as Toyota, for example, as we have seen above, used the word 'customer' sixty-five times in its annual report yet 'client' appeared once. Client was used in connection with other companies with whom Toyota was prepared to do business.

The Royal Dutch Shell chairman, Jorma Ollila, remarked that the company would create value for customers, partners and investors. Customers were placed above investors in the stakeholder hierarchy.

## Employees

Stakeholders can affect or be affected by corporate activity. A drop in a share price or a reduction in activity may mean a reduction in a company's workforce. Businesses tend to have a nineteenth-century view of labour – it is easily got rid of and just as easily acquired again when necessary. Employees are therefore stakeholders perceived to hold less value for the corporation. Yet internal stakeholders, such as employees, can be an important component in reputation management, image and brand recognition. Companies have turned from advertising products and services directly to indirect images showing people and specifically employees as being their most important tactical advantage. Shell chose to use a mugshot (head and shoulders) of a male employee on the cover of its annual report. The man was wearing a white shirt, red tie and spectacles. On the inside front cover the subject of the photo was described as a Shell employee at Shell Technology Centre, Amsterdam. He represented another element of the Shell stakeholder hierarchy. The image of an employee on the front cover implied that they were important stakeholders. But sadly he was not important enough to be named.

## Managers

Like employees, managers are internal stakeholders. They run companies on behalf of shareholders. Managers create business strategies that will benefit owners. Managers are the stakeholders given responsibility by owners and boards of directors to manage a corporation so that it remains sustainable and profitable. A manager as stakeholder has a certain amount of power. Such power must be exercised in a Weberian sense that an actor in a social relationship is in a position to carry out his own will despite resistance (Weber, 1947). Managers have a stake in creating and projecting the strategy of the organization onto other stakeholders in the relationship. They are therefore charged with communicating the corporate strategy and, as such, are the lead stakeholders in any communicative action. They also hold power in the sense that Dahl recounted: as a relationship in which one actor can get another actor to do something they might not otherwise have done (Dahl, 1957).

## Boards of directors

Directors of corporations are responsible for the governance of their corporations. They are generally appointed to act on behalf of shareholders. The chairman or president of the board is the lead director. A chairman's or president's message will lead the narrative in an annual report as we have seen for Toyota and Shell. A board of directors consists of executive and non-executive members. Boards of directors are responsible for the publication of the annual report and company accounts. They can delegate power within the corporation, oversee regulatory and legislative compliance, assess management performance, monitor company performance, control significant mergers or acquisitions, approve company policies and make decisions on behalf of the owners of the corporation. They may themselves be shareholders or other stakeholders such as customers, suppliers or creditors.

## Suppliers

Corporations need inputs. Large and small businesses supply each other with components, raw materials and intellectual property. Everything that is labelled by a corporate entity is not necessarily made by it. Suppliers as stakeholders ought to be at or near the top of a corporate hierarchy for without their inputs a corporation has nothing to offer. In business the term *supply chain* holds an important place in the strategic direction of a company. Supply chain refers to the ways in which raw materials, components or other elements of a product or service find their way into the mix. Historically, suppliers have been viewed as marginal stakeholders – if one fails another will be available to take its place. A view of suppliers was therefore tactical – screw them for the best price, make sure delivery was always solid and expect them to provide instant and accurate service. A corporation with thousands of computers, for example, would change suppliers if they were unhappy with some aspect of the technology, rather than have a two-way conversation with the supplier. The supplier then would behave in a similar way, knowing there was always the chance they would be shut out. Corporations today are far more likely to build a better stakeholder relationship with a supplier. There is less 'order processing' and more integration into the corporate strategy.

## Distributors

Delivery of goods and services was once a simple act of shipping them from one street in one town or from one town to another by road or rail. In the nineteenth century countries built large rail networks to achieve better distribution of goods and services across their countries and, in the cases of Europe and Asia, across borders. The invention of globalization altered distribution patterns to the extent that corporate activity was able to shift itself across borders; building cars in the United Kingdom and Australia for local markets was no longer necessary. The manufacture of textiles, clothing and footwear could all be achieved at lower cost in Asia as long as distribution patterns could be maintained cost effectively.

Distributors of other products such as energy were also seen as important stakeholders when energy such as oil or gas was shipped long distances across oceans. High-quality coking coal, a critical input to the production of iron and steel in Japan, Korea and China, could be sourced relatively cheaply in Australia. Distribution became a vital aspect of the supply chain. New deep-water harbours were built, rail lines constructed and larger ships assembled so that coal from Australia could fire the blast furnaces in Japan. Australia's own iron and steel manufacturing went stone-cold dead. Corporations that had previously been involved in the production process shifted their resources to shipping. Part of the problem for suppliers and their corporate customers related to the asymmetrical nature of how they viewed the corporation they were supplying. They were unprepared to adjust their products or services to fit the requirements of their customers.

## Unions

In most western countries trade unions or unionized labour play a major role in all sectors of the economy, from primary extractive industries through construction and housing to manufacturing, engineering, sales and marketing. Corporations attempt to reduce trade union influence through a variety of negotiating practices but in most companies where there are large labour components trade unions will be attempting to influence wage and other outcomes on behalf of their members.

Trade unions are effectively stakeholders in the corporate sense but their members are dual stakeholders; they look to the union for wage negotiation and work condition support but they look to the corporation for continued work and a continuing wage.

Historically, trade unions and corporations have not had good stakeholder-to-stakeholder relationships. The struggle for wages and conditions for union members has led to conflict rather than to a solidary societal relationship – to asymmetrical communication. Corporations and governments have worked together in many places to reduce the power and influence of trade unions, most notably in the United States.

## Creditors

Lines of credit from banks and other financial institutions, large or small loans, are provided to corporations that continue to be successful and to make a profit. Creditors remain stakeholders while ever corporations continue to repay loans or interest on loans. Corporations consider their shareholders to be their main stakeholders. They view creditors as their second most important. Lines of credit and lines of communication are kept open. Like the corporation itself, creditors have a strong interest in ensuring its liquidity and thus its viability. Throughout the GFC the United States government became a major creditor of some of that country's largest public corporations including General Motors and Bank of America. The 'too big to fail' mantra was invoked so government and other creditors came to the aid of the failing entities.

## Business partners

Corporations refer to a variety of their stakeholder relationships as business partnerships. The terms are not synonymous but they are closely linked. The changing nature of corporate strategy in the twenty-first century has altered the nature of business partnerships. Arrangements that are termed business partnerships usually involve some type of voluntary agreement and structure, clear accountabilities and outcomes for all parties, shared objectives and value adding arrangements that might not be reached without the partnership. The Toyota annual report presents evidence of a business partnership that might also be a stakeholder relationship. It entered a three-year car-sharing experiment in France with partners Grenoble City, EDF Group, Citélib and Grenoble-Alpes Métropole to supply electric cars to reduce traffic congestion. It is not unusual for corporations to build business partnerships that are mutually financially beneficial or, in the case of Toyota, have potential financial benefits but require an initial outlay. Business partnerships are less frequently established between corporations and other power entities such as governments outside Europe where corporatization has been diffuse and for the most part successful.

## Media

Corporations are reticent to attempt to establish stakeholder relationships with media. The uncontrolled nature of the communication that results has too frequently impacted negatively on corporate activity. Media are complex and diverse in nature and frequently they are ideologically motivated. News- and current affairs-based reporting structures are institutionalized to investigate corporate activity. Reporting is seldom positive. News is not news if it does not have an impact. Corporations doing good rather than evil is not newsworthy. It is difficult for corporations to establish symmetrical communication stakeholder relationships with media despite media being reliant on corporations to fill news bulletins. Relationships are built within other media sectors, most notably 'trade publications', both print and online where reporting corporate activity is tied directly to the investment in advertising a corporation might make with the publication or media owner. The shift towards so-called 'citizen journalism' has had a positive effect on corporate activity. If a corporation is aware that every individual with a smartphone is potentially a citizen journalist who will show no hesitation in uploading pictures and text to media sites such as Facebook and Twitter then they are less likely to act inappropriately. Media accessibility requires corporations to consider seriously how they develop stakeholder relationships with them.

## Non-government organizations

As the role of governments monitoring corporate accountability has diminished in recent years, NGOs, to fill the gap, have risen and multiplied like the walking dead. It would be difficult to count the number of NGOs in existence. They act as part of what is termed 'civil society' and they take responsibility for monitoring and reporting on every detail of corporate, government and private activity that exists within societies. A corporation that ignores NGOs does so at its peril. NGOs campaign using strategies and tactics that are professional and well resourced. They focus on corporate activity across borders, with their main objective to monitor and halt environmental and social damage caused by corporate activity. NGOs view themselves as adversarial stakeholders.

## Government agencies

The role of the government agency as a stakeholder of a corporation is fraught. Agencies act to regulate corporate activity but they also act on behalf of corporations. Trade agencies, for example, are set up to promote the external objectives of corporations within their sovereign boundaries. Governments fund such agencies for the promotion of trade and investment but it is the trade and investment of the corporate entities that reside within its sovereign borders that benefit from the boosterism. The development of a stakeholder relationship between a corporation and a government agency is complicated by internal processes; corporations as profit-seekers attempt to be streamlined and non-bureaucratic, while government agencies as rent-seekers tend towards top-heavy bureaucracies in which channels of communication are less evident and painfully slow to negotiate.

## Not for profits

Organizations which do not seek to make profit are incorporated differently. The function of the not for profits (NFPs) is charitable and the focus is towards society and social justice. NFPs refer to their stakeholder relationships with corporations in soft terms such as 'collaborative', seeking 'shared values', looking for 'sustainability'. But the drive is to secure long-term funding so that the NFP can sustain its own strategy. NFPs rely on funding from a variety of sources and it is only recently that they have turned to the corporate world. Governments and individuals were their traditional sources. Organizations working in global health and welfare, for example, seek donations from private individuals to maintain their work. In some circumstances it is impossible for corporations to build stakeholder relationships with NGOs. Médecins Sans Frontières, for example, a global health organization, claims it does not accept donations from pharmaceutical or biotechnology corporations nor from arms manufacturers, oil or gas companies, or tobacco and alcohol corporations.

Corporations in some parts of the world have philanthropic views which allow them to create stakeholder relationships with NFPs. US corporations are the most prolific givers. As part of their strategies corporations are learning that it is more valuable to create relationships with NFPs that are aligned with their own objectives rather than simply providing grants or cash. NFPs are responding slowly.

## Redemptive agencies

This is an unusual stakeholder which is more often confused with NFPs or NGOs or government agencies. Redemptive agencies are those which place the individual squarely at the centre of institutionalized civil society. They attempt to locate the individual in society as the most valued or important element. They look to the welfare and equity of the individual in society as paramount. Redemptive agencies can be collective or singular. They are the foundation of what have become known as 'community' groups and activists, collectively or individually positioned, that attempt to seek advantage within a socioeconomic system through a number of strategies and a variety of tactics not least of which is absolute opposition to all corporate activity. Redemptive agents have carved a space in society which appears to be between governments and corporations. Despite having no legitimate authority, they have instilled fear into governments and halted corporate economic activity. In terms of their capacity for destructive influence they are the most important stakeholder a corporation can have.

## Financial analysts

The job of a financial analyst is to undertake research into economic and financial data for the purposes of making recommendations to businesses. Financial analysts are also called equities analysts, investment analysts and securities analysts. If they are employed directly by corporations they are also employee stakeholders. If they are external they may be connected as business partner stakeholders. Analysts work within corporations or for brokerage firms or investment firms or both. Financial analysts parallel communication analysts in that they perform research on public corporate records, mining them for financial data that will help their own clients make investment decisions.

## Stockbrokers

Like financial analysts the stockbroker analyses publicly listed companies and makes recommendations to clients on investing. Stockbrokers receive briefings from corporations so they are important stakeholders for both the corporate entity and the investor. They buy and sell shares for institutional and retail clients. They are regulated by governments in most western countries. In the United States they are called brokers or financial advisers but they must be employed with a registered broking firm before they can trade.

Stockbrokers tend to ignore all social and environmental aspects of corporate activity. They concentrate on the price of the share that they recommend their clients buy, hold or sell. This does not imply that brokers are unethical. It means they are focused on the movement of the price of shares and all that entails on a daily, hourly or minute basis. Stockbrokers are also business partners but the partnership may be short-lived if they recommend shares in the corporation be sold.

## Loyalty programmes

This is an unusual entry in the taxonomy of stakeholders yet it is one with a growing interest for both loyalty holders and for the corporations that issue loyalties. Loyalty programmes are offered to customers, so one who holds some form of loyalty redemption certificate will be a dual stakeholder. They may also be an employee or a supplier, or any other manifestation of association. But as loyalty rewards accumulate, their stakeholder status also changes. A frequent mile passenger with an airline, for example, may have accumulated so many flyer miles that their loyalty card is at bursting point. Like a financial bubble, the loyalty customer will be concerned that the accumulation of rewards may never be able to be redeemed. The corporation is now important to them.

Loyalty programmes extend downward into reward points for shopping at the grocery market to a free cup of coffee after six paid-for cups. They are mechanisms of structured marketing designed to promote continued use. As such, they create a stakeholder relationship between the product or service and the customer.

## AWAY FROM A STAKEHOLDER HIERARCHY

Now that we have mapped the various interests of stakeholders as they relate to the corporation, we are in a position to think about a hierarchy. Corporations need to know precise information about their stakeholders not only so they can understand their behaviour – what colour a customer likes – but so they can make predictions about where they fit with the company's grand strategy. We will discuss grand strategy in detail in Chapter 6.

A stakeholder hierarchy assists a corporation to know when, where and how it might respond to the particular stakeholder in question. It would be impossible for a corporation to engage all of its stakeholders at the same time over a sustained period. There have been cases of stakeholder vectors overcoming available resources. Such situations have caused share market collapses. Natural disasters have also combined with stakeholder sentiment to cause corporate grief.

Much of the literature and modelling on stakeholder hierarchy argues in favour of it being consistent with stakeholder management. These premises neglect the notion that stakeholders are diverse and complex entities or individuals. It is an archaic argument that continues to promote the separation of stakeholders into primary and secondary and to offer management solutions that are underpinned by asymmetrical communication. There is evidence that a number of the world's largest corporations apply such a model. Rhetoric pervades this model and there is sufficient evidence that it is substantially ineffective in delivering desirable communication outcomes. Traditional hierarchies are vertical integrations in which layers of stakeholders are distilled through portals from top to bottom. Top layers represent important stakeholders while lower layers represent those who are less important. Hierarchy in scientific or logical terms means to be ranked in order, grade or class.

## TOWARDS A STAKEHOLDER ALTERNATIVE: DIFFERENTIAL TRANSMISSION OF COMMUNICATION

Corporations need to abandon the idea of a vertical structure to represent their stakeholders. The vertical structure privileges, and once privileged it is difficult for a corporation to retract. Globalization causes rapid change. To stay ahead of the change curve a corporation must look to the stakeholders who are immediately adjacent to them on the curve. If this means 'getting in to bed' with environmentalists or acquiescing to the persuasive arguments of unions then corporations that are prepared to establish and maintain a symmetrical discourse will succeed.

A stakeholder hierarchy may have some advantages. It is a transparent mechanism for the development of different tactics. The problems, however, are often greater than the advantage. A corporation cannot engage all of its stakeholders all of the time nor for that matter can it engage all of them at one moment in time with the same tactics. The differentials that must be applied are similar to the gearing of the drive train in the car that is being reverse engineered for competitive purposes. When Toyota takes apart a Lamborghini it looks closely at the pattern of the gears, the ratio of the gears and how the transmission shifts them smoothly. It examines the gear train, or speed ratio. It wants to see what Lamborghini has as its *mechanical advantage* – the way the gear ratio is set so that the vehicle achieves its maximum 'torque' in each gear.

If we look in the same way at stakeholders we will see there is a clear need for a *differential transmission of communication*. Corporations need to set their *communicative mechanical advantage* by creating gear ratios for stakeholders so they can get maximum torque – torque being the influence they apply to a stakeholder to change the stakeholders rotational motion. These terms from the physics of engineering are highly relevant to the direction corporations must take to engage stakeholders with meaningful communication. Rotational motion, or torque, is the rotation of an object around its central mass. The metaphor provides a clear image of the corporation at the centre of the action while the stakeholders rotate – at different velocities at different times – around the action.

An alternative corporate stakeholder engagement model is:

---

the ratio of communicative mechanical advantage (cma)
multiplied by
the differential transmission of communication (dtc)
cma × dtc = degree of advantage

cma = known stakeholder actions
dtc = the tactics applied to the actions at specific points in time.

---

The velocity at which the tactics are applied will determine the degree of advantage. Corporations consider the probability that the application of rhetorical devices to their stakeholder communication will be an absorption rate equal to or greater than the suspension of disbelief. The term *cognitive estrangement*, most often applied to fiction and an individual ignorance which leads to suspended judgment or disbelief, can also be applied to corporate communication. Technical knowledge embedded in a narrative will create the same set of circumstances in which partial truth embedded in literary or science fiction allows for the suspension of disbelief so that the narrative can be followed and enjoyed. The problem for the corporate communication lies in the reduction of the knowledge gap that has been a product of diffuse information technology. Cognitive estrangement is easily overcome by access to a search engine; corporations can no longer have an expectation that the embedding of technical details within their rhetoric will create a suspension of disbelief in a stakeholder. Nonetheless, corporations continue to use rhetorical devices – words and phrases they think will resonate even if they are not being applied – in all types of communication. It is no coincidence that Toyota in its annual report used the word 'society' forty-two times, or 'environment(al)' sixty-one times.

Nor is it coincidental or serendipitous that the world's largest corporation, Bank of China, used the word 'society' on the outside front cover of its 2014 annual report (Bank of China, 2014). On page two it uses it again twice – first to present its strategic goal of 'serving society, delivering excellence' and then as part of its overall requirement of its development strategy which was:

> To build Bank of China into an excellent bank driven by the pursuit of noble values, a bank that shoulders significant responsibility for the nation's revival, a bank that possesses competitive edges in the globalization process, a bank that leads lifestyle changes in technological innovations, a bank that earns customer loyalty in market competition and a bank that meets the expectations of shareholders, employees and society in the course of its sustained development.
>
> (Bank of China, 2014, p. 2)

Bank of China points directly to its most important stakeholders – customers, shareholders and employees. But it does so by embedding them in the society in which the bank operates – China. In its introduction on page one it inflates the rhetoric further by suggesting that:

> Faced with new historic opportunities, the Bank will meet its social responsibilities, strive for excellence, and make further contributions to achieving the China Dream and the great rejuvenation of the Chinese nation.
>
> (Bank of China, 2014, p. 1)

If a western corporation were to use such expansive rhetoric to describe its goals and aspirations it might be difficult to suspend disbelief. China and Chinese corporations, however, provide a differential transmission of communication that assists in breaking apart earlier theories of stakeholder hierarchy. By way of explanation, which we will examine in greater detail in the following chapters, it is clear that the Chinese state and its instruments are and have always been rigidly hierarchical. Not so the corporation in the state-based capitalist system. Chinese corporate entities adopted a new and highly desirable strategy, with the imprimatur of the government, as Y. Y. Kueh points out, 'of growth imperatives, economic efficiency and optimum decentralization' (Kueh, 2008, p. 162).

In its 2014 annual report the message from the chairman, Tian Guoli, presented clear indications of the way in which the corporation viewed its stakeholders:

> We continued to honour our social responsibilities within the broad tide of social development, taking the initiative to contribute to the nation and benefit the people's livelihood. We further perfected its service offer for micro, small and medium-sized enterprises in order to help them to overcome the "difficult and unaffordable financing" problem. We explored a cross-border matching mechanism for small and medium-sized enterprises and successfully held forums and matchmaking meetings for Chinese and foreign SMEs in Paris, Milan, Frankfurt and Chengdu, reaping positive results. In a smooth transition, we made 58 thousand external contractual employees into contract employees of the Bank, a move that was highly appreciated by the employees and their families and was thus recognised as a "Heart Warming Project". Earnestly maintaining ethnic solidarity, we stepped up support for Xinjiang and Tibet and dispatched our top managers to launch the "visiting people, benefiting livelihood, uniting hearts" programme.'
>
> (Bank of China, 2014, p. 13)

The chairman concludes his message with the assurance that 'the bank will reward the trust and support of our shareholders and the public with outstanding performance' (Bank of China, 2014, p. 14). We will return to the idea of *public* or publics paralleling stakeholders in Chapter 8 in which community is discussed.

Finally, in supporting the chairman's message in the Bank of China annual report, the president, Chen Siqing, allowed another potential stakeholder group to surface. Chen thanked a number of stakeholders including those we have discussed above – employees, directors, supervisors, customers and investors. He then added 'friends', thanking them for their support as the bank was 'unremittingly marching towards our strategic goal of serving society, delivering excellence' (Bank of China, 2014, p. 18). 'Friend' is a word not frequently used in the west to describe stakeholders in corporate activity. It is defined by the *OED* as 'a person joined by affection and intimacy to another, independently of sexual or family love'. It is also defined as a supporter of an institution but considered to be one who 'regularly contributes money or other help'. We will assume it is the latter use that is being applied by the bank. We will differentiate it from shareholders and apply it to those who provide non-financial support. We will discuss the possibility of friend as stakeholder in Chapter 5 as part of our analysis of community and its relationship to the corporation.

## CONCLUSION

Identification of stakeholders assists in the task of reverse engineering a corporate communication strategy. Corporations need to abandon the idea of a vertical stakeholder structure. A corporation cannot engage all of its stakeholders all of the time. It must apply differentials. Stakeholder engagement requires a differential transmission of communication.

An alternative corporate stakeholder engagement model is the ratio of communicative mechanical advantage multiplied by the differential transmission of communication.

Stakeholder mapping allows corporations to understand the various interests of stakeholders and to shape communication that has relevance to them.

Widespread technology has reduced knowledge gaps so that stakeholders no longer demonstrate deep cognitive estrangement and suspension of disbelief when confronted with corporate communication.

 **DISCUSSION QUESTIONS**

1 Who are corporate stakeholders?
2 How does a corporation identify its stakeholders?
3 Are some stakeholders more important than others?
4 Do corporations conceptualize different communication strategies for different stakeholders?

## CASE STUDY: Kreditech Holding SSL GmbH

### A digital bank for everyone

*Anna Friedrich, Head of Communications, Hamburg Germany*

Kreditech Group is a technology company that delivers a range of custom-tailored financial services with a focus on underbanked consumers across the globe. Kreditech uses big data, proprietary algorithms and automated workflows to acquire, identify and underwrite customers within seconds. Automated processes combined with self-learning algorithms ensure fast and convenient customer service, minimizing cost and human error while continually improving by incorporating new customer data. Since its founding, Kreditech has scored more than 2 million individual loan applications, using up to 20,000 data points per application. Kreditech's global subsidiaries offer products from individually tailored instalment loans and micro-loans to payment and other financial services. Kreditech's Monedo brand provides an integrated suite of financial products, including a digital wallet and a personal finance manager designed to help customers manage their credit score and plan their spending. Founded in 2012 by Sebastian Diemer and Alexander Graubner-Müller, Kreditech Group has a team of over two hundred passionate employees with over forty nationalities.

### Aims and objectives of the corporate communication strategy

While Kreditech has positioned itself on a very 'cool' technology perception in the past, it is aiming to strengthen its position as an 'innovative technology firm with own front-end banking operation'. The clear goal of painting a picture of a high-quality technology company that gives access to banking to everyone worldwide is in line with the strategic exit of the micro-loan sector. While giving out short-term loans to customers was necessary for building up the technology, the algorithms are now well trained to be applied to more complex financial services and products. The launch of an integrated financial services platform in all nine active markets worldwide supports the brand's repositioning to re-enforce the perception as a digital, algorithm-based bank of the future.

The realization of a 'digital bank' for everyone has been achieved through the development of a unique combination of proprietary technology (e.g. algorithm), the Group's digitalization competence, and its clear focus on the front-end customer experience provided via subsidiaries to the end customer. Key messages in communications are derived from Kreditech's unique selling points: (1) an outstanding competence in digitalization of business processes; (2) a unique proprietary technology based on algorithms; (3) a new customer experience within a custom-tailored financial services platform; and (4) a highly competitive product offering in its markets.

To increase effectiveness of communication and to reduce 'avoidable mistakes' our integrated and coordinated communications strategy focuses on defining which messages are communicated to whom and by whom. They are based on specific numbers (KPIs) and on 'ideal' timing. The Group Communications Strategy is a guideline for all stakeholders within the company. It requires internal stakeholders to stay within key messaging and set KPIs in order to transport a compelling story of Kreditech to its public.

*(Continued)*

Our aim is no longer to simply address the 4 billion people worldwide who do not have a credit score. It is to focus on everyone who seeks better banking online. Kreditech is moving forward to position itself as a 'Digital Bank for Everyone'. In the near future we will also be offering non-lending products.

Our communication focuses on two different layers: (1) the product, an integrated financial services platform; and (2) Kreditech itself with its technology, and focus on investors as a legally binding entity. A clear differentiation is made when moving within and between both layers of communication.

In line with the communication layers, the two 'entities' also address different stakeholders (we approach stakeholders with key messages suitable for each one of our focus layers: The Kreditech Group as well as the product and our integrated financial services platform).

The chief executive officer (CEO) is the public face of the company. The CEO is also the key contact person for the business media. Our chief technical officer (CTO) provides the focus for the technological strengths of the company and the chief financial officer (CFO) is the public face when it comes to the financial expertise of our growing fintech company.

As Head of Communication, I work directly under the CEO. As Head of Communication, I am also being closely aligned with the rest of the management team as well as the Country Managers.

### Kreditech corporate social responsibility policy

Kreditech has a small track record in corporate social responsibility (CSR) activities. We focus on supporting local projects in and around our headquarters in Hamburg. As an international company with more than forty nationalities, we are pursuing more involvement in social and economic globalization issues such as refugees. Also, with a reputation in some parts of the media as the 'bad loan shark' our aim is to improve our reputation, image and brand through actions that take us in the opposite direction.

Kreditech stands for a 'bright elite' of people who know how to treat everyone worldwide fairly and with respect. We are a company that enables the 'underbanked' to gain access to financing. If we can transfer our objectives to the refugee and migrant issue we may assist in enabling the neglected from within their original societies to establish a life and a living in a foreign country. We may be able to assist them with access to a new culture and with navigation tools to understand different bureaucracies, politics and behaviours.

With the specialized target group, the local business media and the blogger scene as well as the German start-up scene, we recently began an initiative to support refugees in Hamburg. These CSR activities cover quick wins such as donations and man-day support in camps. We are also considering mid and long-term involvement of the company in this area – most of which will be defined according to current initiatives and events going on in and around Hamburg. Together with the authentic personal engagement of Kreditech's employees and management, this is the only way to establish a reputation as a sustainable, reliable company that cares about its society and its environment.

Meanwhile, corporate social responsibility activities do not prioritize in communication but in the impact of the support they achieve. While internally CSR projects such as the refugee initiative support team-building and strengthen team commitment, they are externally supported by social media engagement and blog posts commenting on the activities.

For a small company like Kreditech, our own initiatives are only part of the CSR mix. It is also important to jump on other projects and support waves. This is not only due to budget restraints. Support for other networks in their initiatives strengthens the social component and collaboration of Kreditech. Support for existing high-reach events will give Kreditech a larger 'radar' and better positioning us for our engagement with the issue of migrants and refugees.

**Kreditech**

|  | Interests | Influence | Access to resources |
|---|---|---|---|
| Employees HQ & worldwide | Strategy Results Updates | Medium | Newsletter Weekly team meetings Internal website |
| Investors | Strategy Results Updates | High | Monthly board meetings Email updates |
| Media (B2B, B2C) | News Strategy | High | 1:1 with CEO/CFO Press releases Events |
| Start-up & tech scene | News | Low | Media Word of mouth |

## Stakeholders and stakeholder attributes

Our most important stakeholders are investors and the media. Our focus is on the markets in Germany, the United Kingdom and the United States in business-to-business (B2B) communication. We also focus on Spain and Poland as well as all other subsidiary companies for all business-to-consumer (B2C) topics.

## The importance of stakeholders

One of our communication strategies we developed was part of our announcement of our Series C funding of $US82.5 million. Our main stakeholders in this strategy were media – journalists in Germany, the United Kingdom and the United States. In order to roll out the media release, we arranged preliminary and exclusive talks for targeted media which we coordinated through a large international news agency based in Germany. We arranged similar activities through a high-reach medium in the United Kingdom and the United States as well as placing the issue with one special-interest magazine. The sole focus of the special-interest magazine communication tactic was on investors.

*(Continued)*

The 'exclusives' and sticking to our invited embargo, served effectively as satellites when we were distributing the release. They also assisted us in gaining public interest in the issue. Once the media release was distributed and taken up by three publications for different target media, further in-depth interviews and background talks were organized. With exclusives as a general 'radar' further distribution was easier and had a broader reach – especially as the reputation, image and brand of the company were not well known and it was very specialized in its field.

# STAKEHOLDER ENGAGEMENT AND MANAGEMENT

This chapter provides practical explanations of the various methods available to analyse stakeholders including focus groups and surveys. It develops a deeper understanding of how reverse engineering is employed once surveys and focus groups are completed. It demonstrates how to best interpret the raw data into stakeholder profiles. It provides a calculus of corporate contemplation on stakeholders and presents evidence of how corporations create stakeholder maps. It explains the processes in the development of a stakeholder map and what functions it might serve in the conceptualization of an effective strategy.

In continuing the agriculture metaphor from previous chapters, a country's agricultural sector has a vertical hierarchy of stakeholders who can be separated into primary, secondary and tertiary. While it is longitudinal it is also latitudinal in that stakeholder branches within each of the three vertical groups wander horizontally across the landscape. Communication strategies of corporations directed at agricultural sectors are most frequently framed by longitudinal fixed attributes while ignoring the dynamism of the horizontal or latitudinal stakeholders and their situational variables. These stakeholders surface and submerge with far greater frequency than those on the vertical axis – which is why government communication policies for the sector are normative constructs; they follow the dictum of how communication strategies *should* be framed rather than how they *are framed in practice* – narrow and ineffective, unrepresentative and exclusive.

In a New Zealand example the grand strategy for the agriculture sector was framed against *static* stakeholder attributes. It ignored external environmental factors such as activist groups. Stakeholder attributes in the agricultural sector vary across strategies thus their attributes should be directly related to the construction of communication strategies. Sectoral stakeholders range across economic, political and social boundaries. They include:

1  farmers, contractors and employees, transport drivers, handlers, suppliers and growers;
2  governments and elected representatives;
3  manufacturers and packagers;
4  wholesalers, retailers, consumers and customers;
5  international and local corporations, banks, financiers, advisers and strategists;
6  shareholders and investors; and
7  indigenous interest groups and communities.

Stakeholder attributes should also be related to the perceived effectiveness of strategic corporate communication in achieving grand strategy objectives. We will discuss grand strategy in the next chapter.

## STAKEHOLDER ATTRIBUTES

In the previous chapter we identified a variety of corporate stakeholders which included the possibility that we might examine the new category of 'friend' as corporate stakeholder. To a large percentage of other stakeholders, most notably externals such as environmentalists, distributors, suppliers, stockbrokers, NGOs, media and creditors, 'friend' might not be a word to be applied liberally to the relationship. On the other hand, the Bank of China was very clear in its vision that friends were a strategic part of its future.

The question that friends raises is, what are the attributes of stakeholders and if a corporation can have friends and friend is a primary attribute in itself, what are the attributes of other stakeholders? Stakeholder attributes are derived from the public relations work that investigated the attributes of publics, most notable of which was undertaken by Hazleton (1992) and Hazleton and Long (1985, 1988). Four primary attributes were developed: problem recognition, level of involvement, constraint recognition and goal compatibility. Hazleton acknowledged that the first three were derived from Grunig and Hunt's (1984) situational theory of publics in that behaviour can be understood by measuring public perceptions of the consequences of actions. Grunig and Hunt were interested in all types of organizations. We can extrapolate specifically into corporate activity and argue that publics can be subdivided into stakeholders who demonstrate certain types of behaviour after or before they have been exposed to corporate activity. We will look more closely at this as part of our understanding of focus groups later in this chapter.

Corporations are interested in the attributes of stakeholders so that they can create or adjust communicative actions. They are interested in whether their communication inspires *passive responses* or *active responses* in their stakeholders. If a corporation pitches a communication at a shareholder, for example, the shareholder can react actively or passively. A shareholder may buy or sell a share – effectively an active reaction to information or news. Or the shareholder may act passively by holding the share, neither buying nor selling. A supplier may react passively to a company announcement that they are unwilling to continue to pay the asking price for a good or service. The supplier may continue to supply at the reduced rate. Or they may actively seek to sever the relationship or attempt to negotiate for the existing rate of payment. An environmentalist, while perceived to be an activist at all times against a corporation, may act passively if a corporation adjusts its activity in favour of the environmentalist's concerns or objections. Stakeholders' reactions will be active or passive depending upon the level and type of information or news they obtain before or after an event depending upon their relationship with the corporation. The four primary attributes framed by Hazleton have their bases in the quality of information or news a stakeholder receives and what they do with it. A negative business story in a left-of-centre newspaper, for example, may not provoke a shareholder into selling shares. It was the ideological position of the newspaper that drove it to report a corporate activity in a particular way. The shareholder may obtain more or different information from a conservative newspaper.

## REFRAMING ATTRIBUTES

For the purpose of representing stakeholder attributes less generally and therefore more specifically we need to reframe the four primary attributes identified above and to examine whether there is a requirement for additional primary attributes to be put into play. Hazleton (1993) argues organizational selection and use of communication strategies is effective when attributes of publics are recognized and adopted within the strategic communication frame. There is evidence that many stakeholders' standpoint is limited to problem-based relationships. For some stakeholders the corporation is itself problematic. While Hazleton and Grunig provided concrete underpinnings for the development of attributes of publics they were not futuristic in their expansion of publics into categories that confront today's corporations and their communication with stakeholders. They were, as we know, dealing with organizations more generally rather than anticipating the exclusivity required of corporate communication. Indeed, the frame adopted by Hazleton in an empirical quest for the development of an array of communication strategies (which we will come to in the next chapter) was narrowed to a not-for-profit organization within arm's reach. We agree with Hazleton that the likely outcome of the adoption of a particular strategy may be more successful when attributes of stakeholders are well known to the corporate entity. But we argue that the narrowness of the existing frame precludes the corporation from adopting optimal strategies. Let's examine the four primary attributes posited by Grunig and supported by Hazleton before we consider how we might expand or develop them further.

## Problem recognition

When we think of problem recognition we must assume that there is a problem. But such an assumption might narrow our stakeholder focus. Not all stakeholders might consistently believe there to be problems with the corporation with which they are engaged. Or they may wish to look at a problem as a short-, medium- or long-term consideration. For a stakeholder engaging with a corporation in the short term, there may never be a problem. A natural disaster, a stock market collapse – big problems that might affect the corporate entity – live either side of our stakeholder's engagement. In this case it may be five years between the events. Our stakeholder may have engaged for four years and six months in some capacity, employee, shareholder, supplier, whatever the relationship, without it being problem-based. At the other end, looking at the corporation over a period of one hundred years, every stakeholder would be entitled to assume a problem will eventuate. Some stakeholders will find problems wherever they look. Customers nitpick, employees complain about pay rates, news media look for negative story angles. Corporations can create strategic communication as counter-measures to such problems but they will never eliminate them.

The problem for the corporation lies not in the application of a counter-measure but in the knowledge that the stakeholder is aware of a problem. For Grunig and Hunt, problem recognition led to a realization that there were consequences for the stakeholder and that in itself led to the desire to acquire more detailed information. Recognition of the problem anticipated the desire for increased knowledge about the problem. The stakeholder desire for increased information was a result of wanting to resolve the problem so it would not impact directly on the stakeholder.

This was occurring in countries where shale-bed methane was being extracted by gas companies – land-owning stakeholders who did not have sufficient good quality information became agitated, which led to behaviour that they may not normally have exhibited, including criminal acts.

We suggest altering the primary attribute of *problem recognition* so that it becomes *issue recognition*. That way there is potential for stakeholders to recognize both positive and negative aspects of any situation rather than focusing solely on the negative or problem side.

## Constraint recognition

This is an interesting primary attribute. A stakeholder can be constrained in a number of ways. Similarly, recognition of the obstacle or constraint placed upon them will determine the level of information they seek and need to overcome or manage the obstacle or hurdle. A rock face, for example, is a large physical obstacle that may require the use of a rope, some quickdraws and cams before it can be overcome. Physical obstacles and hurdles are translatable into metaphorical barriers. Much of the vocabulary of business is involved with creating metaphors such as *coal face* or *value proposition*.

Grunig and Hunt argued that constraint recognition represented the framework in which stakeholders viewed hurdles that limited their freedoms and their capacity to act in ways they wished to act (Grunig and Hunt, 1984). We might look to most of the actions of corporations as being conceived to constrain individual human behaviour – the prescribed pattern of consumption of all manner of goods and services, for example. A national grocery market in which a number of global competitors operate diminishes the availability of independent grocers and thus provides the perception that there is a constraint on freedom to choose. A belief that governments act to place limitations on individual freedoms is played out through actions such as increasing taxes and reducing welfare benefits. Constraint recognition can be applied to any number of corporate-controlled activities that involve a financial cost – air travel or luxury cars. Constraint recognition can be scaled from high to low. Low constraint recognition means a stakeholder is more likely to seek information from a corporation or be open to the interpretation of information supplied by a corporation. A brochure or flyer for the sale of a luxury apartment appearing in a mailbox of a low-income family is unlikely to receive attention because of the high level of constraint placed on the family by their low income; they are unable to consider the purchase of a luxury apartment. Their constraint recognition is high so their information processing is low. The same brochure in the hands of a high-income, single, non-home-owning individual may elicit a different behaviour.

## Level of involvement

The application of this primary attribute works well for a variety of organizations including NFPs and NGOs. When applied to corporations it is not as sound. Public and private corporate entities by their nature are exclusive. They do not embrace the 'share the love' mantra. There are good reasons for this. Widespread public access to corporate information would have the potential to impact adversely on an entity's comparative advantage. As we have seen above, legislation frames intellectual property and trade secrets. If corporate information were freely available we would have no use for patents nor the concept of reverse engineering.

Stakeholders have a wide range of perceived level of involvement with a corporation. Level of involvement can be as clear as the purchase of goods or services. Or the acquisition and accumulation of shares. Or employment. Corporations work hard to engage stakeholders so that they perceive their level of involvement to be higher than it might be in reality. There are many rhetorical devices available, including glossy advertising and expensive sponsorship of professional sporting events. Corporate names that have been synonymous with major sporting fixtures include the car companies Toyota and Volvo, Swiss watchmaker Rolex, sports clothing and equipment manufacturers Nike and Fila, the bank Barclays and airlines Emirates and Qantas. In the UK football league, sporting goods manufacturers provide sponsorship of club 'kit' where values include £34 million to Arsenal from Puma, £70 million for Manchester United and £30 million for Chelsea from Adidas, and £25 million for Liverpool provided by New Balance. Sports sponsorship in 2015 was $US145 billion (PwC, 2015).

## Goal compatibility

As humans we seek to engage in compatible behaviour with others. We seek out the actions and activities that we believe we are best suited to. The natural instincts of humans are to work with and associate with others who have the same goals, aims and objectives. Social, religious and cultural institutions receive warmly those who abide by their principles and precepts and who have the same aims and goals.

Goal compatibility underpins the rhetoric of the corporation as it seeks to align itself in society. It seeks to encourage individuals to recognize goal compatibility between it and them. We will discuss the issue of non-compatibility in the next chapter.

Corporations can distinguish easily which stakeholders are likely to be more goal-compatible with them than others. Shareholders are obviously the most goal-compatible. They have sufficient information about the corporation to make investment decisions. Shareholders do not invest for fun. So the importance of compatible goals and objectives is paramount. We need to include objectives in this because objectives are measurable quantities. Shareholders like to know specifically what it is the corporation is planning and how it will strategically act to make those plans work. Similarly the compatibility of the creditor with the goals of the corporation are most often in alignment. Creditors and corporations have the same goal – profit. Goal compatibility and constraint recognition are attributes that frequently combine to enhance the value of the corporation. If a corporation communicates its goals within a narrowly constrained environment and those goals are compatible with a majority of stakeholders, then the capacity of the corporation to achieve its goals is enhanced in the short and possibly the longer term.

Governments and political candidates combine goal compatibility with constraint recognition when attempting to persuade corporations to do business on their turf. They offer goal-compatible tax breaks and unconstrained property access. They cannot, however, promise in their persuasive marketing arguments the inclusion of stakeholders who are not goal compatible with them or those who have low constraint recognition of the proposed corporate activity – unions, for example, or NGOs.

## Additional stakeholder attributes relevant to the corporation

The four primary attributes of stakeholders – problem recognition, level of involvement, constraint recognition and goal compatibility – underpin the corporate strategic view of stakeholder communication. And while they should form the basis of any communication strategy there are some additional attributes that ought to be recognizable and applied as an overlay to the primary attributes. By way of empirical observation we have concluded that secondary stakeholder behavioural attributes or competencies relevant to corporate communication might include *research techniques, resource accumulations* and *anticipatory actions*. Stakeholders vary in their capacity for engagement. Customers buy goods and services but they do not spend their days thinking about what they have bought. They buy food, put it in the refrigerator or cupboard and then get it out when they want to eat. They buy energy, water and other utilities but rarely invest time thinking about them. They switch on a light, turn on a tap, click the remote. But they have at their disposal the research techniques (search engines), resource accumulations (smartphones and tablets) and anticipatory actions (lining up to buy the latest smartphone or tablet) to engage with the corporations who supply the goods and services. The question is why they do not do so more frequently and at a deeper level. This is something that occupies the communication research departments of corporations. For all stakeholders are not customers. The secondary attributes are activated more commonly within other stakeholders such as suppliers, distributors and business partners on one side, and NGOs, regulators and media on the opposite side.

The paradox that appears in the development of a serious framework or taxonomy of stakeholders, no matter what their attributes and behaviour, is irrelevant in the face of the cold hard reality on the opposite side of the corporation: its finances. The early view of the firm from inside its walls was that raw material came in from suppliers, was turned into goods and services, and shipped out the front door through distributors to customers. A little later at the beginning of the professional era the picture altered marginally when it became a managerial view of what the firm should be seen to be, with environment wrapped around the outside and the corporation and management at the centre with four satellites – owners, suppliers, customers and employees – revolving around the core. The shift, according to Edward Freeman (1984) in his landmark work on the identification of stakeholders, heralded a conceptual void in which managers had no idea how to manage the newly minted stakeholders known as owners and employees. For the new system to work it required what Freeman termed a *conceptual shift* – new concepts and new ideas which 'dealt with owners and employees as a matter of everyday occurrence rather than as an exception' (Freeman, 1984, p. 7). The folly of ignoring the conceptual shift still haunts some corporate entities. Many global multinationals are unable or unwilling to adapt to practices which deal with established and emerging stakeholders on an everyday basis. The folly lies in the belief that shareholders (stockholders) are prime and that all others are the exception. Freeman also considered the oppositional discourses in which business and ethics never merged. The theory of shareholders and the theory of stakeholders, he argued, should cease to exist and the theory of stockholders should either lie down and die or be merged for normative purposes with the theory of stakeholders. Freeman's later arguments concern new narratives which recognize certain effects of the firm on stakeholders other than owners and the idea that the firm is all about value creation and the maximization of the greatest good for the greatest number (Freeman 1994).

# TWO ADDITIONAL ELEMENTS TO CONSIDER BEFORE ENGAGING WITH STAKEHOLDERS

From within the corporation the mapping of stakeholders and the identification of stakeholder attributes provide a substantial basis for engagement. But there are two additional elements that contribute to the validity and consequent success of a communication strategy: the application of information from focus groups and the application of data from surveys. Focus groups can be used to design surveys.

## Focus groups

Focus groups assist in identifying issues, reducing risks and avoiding direct responses from publics. They are a qualitative method of obtaining information about perceptions or beliefs or attitudes towards issues and objects. Focus group research can discover stimulating themes that are amplified as group members influence each other. Participants feel encouraged to state opinions they would not normally share with an anonymous pollster. Once articulated by a respectable group member (prolocutor) a questionable line of rhetoric can become legitimized by its very use. The extensive use of focus groups as a means of finding and testing themes has predictable consequences: it changes the terms of public discussion and magnifies the importance of themes that appeal to 'opinion swingers'.

Corporate communication strategy selection is closely linked to an attempt to identify issues that will work in an entity's favour without regard to underlying sociopolitical problems. A differentiated category of issues is created which 'focus' on the issue as a strategic tool rather than a substantive presence. The degree of structure or non-structure of a focus group is relevant to the design and construction of stakeholder surveys for content analysis purposes.

There are various ways to run focus groups:

- Two-way focus – one group of actors observes another and reports on the interplay of the group. The action is then reversed and repeated.
- Check-and-balance focus – one facilitator runs the group while another facilitator checks against topic.
- Duelling-banjos focus – two facilitators take opposing sides of the topic.
- Client-embedded focus – one or more clients are part of the group either known or unknown to others.

Groupthink or the group effect assists in stimulating ideas as one side or the other of a focus group frame their experiences. This in turn means the integrity of a focus group is marginal. But it is important to keep in mind that it is worthwhile as a base for setting up a more valid test in the analysis of survey data which is quantitative and qualitative. There is no reason to privilege quantitative analysis. The analysis of corporate strategic communication, as we have argued above, is for the purpose of establishing and investigating the relationship between the corporation and the society in which it operates. Corporations apply quantitative analysis methods to internal and external problems and issues. It is sufficient for the purposes of a reverse engineering analysis to adopt qualitative data if quantitative data is unavailable.

## Analysing focus group data

Data collected from a focus group can be analysed collectively or individually. A respondent may hold strong opinions that separate them from the group. Or the group may frame a position that is unable to be subdivided. It is important to restate that in the context of a corporate strategic communication, the focus group is a method of determining how to structure a survey questionnaire. It is not being used to analyse matter or to create concepts for new products or services, nor is it being set up to get feedback on old products or services.

Analysis of the data will be dependent upon the method of collection. A small number of people in a group discussion are managed either by voice recording or voice and video recording. A small group of six to twelve is manageable and should have a timing of between one to two hours. If a facilitator is present, and there is an assumption that for corporate use this would be essential, then note-taking may stimulate additional ideas and questions that did not surface in the original plan.

A transcript of the session is the most exhaustive method of analysis. Yet this may extend to a large number of pages of text, fifty or more, for a one-hour session, for example. An abridged transcript is an alternative in which a facilitator listens to the audio and ascribes meaning to sections.

It is most likely that a focus group used for the purpose of establishing a survey will be a single activity from which either a content analysis or a discourse analysis may be employed. We recommend discourse analysis as the preferred method. Discourse analysis is 'concerned with the detail of passages of discourse, however fragmented and contradictory, and with what is actually said or written' (Potter and Wetherell, 1987, p. 169) rather than a generalized notion of what might be intended. Discourse analysis searches for a pattern in any matter under investigation. It is the role of the observer to look for patterns that might include both consistency and variation.

# WHY DISCOURSE ANALYSIS IS GOOD

The most useful methodology for analysing focus groups is Potter and Wetherell's (1987) discourse analysis for the reasons presented above – that discourse analysis searches for a pattern in any matter under investigation. Was there consistency, for example, in the focus group discussion around the topic at hand? This model provides a causal link to focus group actions.

Discourse analysis provides a broad theoretical framework for the observation of the functional and constructive dimensions of focus groups – those elements which formed the basis of the sessions in a traditional normative sense. Discourse analysis relies for its validation on the orientation of the participants. Resonance and dissonance for facilitators as observers are a function of the orientation of the specific actors. An analysis of discourse also requires, as Paul Chilton (2004) observed, the presence of promotion of representations which in turn are comprised of a variety of communicative devices that must be evidential, authoritative and truthful – or legitimate (Chilton, 2004, p. 23). Elements that form the basis of the analysis of focus groups must therefore represent *evidence, authority* and *truth*. Chilton's model resonates with Leon Mayhew's claim that 'influence becomes inflated when it is perceived to be backed by money (power) rather than trustworthy argument' (Mayhew, 1997, p. 227). This is an argument we will come to in the following chapters.

## Surveys

Surveys or polls involve asking standard questions of respondents and comparing responses. They are appropriate for description, analysis and prediction. Limitations can occur with inadequate samples or poorly worded questions.

There are a number of ways a corporation can implement surveys. In-house software provides the highest level of security. Engaging a third-party provider is the next best solution. Use of public or free online software is not recommended.

Corporations use surveys for a variety of reasons, most notably to measure customer satisfaction levels and employee experiences and satisfaction. They use surveys to gauge perceptions about proposed actions – community group or environmental group thinking about a proposed new high-rise housing construction or a new open-cut coal mine, for example.

Corporations invest in survey data for short-term and long-term measurement. A short-term survey by a multinational retailer might provide data about the location of a new supermarket, for example, while long-term surveys might provide data about how certain new products will fit into the new supermarket.

Surveys must be undertaken against measurable objectives. Questions that emerge when thinking about objectives are:

- Will the information feedback assist in the reinforcement of objectives?
- How much information is required to assist in framing the objectives?

Surveying a representative sample of stakeholders with the right questions can be of enormous benefit to a corporation. Objectives and goals that were framed internally by management and paid consultants can be overlaid with survey data so that the objectives can be finely calibrated for optimum effect.

The survey is an integral component of reverse engineering. Let's think about what we need to do to create an effective survey that will enhance our reverse engineering:

- What is the purpose of the survey?
- Where will we find our survey respondents?
- When should we administer the survey?
- How will we frame the survey?

For a corporation, these questions are less difficult than they are for an entity attempting to embed survey data in a reverse engineering strategy. A corporation might answer that the purpose of the survey questions are:

- to identify a new product or service;
- to consider changing employee benefits; or
- to seek community support for new exploration.

Accessibility to survey respondents is a relatively easy task. Customer databases, employee databases and community databases are maintained by corporations for just such purposes. The timing of the administration of the survey is also relatively straightforward. The corporation will seek to survey customers when it is conceptualizing a new product or service. It will survey employees when it is financially able to change benefits. And it will survey community groups well before it sets foot on the ground where its exploration will take place. Corporations can use third parties to undertake these surveys. They should be aware, however, that such an action may ignite attributes that might have been better remaining dormant. A third-party approach may bring out a lack of goal compatibility, a high level of problem recognition and a low constraint recognition. The stakeholders may then exhibit behaviour that the survey results were designed to suppress.

For the purpose of reverse engineering a corporate strategic communication campaign the survey must look to respondents who are accessible and voluntary. The discovery objective must be ethical.

Surveys can be administered in a number of ways:

- Telephone
- mail
- personal interviews
- online.

### Conducting the survey

Specifics need to be considered when setting up and administering surveys.

1  Identify the topic or issue
   Identification of the issue under observation must align with the objective. Set out the objective by knowing how and why the topic or issue relates to it. Redefine or narrow the frame if necessary.

2  Select a sample
   *Reliability + time + cost.* Your sample must be an accurate representation of the stakeholders under observation. Additional questions at this stage might include whether a stakeholder being surveyed cuts across other stakeholder groupings – is a customer also a shareholder? It may be necessary to probe a stakeholder more deeply when asking initial demographic questions.

3  Write out questions
   *Short questions = better response rates.* If the survey is written allow for respondents to apprehend the questions easily and quickly. More assumptions does not mean a more predictable outcome.

4  Decide on delivery method
   *Respondent or pollster?* If the survey questionnaire is face to face there is a choice between allowing the respondent to fill in the questions or you (the pollster) filling them in when respondents provide answers. There is no rule that says one way is better than the other. It is a matter of judgment for you at the time. If a respondent is being asked about grocery preferences as she emerges from the supermarket it will be clear that it would be more appropriate for you to fill in the details as the respondent may be pushing a supermarket trolley or carrying armloads of groceries.

5  Test questionnaire
   *Small sample group.* Valuable feedback can be provided by the selection of a small sample group who act as test respondents before the real survey is distributed. Test respondents in a small sample group will allow you to refine questions provided they remain within the frame of reference relative to the objectives.

6  Modify questionnaire
   *Changes from small sample test group.* Sample respondents may offer specific advice on questions and how they might be framed or they may exhibit behaviour that allows

you to make a judgment about the questions. A negative facial expression or a head scratch may indicate a respondent is not understanding the question. Modifications to the questionnaire must remain within the framework of the objectives of the survey.

7   Work the field
    *Stakeholders are widespread*. Do not rely on a sample for accuracy if it has been extracted from a subjective pool. Fieldwork research that identifies stakeholder variety is essential to a strong data set.

## Questionnaires

*Introductory remarks*. An introductory statement identifies you, (the pollster), the corporation and the issue. These introductory remarks in all survey forms – online, face to face, telephone – are the 'hooks' needed to catch the respondent. An introductory remark must be applied in an open, friendly, non-threatening manner, either written or spoken. It must draw in the potential respondent with an underlying component of curiosity.

## Hierarchy of objectives

- Awareness (knowledge of and retention of information)
- Acceptance (interest or attitude)
- Action (opinion or behaviour)
- Demography (background and environment).

Introductory remarks will open the way to a respondent working with you to reach your objectives which are:

- To create awareness in the respondent about the issue
- To allow the respondent to accept that they are interested in the issue
- If not interested then to open to the prospect of becoming interested
- To elicit an opinion on the issue through the respondent filling in the survey.

If a relationship has been built between you and the respondent, then the respondent will be also willing to provide personal information such as age, employment and marital status. Some of the demographic information may not be relevant to the survey objectives but it allows the respondent to perceive that there is a relationship because of what is being asked of them.

In setting out the survey:

- Use short questions
- Use clear simple words and phrases
- Be specific and avoid ambiguity
- Ask only questions relevant to the issue or topic
- Create a logical sequence
- Arrange sentences in positive constructions
- Use words with clear meaning
- Avoid double-barrelled questions.

All of this is self-explanatory. Respondents are not invested with the survey. They may provide you with a wedge of their time but it will not be a large wedge. Adhere to the dictum of short is sweet, active voice, present tense.

Special considerations when seeking opinion or attitude include

- Don't ask opinions on matters of fact
- Avoid speculative or hypothetical questions
- Avoid terms that call for subjective judgment
- Be careful about mixing fact and opinion.

Facts and opinions are different. An opinion may have its basis in fact but for the purposes of surveys and corporate objectives we are interested in what stakeholders know to be factual. An environmentalist will hold an ideological position. They will be opposed to most or all of the activities of the corporation. They will hold strong opinions about what corporations do and do not do, some elements of which will have their bases in fact while others are purely ideological. It is axiomatic that an environmentalist will opine about the issue or topic so it will be critical to differentiate between whether the survey seeks opinion or attitude.

Speculative or leading questions will be of no value when overlaid onto objectives. Avoid leading questions. Journalists and reporters seek angles to their stories which present leading questions designed to elicit known responses that confirm their story angles. Avoid journalistic tactics. Avoid emotive words and phrases that a respondent can connect with. A survey littered with subjective data is useless. When dealing with stakeholders do not always assume they are ignorant of issues and topics but take care when seeking information on facts to ensure they are not confused with opinion.

Special considerations about action/behaviour:

- Make sure you are asking for relevant behaviours
- Don't word question to assume a particular answer
- Make sure the questions can be reasonably answered
- Make sure the topic is within the respondent's relevant experience
- Avoid intrusive questions.

Take special care when drafting survey questions. Seek from the respondent an appropriate response mechanism so that it is clear the respondent can answer the questions effectively and accurately. Keep questions within a framework that is unobtrusive but at the same time capable of obtaining information that will be relevant.

*Impartiality*

- Keep wording neutral
- Don't signal your own bias
- Don't employ terms with different meanings
- Avoid prestige bias in making associations with known figures.

Whether the survey is online, face to face, by telephone or in some other format it is crucial to maintain impartiality. A pollster may have an inbuilt bias, and in the case of acting on behalf of a corporation the perception may be that the pollster is in favour of the actions of the corporate entity in question. Whatever the case it is important that the behaviour exhibited by the pollster does not translate into a perceived bias that could be picked up by the respondent.

*Demographics*

- Divide income/age into ranges
- Tailor educational levels to target populations
- Tailor demographic information to research needs.

When seeking information from the respondent related to age, status and so on take care to offer non-specific ranges for the data. Ages might be 20–25, 26–30, 31–34, rather than asking for a specific year. Income, too, should be offered in a range that can then be extrapolated.

When seeking information about levels of education do so by avoiding embarrassing the respondent. If the respondent has a lesser qualification than that which you are asking about they may embellish their answers to suit your requirements.

*Types of questionnaire*

- Multiple choice – must be comprehensive and exclusive
- Checklist items
- Forced choice – two or more statements.

There are numerous ways to structure questions. If the survey uses multiple choice make sure it is exhaustive. Do not leave room for a 'don't know' answer.

Rating scales:

1   Likert bipolar
- Poor–Good
  1-2-3-4-5, where 1= bad; 5= good
- Endorsement (true/false)
- Frequency (always/never)
- Intensity (none/severe)
- Influence (big problem/little problem)
- Comparison (much more/much less).

2   Semantic differential
- Two opposing positions
- Interesting/uninteresting
- Enjoyable/horrible.

## Collection and analysis of survey data

Here are some question points to consider when conceptualizing a survey summary.

1   The survey
    Was it constructed well enough to be useful?

2   The questionnaire
    Was the response rate acceptable?

3   The sample
    Did the sample represent the general population?

4   The stakeholders
    Was there a link to the hypotheses drawn between stakeholder groups?

### Questions relating to the surveys

1   Do corporations sometimes choose inappropriate strategies for goal achievement?
2   Are attributes of stakeholders for a particular strategy reflective of that stakeholder group or would they be better reached through an alternative strategy?
3   Do stakeholder attributes vary across strategies?
4   Do the survey results provide evidence that the corporation under investigation uses other strategies outside the chosen frame?

## CONCLUSION

Stakeholder attributes create or adjust communicative actions. Corporate communication inspires passive responses or active responses in stakeholders. Stakeholder reactions will be active or passive depending upon the level and type of information or news they obtain before or after an event based upon their relationship with the corporation.

Four primary attributes – problem recognition, level of involvement, constraint recognition and goal compatibility – underpin the corporate strategic view of stakeholder communication.

Additional attributes that are recognizable and can be applied as an overlay to the primary attributes are research techniques, resource accumulations and anticipatory actions.

Mapping stakeholders and the identification of stakeholder attributes provide a substantial basis for corporate engagement. Two additional elements contribute to the validity and success of communication strategies: information from focus groups and data from surveys.

 **DISCUSSION QUESTIONS**

1   How important is it for corporations to identify different stakeholder groups?
2   Why do corporations need to consider the different needs of stakeholders?

# GRAND STRATEGY, NARRATIVE THEORY AND TAXONOMIES OF CORPORATE STRATEGY SELECTION

This chapter explains the concept of narrative theory as it applies to corporate communication. It explains the various aspects of narrative theory. It describes the historical narrative of the corporation as one which has led to a contemporary asymmetrical approach
to corporate communication strategy. It extends into corporation communication Carl
Botan's definition of grand strategy which is interpreted as policy-level decisions being
made about goals, alignments, ethics and relationships with publics and other forces in the
environment (Botan & Hazleton, 2006). It expands Vincent Hazleton's work in developing
a taxonomy of corporate strategy selection. It argues that while there are other models
available, Hazleton's taxonomies provide an important underpinning from which to investigate and analyse corporate stakeholder communication and engagement. It provides an
extensive evaluation of Hazleton's taxonomies and adds a significant dimension to them by
demonstrating ways in which additional categories are conceptualized and function.

## GRAND STRATEGY

Grand strategy has its origins in conflict. It has been described by US scholar Peter Feaver
(2009) as the art of reconciling ends and means and that it involves *purposive action*.
He described it as a collection of plans and policies that comprise a state's deliberate
efforts to harness political, military, diplomatic and economic tools to advance national
interest (Feaver, 2009) and where leaders mobilize and deploy resources and capabilities,
military and non-military, to reach national goals (Feaver and Popescu, 2012). Countries,
therefore, are meant to construct grand strategies. But as we know many of the world's
largest corporations are larger than some of the world's medium-sized countries and much
larger than some of the smaller ones in both capital and populations. It would be difficult
to recognize the grand strategies of most countries. Even the United States of America and
the People's Republic of China demonstrate no clear grand strategy.

The elements of grand strategy for nations can be examined so that we get a good idea
of how a grand strategy plays out for a corporation. A grand strategy implies control and
the maintenance of order. In global political terms, for the second half of the twentieth
century, the grand strategy of the United States was to maintain international order
through a selective employment of military and economic 'hard' power coupled with
less effective diplomatic and political 'soft' power. Since the beginning of the twenty-first
century there has been a perceptible shift in ownership of grand strategy on a global
scale. The emergence of China as an alternative global power has created a struggle for
supremacy between the world's two most powerful nations. Not unlike the competitive

struggles which categorize corporate power plays, China and the United States appeared after the first decade of the twenty-first century to be headed towards a conflict based upon very different notions of grand strategy. (For an alternative view of US and Chinese grand strategies see Karabell, 2009). In 2011 China published a white paper entitled *China's Peaceful Development* which comprised six core elements (core here is similar to core competences for a corporation): state sovereignty; national security; territorial integrity; national re-unification; constitutional, political and social stability; and sustainable social and economic development.

A similar set of grand strategy principles can be laid down for a corporation: corporate sovereignty; corporate security; territorial integrity; unified business interests; legal, political and social stability; and sustainable development. Corporate sovereignty would be the ability of the corporation to act in its own best interests without political or military interference from other corporations or from states. Corporate security is self-evident; it would be both the security of trade secrets or intellectual property and the security of property and capital against physical or cyber attack. Territorial integrity would refer to the ability to maintain physical property rights. In state terms this would be considered against the possibility of external attack from other states. In the corporate sense it could be considered against any erosion of property rights that may be initiated by a state. Examples might be the contraction of gas exploration leases or the conversion of fishing grounds to state marine parks. Unification of a corporation's business interests could occur under new ownership. They might also be subject to merger or acquisition. Legal, political and social security would refer to the ability of a corporation to do business within state boundaries that were unlikely to suffer from the upheaval of war or revolution. In many African nations, social and political instability has historically proscribed corporate development. Sustainable development is also self-evident. A corporation like a state has as a priority goal long-term existence. China's ruling communist party has enunciated a desire for long-term social and economic development at sustainable levels rather than overexuberant levels. Corporations, too, look to the long-term profitability of their enterprises as a goal of sustainability.

There are arguments on both sides concerning a grand strategy for the United States. With China's adoption of a position that claimed to want to secure a 'new type of great power relationship' the United States was forced to reconsider its own position. Such a demand by a perceived potential enemy was not taken lightly. The United States had taken a leadership role in the aftermath of the Second World War and had dominated global diplomacy in both hard and soft power relationship development. With the surfacing of China as a potential competitor to US hegemony it was forced to reconsider a number of elements of its own grand strategy: its global leadership; its capacity for building rather than defending and preventing; its domestic support for global leadership; and its global relationships and their relative strengths and weaknesses.

Corporations can look to structuring or restructuring their grand strategies along the same lines. In much the same way that states are in global competition for leadership and power dominance, corporations are in competition for brand, image and reputation dominance. A corporation will look to fill a competition vacuum in the same way a state will fill a power vacuum. Corporations use similar rhetoric to states – global leadership, building, domestic brand loyalty, and fostering strong relationships. The rhetoric of grand strategy must have tangible meaning if it is to enhance the long-term entity of state or corporation.

# HOW DOES A CORPORATION GET A GRAND STRATEGY?

If, as we argue above, a grand strategy is overarching – if it is the assembly of policies and plans that are purposive and converted to action – then it must be enunciated clearly and concisely. US analyst Carl Botan provides a clear and concise definition of grand strategy. It is the 'policy level decisions an organization makes about goals, alignments, ethics and relationships with publics and other forces in its environment' (Botan and Hazleton, 2006, p. 225). Botan suggests corporations and other organizations have grand strategies that are 'analogous to, but fundamentally different from the grand strategies of nations' (Botan and Hazleton, 2006, p. 225). General Motors (GM), he adds, maintains different marketing strategies for its automotive brands (Buick, Chevrolet, Cadillac and GMC). (Pontiac ceased production in 2009 following the GFC though Botan refers to this as the fifth division in his 2006 work.) Grand strategy works at a level above campaign strategy and is defined by its capacity to constrain or limit campaign strategies, Botan argues. We might look more closely at Botan's definition to see if it fits with our framework of corporate strategic communication.

For Botan, grand strategy sits at policy-level decision-making within organizations. Given that Botan described organizations more generally, we need to contextualize the term policy-level decision-making for corporations. Where and at what level does policy get framed? Corporate policies are the guiding principles upon which the corporation is founded. Policy is most often conceptualized and framed by the board of directors. Policy embraces the goals and objectives of the firm. It also frames the operations of the firm – how employees carry out their work and authorization levels of activities. When we hear someone say, 'it's company policy to do it this way' we may not discover why the policy does it that way but we can rest assured it will be done that way. Once a policy has been set there is little in the way of flexibility. Policy is an interesting word that really means principles, or guidelines. It can be used for any number of actions including those of an individual. One may have a 'policy' for never driving a car while texting or taking selfies. Or one may have an 'insurance' policy that covers driving a car but not driving and texting at the same time. It is derived from the Greek *politeria* which means 'citizenship' or 'government'. It can be any course of action adopted or proposed that is expedient or advantageous. This means policy should not be created if it is going to be inexpedient or disadvantageous but in corporate terms the competitive environment means all policy must by its nature disadvantage those competing against it. This is the core reason why not all stakeholders see corporate activity from the standpoint of the corporation. If corporate policy is designed to benefit, to create an advantage and be expedient, it does so for those closest to it: shareholders. It may look to be beneficial to a range of other stakeholders but, again, by its nature it cannot benefit all stakeholders all of the time.

Governments create a variety of policies for the different elements of a society under their control. They create health policy, defence policy, communication policy, foreign policy, economic policy, financial policy and education policy, among others. Corporations create overarching policies for different divisions and different levels of activities within the corporate structure. As Botan remarks, GM created different marketing strategies for each of its divisions but its grand strategy lay across the top of the whole enterprise. Grand strategy relies for its success on a set of principles that combine to make up the company policy. So we can say that a corporation has a grand strategy *if it adopts and adheres to the deliberate set of principles it puts in place to guide its actions and achieve rational objectives*. The success of corporate policy is based on rational rather than irrational objectives and outcomes and therefore rational policy leads to the achievement of rational objectives. It is only when policy is set outside rational guidelines that it goes astray.

The same does not hold for governments. They create policy based upon additional factors including the franchise. A conservative government will never create a broad-based welfare policy, while a progressive government will never create a tax policy that favours the wealthy. Corporations have a different standpoint. Shareholders are their primary voting publics; secondary voters might include creditors and employees.

A corporation gets a grand strategy when its policies align with the greatest number of stakeholders. As we have seen above the idea that shareholders are the primary focus for the corporation has been set aside in favour of a more inclusive arrangement. We have seen from the various annual reports described in earlier chapters that some of the world's largest companies have grand strategies that embrace sustainability and as such they create policies that are directed at different stakeholders. What we are now interested in is the way in which they create their grand strategies and their policies so that they can include the greatest number of stakeholders in their actions and still achieve what they set out to achieve: to be profitable to their shareholders.

# THE PLACE OF NARRATIVE IN THE CORPORATE STORY

Narrative and narrative theory underpin the corporate 'story'. How a corporation tells its story and how successful it is at telling it bears a direct relationship to how it conceptualizes and operationalizes its grand strategy. Grand strategy and narrative are inexorably interwoven throughout corporate history. Corporations sometimes tell their story by creating a book-length work, authored by a professional writer, who creates a non-fiction narrative filled with characters, plots and intrigue in the same way as a television drama or an old-fashioned murder mystery.

A narrative is a series of events or actions that are interconnected and set out in the form of a story. In book or televisual form a narrative story requires the interposing of a narrator. A narrator is one who conveys to an audience the actions or events that occur in the story. A corporate story, or narrative, also requires a narrator. Much of the matter constructed by a corporation is done so by professional communicators such as public relationists, marketers and copywriters. They write stories that become advertising, press releases and point-of-sale brochures. But they are not the narrators of the corporate story. Let's look at what a narrator might be in the corporate sense.

## The narrative voice: real or implied

A storyteller is a vital part of any story including the corporate story. A narrative voice conveys meaning from the story to readers and audiences. But stakeholders in the corporate story are more complex than readers and audiences. Readers and audiences are part of the mosaic of the story but they are passive in that they absorb without taking action. Readers and audiences are stakeholders in the sense that they invest monetarily in being readers or audiences but they are not active stakeholders in the sense that they were not a part of the action that created the narrative. A corporate story is created because of, not in spite of, its stakeholders. Corporate stakeholders drive the corporate story. They are not passive because they are viewed by the corporation as integral to the story.

Narrative voice is the standpoint of the story; it is the way in which character, plot and setting are determined and it is the lens through which the story projects itself onto its readers, audiences or stakeholders. Journalists refer to this as the angle of the story. The angle from which the story is told determines how it is received. Annual reports are the narratives that drive corporate activity. All other narratives and stories emanate from the annual report. The annual report has a narrative voice. It chooses its narrative voice by deciding the standpoint of the company. When the standpoint is decided the narrative voice becomes clear. Standpoint can be:

1  outside the company;
2  inside the company; or
3  dramatic independent.

If it is a dramatic standpoint no single individual represents the narrative voice. Corporations that publish books and make movies about their work use either the outsider or the dramatic. Annual reports use the insider, the first-person, usually in the form of the chairman, president or chief executive, to set the tone for the plot, setting and characters.

How do corporations decide on the narrative voice for specific stories? In the two or three decades before the turn of the twenty-first century the corporate book was the popular choice. The world's largest corporations turned to professional writers to author hardback brick-sized works that set out their story through a series of events and actions that were interconnected but most often had as their central character the chief executive who had driven the success of the company. Sony, General Electric, IBM, Apple and Microsoft all churned out narratives that looked more like Mills & Boon than the reality of the mundane day-to-day work of running a corporation. General Electric commissioned Robert Slater to write the 328-page glossy hardback, *Jack Welch and the GE Way: Management Insights and Leadership Secrets of the Legendary CEO*, which was published in 1999 by McGraw-Hill. In the same year Sony commissioned John Nathan to write *Sony: The Private Life*, a 348-page glossy published by HarperCollins. Slater and Nathan provided an independent or *omniscient standpoint*, one which was outside the corporation and therefore appeared to be more objective than if the works had been written by insiders. This works well for corporate entities. The external or omniscient narrative voice provides reinforcement, or *third-person endorsement*.

## Implied author

There is one other aspect of narrative voice that is relevant to the corporation. A concept known as the implied author was first enunciated by US rhetorician Wayne Booth in 1961. Booth believed an author discovered him- or herself as they wrote. It was the discovery of the other presence, the official scribe or second self, that Booth argued was crucial and that it occurred when a writer wrote (Booth, 1961, p. 71). With this discovery came the realization that a reader or audience identified not with the actual or real author but with the *implied author* or the official scribe. The implied author, or second self, differed to the real author, or first self, by the way the writing took shape, the standpoint or angle it took. Journalists and reporters when writing about corporations adopt an angle and a second self or official scribe position. They provide a standpoint but that itself is checked against the reality of what the corporation does by editors and subeditors who stand between the journalist and the ultimate representation of the story.

For Booth, the implied author encoded the story and the reader decoded it. Corporate communication is encoded by an implied author, such as the chairman, and decoded by stakeholders. The textual choices made by the corporate author in the encoding process will be decoded by stakeholders using known inferences that allow them to construct an image of the corporation in ways that do not necessarily accord with what the author intended to be inferred. This is the point of departure for corporate communication. It can be constructed without being underpinned by the policies that inform a grand strategy, or it can be constructed around the rational objectives of policy.

## NARRATIVE THEORY INFORMS CORPORATE STRATEGIC COMMUNICATION

If we seek to apply a definition of narrative to the communications produced by corporation a good starting point is the functional approach argued by Lucaites and Condit (1985). They argue that narrative voice pervades every genre or medium of human discourse and, as such, requires a broader theory based upon 'recursive interaction of the multiple forms and functions of narrative as they are materialized in the discourse of everyday life' (Lucaites and Condit, 1985, p. 91). Discourse, they argue, is served by a wide range of narrative functions. The most relevant to the corporation under discussion is the rhetorical function. The goal of *rhetorical discourse* is a persuasive end that assumes controlling interests and the presumption of power. Rhetorical narratives aim to achieve something beyond their own existence. They are produced with an end goal in mind which means they are set up as a function of corporate strategic communication rather than as something which has, as its goal, form and content. Lucaites and Condit differenti-ate rhetoric in this way because most narrative theory has its basis in the study of poetry where form and content are end goals. For the corporate entity, the poetic is valueless as it provides no advantage in terms of interests and power. The origin of the rhetorical narrative lay in the persuasive argument of an orator who prepared a case before court. Some of the best orators are those members of parliaments who have spent time in the legal profession, particularly at the bar where they advocated decisively on behalf of their client stakeholders.

The corporation of the twenty-first century has not abandoned entirely the principles of form and content in rhetorical narrative. In fact corporations have embraced them in the way they present their annual reports, corporate histories and YouTube videos so that form, content and function are interwoven seamlessly with the idea of implied author. Stakeholders can but marvel at the result. But all corporate rhetorical narratives are not dominant. A *dominant narrative*, according to US scholar Hugh Miller, if it is institutional-ized, 'defines the status quo way of understanding problems in its domain' (Miller, 2014, p. 287). An entrenched or *institutionalized narrative* is more easily defended against competing narratives. If we apply this in a corporate context we might see that certain industries or economic sectors have become embedded or institutionalized so that the corporations which they serve have a competitive advantage in terms of their communi-cation. News media sources play into this. Once a journalist or reporter has a corporate source they value they tend to return to it for every comment or statement about events and issues across a particular sector. A comment from Shell or British Petroleum (BP) is institutionalized when making reference to global energy, for example. In Europe when an automotive issue is raised, Fiat, Peugeot and Audi are first points of reference.

Corporations need to take care though when attempting to construct a dominant narrative even when it plays to the strengths of its grand strategy. As Miller argues, 'narratives institutionalize certain arrays of meaning and solidify them into a coherent format. This coherence is not necessarily logical coherence. Narratives can be difficult to disengage from. There may be a tipping point where a dominant narrative loses its status and a new narrative takes hold' (Miller, 2014, p. 292). If we use the narrative presented by Toyota in its annual report which we have discussed above, we see that it aligns with the more generally dominant narrative in the global automotive sector that Toyota is heading towards being the world's leading automotive manufacturer. But there are other auto manufacturers who are equally keen to represent their position and to embed their narrative as dominant. It would not take much in the fickle world of car making and buying for Toyota to be knocked off its perch. But which auto maker would represent the dominant narrative in global terms? American manufacturers have large domestic markets and are less interested in global dominance. Does the GM narrative imply its ambition for diffuse global action? What of a European manufacturer. Or Indian? If we examine closely the narratives represented by all the leading auto makers Toyota stands the best chance of institutionalizing its narrative and thus becoming dominant.

Let's look again at our earlier global seafood industry leaders. Japan's Maruha Nichiro constitutes one of the world's largest fishing and fish processing companies. In 2014 a recall of its products was forced on the company because it had poisoned 3000 people. In dominant narrative terms such an incident might lead to a realignment of narratives in which Maruha Nichiro was knocked from the top of the heap by competing corporate seafood narratives. But it was not clear that Maruha Nichiro possessed a dominant narrative. The global seafood business is filled with competing corporate narratives that rely on a changing primary resource focus. Unlike auto manufacturing which can apply a rhetorical narrative directly to car buyers as stakeholders, the fishing business is reliant upon a range of stakeholders to carry the narrative towards a singular standpoint.

## Analysing the corporate narrative: avatars and selves

As discussed above we can approach the corporate narrative using a variety of methods including content analysis or discourse analysis. Whatever we choose we must consider Miller's argument that narrative analysis requires us to contextualize what it is we are investigating (Miller, 2014, p. 293). In most cases corporate narratives will demonstrate similar elements precisely because they are rhetorical in focus.

This leads us to consider Spanish linguist Angeles Martinez's (2014) argument that narrative engagement can be mystifying – it does not always work the same way for all stakeholders; some stakeholders find certain narratives relevant while others are indifferent; stakeholders alter perceptions about narratives over time; and most importantly, 'why do people sometimes wonder at a past self who could find pleasure and self transformative potential in a narrative that their present self cannot feel carried away by at all?' (Martinez, 2014, p. 110).

Corporations want stakeholders to become immersed in the corporate narrative they present. Martinez described immersion in a narrative using traditional metaphors such as 'reading is a journey', 'reading is engaging', 'reading is control', and most importantly to the corporate strategy, 'reading is investment'. If a corporate entity can represent its narrative using matter which is at once engaging and investing, then it will capture a wider array of stakeholders than if the matter is filled with jargon or otherwise disengaging. We have seen in Chapter 3 the differentiated narratives in the annual reports of Toyota and Royal Dutch Shell. We may make determinations on engagement and investment by analysing their respective differentiated narratives.

Analysis of the narrative as discourse is, as Martinez points out, 'an instance of a communicative situation [that] frequently includes several levels of representation' (Martinez, 2014, p. 112). These different levels prevent interaction between participants on other levels but as Martinez argues, this is historically valid when the boundaries between the fictional world and the real world are in play but it has been altered substantially by the invention of the computing avatar. Fictional gaming has pushed these boundaries as 'the real world player is invited to play the role of a fictional world character, who becomes the players avatar' (Martinez, 2014, p. 112). Do corporations employ similar communicative devices that pull stakeholders and their avatars into the narrative representing the corporation? If we think about stakeholders as first and foremost human beings with images of themselves in particular situations we can also locate them in those situations. Martinez uses the image of self to construct a metaphor for narrative analysis. In it the self is a conceptualization of everything one does which is a network of inter-related schemas. These self-schemas act like a computer hard drive by collating and interpreting thoughts, feelings and experiences into compartments. The compartment specifics are brought out when we are put into a space so that we can interact appropriately. We have what Martinez calls *domain-specific* aspects of self derived from past experience which 'influence current behaviours and project domain-specific expectations on future imaginings of self' (Martinez, 2014, p. 118). It is these domain-specific aspects that corporations employ in their narratives to engage stakeholders.

For its legitimacy and control the corporation relies upon a concept of self that is known as *possible selves*. These possible selves are what we project towards. They are what we would like to be at some time in the future. Rather than old and dying when we are eighty, for example, we would like to think that we will continue as we were when we were twenty – young and alive. This is where the corporation has the potential to engineer its narrative so that it resonates with stakeholders who may not have in their existing selves included in their schema being a stakeholder in a corporation. The prospect of increased wealth is the first part of the narrative that corporations apply to potential investor stakeholders; the future possible self cannot resile from that.

An analysis of the corporate narrative should include the anticipation of generational change. It should recognize 'the dynamic nature of the self concept and for its potential for growth and change (Martinez, 2014, p. 119). Perception and motivation are driven by the interaction between the present self and the future self. Patterns of behaviour can highlight for a corporation the possible actions an individual will take. We would normally talk about these elements as part of a behavioural scientific analysis of customers as stakeholders, for example, or how environmental stakeholders might behave in specific situations. Here we are applying the same behavioural principles to the ways in which a corporation should frame its grand strategy as narrative. The grand strategy underpinned by rational policy is the corporate narrative. It is what we are most interested in as the unit of analysis if we are going to successfully reverse engineer the strategic communication of a corporation.

## TAXONOMIES OF CORPORATE COMMUNICATION STRATEGY SELECTION

Corporations choose which communication strategies they will use for which campaigns, when they will use them and which stakeholders they will pitch at. What the strategies look like and how they choose them is less obvious. On one level, corporations make strategy selections based on problems. They wait until a problem is upon them then decide how to communicate with stakeholders to reduce or contain damage. This is known more generally as crisis management. These corporations are like cyclists who say they will never fall off their bikes. When it happens they are surprised. The cyclist who says I will fall off, it's just a matter of time, is prepared for the inevitable. Corporations that look to future problematic issues create communication strategies that are better equipped to deal with the problem when it arises. Not all problems are so severe that they need to be labelled 'crises'.

What is important for corporations is the construction of an array of communication strategies that can be effective across a variety of spaces and places. These strategies can be categorized so that they are easily identifiable and usable. As we have seen in Chapter 5, James Grunig's work on the identification of publics by how they see or don't see a problem can be extrapolated into how corporate stakeholders identify and recognize issues or problems within the corporate world. If we explain it simplistically, Grunig argued that publics looked at things in different ways dependent upon the time of day, how much they knew about a situation and whether they had the capacity to be involved. The same can be said of stakeholders in corporate activity. Here we need to consider two things:

1  What stakeholders are looking at when they look at a corporation;
2  What a corporation looks at when it looks at stakeholders.

By *look at* we mean the metaphorical image that is projected not the act of standing and staring. When a stakeholder looks at a corporation it imagines certain things. Similarly when a corporation looks at a stakeholder it, too, imagines certain things. On the corporate side of the calculus those things need to be translated into effective communication strategies. What does a corporation see when it looks at a stakeholder and how does it conceptualize its strategic communication around what it sees?

One of the more important models for the conceptualization and operationalization of strategic communication was that defined by US academic Vincent Hazleton. In 1999 Hazleton, with colleague Kelly Page, presented an empirical analysis of factors influencing public relations strategy selection and effectiveness. Page and Hazleton (1999) used data from a survey of American Public Relations Institute members to embellish and extend earlier work by Hazleton and Long (1988) which provided an alternative to Grunig's theory of excellence in public relations. Hazleton and Long added environmental factors to Grunig's attributes of publics and demonstrated that a taxonomy of public relations strategies which included message and receiver variables provided a positivist alternative to the normative Grunig model (Page and Hazleton, 1999, p. 4). The analysis of factors influencing strategy selection allowed the further development of the functions of 'messages' at a psychological level that Page and Hazleton thought reflected the way in which communication strategies were developed and employed. There were six functions:

1  facilitate;
2  inform;

3 persuade;
4 coerce;
5 bargain; and
6 resolve.

The first four Hazleton extrapolated from social change theory where organizations plan for change and communicate it accordingly. The two remaining he took from Grunig's ideas about the direction and purpose of communication. Hazleton framed his taxonomies of strategies around the six functions and came up with a model that presented them as:

1 *Informative* – based on the presentation of unbiased facts. A presumption that stakeholders will infer conclusions from accurate data.
2 *Facilitative* – makes resources available to stakeholders which allow them to act in ways in which they are already disposed to act. Best used when stakeholders recognize a problem exists and agree remedial action is necessary.
3 *Persuasive* – characterized by appeals to stakeholder values and emotions. Used when a problem is not recognized or considered important. Used to convince stakeholders to re-allocate resources.
4 *Promise and reward* – employs a coercive function and involves the exercise of power. Implies the source of the message controls an outcome desired by the receiver of the message.
5 *Threat and punishment* – employs negative coercion and the exercise of power and threat. Implies the source controls an outcome feared or disliked by the receiver. Useful when the stakeholder's perceived need for change is low.
6 *Bargaining* – characterized by an exchange of messages between communicators. Employs deception and withholding of information.
7 *Co-operative problem-solving* – jointly defines problems and solutions to problems. Open exchange of information to establish common goals.

As we outlined above Hazleton's work is a strong underpinning. Corporate strategic communication, however, requires a new approach. Our new model removes the persuasive strategy (3) and substitutes for it an empowerment strategy. It places empowerment at the top of the list. The persuasive strategy is overarching and has shifted in importance over time. The empowerment strategy is linked directly to Leon Mayhew's notion that communication with publics requires the instrumental injection of an *educative mechanism* for the communication process to be effective. An empowerment strategy remains dynamic and situational but adds significantly to the flexibility required for corporate strategic communication to be truly effective and societal.

Let's look more closely at Hazleton's taxonomies. They were:

1 An informative strategy based on unbiased facts which did not draw conclusions. We will sidestep the problem of facts and whether or not they can be unbiased for the moment. There was a presumption that stakeholders would make inferences and draw conclusions if they were provided with accurate information. There are numerous problems associated with the idea of information accuracy which we can set aside.
2 A facilitative strategy was one based on the provision of resources such as artefacts or guidelines which reinforced stakeholder actions. This strategy was designed to support stakeholders who could be identified as being themselves supportive of the entity in question.

3 A persuasive strategy was based on appeals to emotion and value. Persuasion is a by-product of rhetoric so this strategy reinforced the rhetorical nature of corporate strategic communication. This strategy was designed to use selective information and to reflect the salience of an issue for the entity rather than for the stakeholder.

4 A promise and reward strategy was based on coercion rather than persuasion. It was designed to reflect the power of the entity and the capacity of it to offer stimulants to action undertaken by stakeholders.

5 A threat and punishment strategy was also based on coercion but it was the mirror image of promise and reward. Threat and punishment also had its basis in the power of the entity but it implied negative denotation. It was denotive rather than connotive because it relied on direct meaning for its effectiveness. Coercion is also used to define propaganda. There is an overlap between propaganda and rhetoric.

6 A bargaining strategy was based on the exchange of information between the entity and stakeholder and the stakeholder and the entity. This did not imply two-way symmetry because the information exchange was selective on both sides.

7 A cooperative problem solving strategy was based on a free and open exchange of information. It was different to the bargaining strategy because entity and stakeholder were supportive of common goals. It implied two-way communication symmetry between the entity and the stakeholder and the stakeholder and the entity.

While there are some important underpinnings within the historical frame of these selections there is a need to acknowledge that they were conceived of as public relations rather than corporate-specific strategies. Hazleton and his colleagues looked for answers to broader relationship issues as they related to a generic public rather than to the specifics of more complex stakeholder categories. So, too, the work of James Grunig in investigating the idea of public and publics as they were imagined by a variety of organizations including corporations. In the intervening time period the shape of the corporation has altered as has the shape and dynamics of publics. Where differentiation was less a part of the calculus in early analysis, now it is paramount. Corporations must differentiate and therefore select strategies that denote deeper meanings in the way they see their stakeholders. A new taxonomy of corporate strategic communication selection is set out below.

## NEW TAXONOMIES FOR CORPORATE STRATEGIC COMMUNICATION SELECTION

While Vincent Hazleton developed and inspired thinking about how to categorize communication strategies by combining attributes of stakeholders with influencing factors he did so in a limited sense. Limitations included confining the empirical analysis to an accessible NFP organization and thinking about power without developing any specific strategy around it. All categorization of communication strategies must by their nature focus on power. It is even more important when considering corporate strategic communication because corporations are most interested in communicating when it accumulates power. By this we mean the accumulation of power for the purposes of profit. But the imperative lies with the capacity of the corporation to develop its strategies around the accumulation of power in the knowledge that power is derived from stakeholders. We will revisit the notion of power accumulation in the following chapters when we discuss the relationship between the corporation and society.

### Power and what it means in corporate strategic communication terms

America's foremost authority on global political power, Joseph Nye, refers historically to two types of power: hard power and soft power (Nye, 2008). Hard power was the power of coercion and payment. Soft power was the persuasive, rhetorical alternative. More recently Nye (2011) has argued that any shift in global power from the dominance of the United States to other global actors, most notably China, focusing on gross national product, was a mistake. Smart power, he argued, was the combination of hard power and soft power and 'power always depends on context' (Nye, 2011, p. 31). He added that power was three-dimensional with unipolar military power at the top, multipolar economic power in the middle, and at the bottom transnational relations that involved non-state actors and operated outside government control. These non-state actors Nye referred to included global corporations. If we add to this the idea that there was a power shift which was two-dimensional, 'a power transition among states and a power diffusion away from all states to non-state actors' (Nye, 2011, p. 33), then we can see why corporations need to consider in much more complex detail how they invest in strategic communication.

The possibility of conceptualizing a new taxonomy from within this paradigm is tantalizing. Nye provides further justification for its existence in a parallel political image:

> [I]n a world where borders are becoming more porous that ever to everything from drugs to infectious disease to terrorism nations must mobilize international coalitions and build institutions to address shared threats and challenges. In this sense, power becomes a positive sum game. It is not enough to think in terms of power over others. We must also think in terms of power with others. On many transnational issues, empowering others can help us to accomplish our own goals.
>
> (Nye, 2011, p. xvi)

It is the last part of this statement that is of most interest in the construction of a new taxonomy of corporate communication strategies. The empowering of others provides the clue. Let's first think about how this might be different in the corporate grand strategy sense to how it would play out in the public grand strategy sense.

When Hazleton constructed his strategy selection taxonomies he did so from a US-centric standpoint. Had he contemplated the nature of strategy selection across state boundaries he may have presented his findings differently. Since the beginning of the twenty-first century, corporations located outside the boundaries of democratic states have charged up the leader board to claim top positions among the world's largest global corporations. They include Chinese banks and Russian energy providers and Middle Eastern airlines. Corporations have an abiding interest in accumulating and holding on to power. The accumulation of power is the buffer that separates profitable corporations from their less profitable competitors. So the contemplation of shared power, or the empowering of others, as Nye argues, can be a difficult transformative action for the corporate entity. But Nye is correct in his assessment. If we take his metaphor out of the public space and locate it in the corporate space we see the inevitability of corporate power sharing.

## NEW TAXONOMIES

Persuasion and persuasive capacity are overarching. They are more than single elements within a corporate strategic communication. They are the rhetorical devices of most relevance to stakeholder engagement. Corporations must be persuasive and they must use their persuasive capacity – financial and emotional – if they are to control stakeholder behaviour. A persuasive strategy categorized by appeals to stakeholder values and emotions is therefore removed from the list and implied as being overarching. In its place is empowerment. An empowerment strategy is characterized by the injection of *educative mechanisms*. We will discuss educative mechanisms in detail in Chapter 7. Educative mechanisms are the triggers that allow stakeholders to grasp the context of corporate actions and behaviours. They provide the empowerment. Most importantly, if a corporation is competent to use an empowerment strategy, in doing so it acknowledges the existence of the reverse engineering model. It says to its stakeholders, here are the resources you need to contextualize what it is we are doing and to be part of it. The empowerment strategy assists stakeholder engagement by reinforcing what it was that was revealed to the stakeholder through their activation of the reverse engineering model.

An empowerment strategy removes the need for a co-operative problem-solving strategy. This last of Hazleton's conceptual approaches was important for governments, for NFPs and community groups keen to engage in discourse that represented a metaphor for the establishment of common goals and purposes and to project them onto unassuming publics. We will discuss in detail in Chapter 8 the idea of co-operation, both legislative and social, within the concept of corporate social responsibility.

A corporate standpoint must also question other strategies within Hazleton's taxonomy. More widespread applications would include an informative strategy and a facilitative strategy, but from the corporate perspective, these strategies are only applicable when dealing with shareholders and other direct investors such as creditors. A threat and punishment strategy is no longer relevant. There are too many exogenous variables acting against a corporate entity for it to measure its success against stakeholder threats or punishments. This does not assume corporations have become accessible or that they have softened their approach to how they communicate their actions. What it states is that there are any number of mechanisms available for stakeholders to broadcast the negative actions of corporations. A communication with an implied threat or punishment will be broadcast, resulting in possible negative reactions against the corporation by any number of powerful stakeholders including governments and shareholders.

A new taxonomy of corporate strategy selection must differentiate between the direct power held by some stakeholders and the indirect power of others. Those with no power must be considered to not be stakeholders. They may be stake-seekers. The empowerment strategy allows the corporation to decide which stakeholders will benefit. The incentive and reward strategy varies and enhances the promise and reward strategy. The negotiation strategy replaces the bargaining and co-operative problem-solving strategies.

## Three strategies

From seven broad communication strategies that could be used by a variety of organizations, we have narrowed and refined Hazleton's taxonomy to three strategies that are directly relevant to the communicative actions of corporations:

1 *Empowerment* – characterized by educative mechanisms that contextualize corporate behaviour and actions. Provides information that would not normally be available to stakeholders. Acknowledges the existence of the reverse engineering process for corporate strategic communication accessibility.

2 *Incentive and reward* – characterized by implicit or overt actions that benefit stakeholders at some time in the future. Used when a corporation perceives a stakeholder holds a low level of power.
3 *Negotiation* – characterized by a desire that all stakeholders involved in an action seek a balanced outcome. Used when a corporation perceives different degrees of power to be held by stakeholders.

The resultant taxonomy of corporate strategy selection locks in an understanding that power is distributed among stakeholders and that a corporation must know precisely where stakeholder power lies and to what degree it might be wielded if it is to communicate its actions effectively and profitably. A restatement of the calculus (system of reasoning) provides that a corporation knows its stakeholders better than its stakeholders know the corporation. It does so by compiling data and information and contextualizing stakeholder behaviour. When it has sufficiently mapped its stakeholders and understands their motivations it can apply a variety of communications to them to achieve its goals and objectives. Conversely, a stakeholder can easily determine what strategies a corporation is applying or intending to apply by reverse engineering the communication artefacts of the corporation. When the stakeholder has unlocked or decoded the strategy it can apply its own communication strategy to other stakeholders to achieve its own goals and objectives. Let's look at some examples.

A corporation wants to get a government to build a large infrastructure project or service project. We are often led to believe that governments are innovative and that they come up with ideas themselves. This is not the case. Most often governments are presented with ideas by corporations. The corporation will enact an empowerment communication strategy, followed by an incentive and reward strategy, and concluded with a negotiation strategy. The stakeholder government will be the subject of three separate rolling communication campaigns with one object: legislate to enact the project. On the opposite side of the project will be other stakeholders of the government who may or may not be in favour of the project. They will include competing corporate entities and activist groups which will impose their own communication campaign strategies upon the government. If they are to be successful in opposing the project they will need to understand how the corporation proposing the activity is communicating with the government. They will gather all the artefacts the bidder puts into the public sphere. They will reverse engineer all three strategies being applied to the government by the bidder. They will use the information they have gained to attempt to influence the government to stop the project. The corporation will need to enact further strategies to counter the opposition strategies. Within the same campaign frame it will create a second empowerment strategy aimed at the activist group to provide an educative mechanism. It will enact an incentive and reward strategy followed by a negotiation strategy to reach a balanced outcome. Strategic communication action by the activist group may be ideological or reasonable, or a combination of both. It is crucial that it be taken seriously and engaged appropriately by the corporation. Exertion of energy emanates from the corporation. Agreement, acquiescence or oppositional reactivity is a product of corporate exertion. Whatever the qualifier, the corporation must represent its interests by conceptualizing and operationalizing strategic communication which allows it to exist within a sustainable socioeconomic environment.

# CONCLUSION

Corporations are in competition for brand, image and reputation dominance the same as states are in global competition for leadership and power dominance. Corporations fill competition vacuums in the same way states fill power vacuums. Corporations use similar rhetoric – global leadership, building, domestic brand loyalty, strong relationships.

Narrative and narrative theory underpin corporate stories. How a corporation tells its story and how successful it is at telling it bears a direct relationship to how it conceptualizes and operationalizes its grand strategy. Grand strategy and narrative are inexorably interwoven throughout corporate history.

Corporations use form and content to shape their rhetorical narratives. Form, content and function are interwoven with the idea of implied author in corporate annual reports, histories and YouTube videos.

Corporations choose which communication strategies they will use for which campaigns, when they will use them and which stakeholders they will pitch at.

Corporations need to construct an array of communication strategies that can be effective across a variety of spaces and places. The strategies must be categorized so that they are identifiable and usable.

All categorizations of communication strategies focus on power. Corporations are most interested in communicating when accumulating power.

Narrative theory underpins corporate stories. Corporate narratives underpin grand strategies. A narrative is a story arc that has a beginning and an ending. Narrative voice conveys meaning from the corporation to the stakeholder. Annual reports are the narratives that drive corporate activity.

Corporate stories are encoded by an implied author such as the chairman or chief executive and decoded by stakeholders who use known inferences to construct an image of the corporation. But storytelling does not always have the desired effect. Narrative engagement does not always work the same way for all stakeholders. Narrative perception can alter over time – what a past self may have liked, a future self will question.

Corporations need to construct an array of communication strategies that are effective in different situations. The strategies need to be categorized so that they are identifiable and usable.

Taxonomies of communication strategies must include an empowerment strategy. Three strategies are relevant to corporate communication – empowerment; incentive and reward; and negotiation.

A corporation must know its stakeholders better than the stakeholders know the corporation.

 **DISCUSSION QUESTIONS**

1   What is a grand strategy and why is it important to corporate communication?
2   Why is narrative important as the primary focus of a corporate story?
3   How are categories of communication strategies selected?
4   When should communication strategies be selected?

*Juan Gonzalez Valero, Head of Public Policy and Sustainability, Syngenta*

*Peter Arkle, Global Stewardship Lead, Syngenta*

### Overview of the corporation

Syngenta is a leading agriculture company helping to improve global food security by enabling millions of farmers to make better use of available resources. Through world-class science and innovative crop solutions, its 28,000 people in more than 90 countries, the company is working to transform how crops are grown. Syngenta is driven by its ambition of 'bringing greater food security in an environmentally sustainable way to an increasing populous world by creating a worldwide step-change in farm productivity'.

### Aims and objectives of the societal, human and environmental strategy

Evolving the global food system to meet the demands of the growing global population is one of the greatest challenges of our time. Never in human history have more people lived in urban areas, depending on the rural economy to provide them with enough nutritious food in the right quality. Food is a contentious and divisive issue. Concerns include: civil unrest that can arise in times of food shortage; the role new agricultural technologies should play in sustainably increasing global farm productivity; and how to cope with the resource constraints of land, water and biodiversity when the consequences of climate change demand fast adaptation.

The need to advance our global food system is pressing. Building societal trust and acceptance of the role agricultural technologies – such as pesticides, high-yielding crop varieties, or genetic modification – can play is a critical pre-condition for an effective global response. Syngenta recognizes that trust and acceptance will only be built through true engagement of stakeholders who have a genuine interest in building a sustainable and resilient global food system. Consequently, the company's engagement strategy is to build and share value by shaping the future together with its stakeholders. In recognition that trust and acceptance depend on measurable action rather than just words, the company's *Good Growth Plan* provides Syngenta with a unique framework to partner and engage with key stakeholders to increase the sustainability of agriculture.

Under the *Good Growth Plan*, Syngenta has committed to:

- Make crops more efficient: increase the average productivity of the world's major crops by 20 per cent without using more land, water or inputs
- Rescue more farmland: improve the fertility of 10 million hectares of farmland on the brink of degradation
- Help biodiversity flourish: enhance biodiversity on 5 million hectares of farmland
- Empower smallholders: reach 20 million smallholders and enable them to increase productivity by 50 per cent
- Help people stay safe: train 20 million farm workers on labour safety, especially in developing countries

- Look after every worker: strive for fair labour conditions throughout its entire supply chain network.

Syngenta wants stakeholders to be active participants in what the company is trying to accomplish and has already developed a range of partnerships in support of each of the six commitments. The *Good Growth Plan* is built on a foundation of openness and transparency, underpinned by a unique framework for measurement. This relies on internal and third-party data collection and validation, as well as assurance by independent auditors. The auditing standards of the *Good Growth Plan* are now at the same level as a full financial audit – making Syngenta one of the very few companies in the world in any sector to strive for such rigour in auditing sustainability performance.

Syngenta's business strategy is focused on sustainable agriculture, and the *Good Growth Plan* is integrally linked to the company's strategy. This is a defining feature of Syngenta's approach. The *Good Growth Plan* is not a stand-alone sustainability strategy or separate corporate responsibility initiative – it is a framework to measure, demonstrate and deepen the sustainability of Syngenta's strategy. Progress towards the company's *Good Growth Plan* commitments is a key metric in performance management across the organization.

### Where the strategy sits within the corporate structure

Stakeholder engagement in support of the *Good Growth Plan* is a responsibility of the company's entire senior management, with Corporate Affairs taking a lead in coordinating and supporting communication and engagement activities. Corporate Affairs is an executive function within Syngenta, with the company's Head of Corporate Affairs sitting on Syngenta's Executive Commission (SEC). The function plays a pivotal role in communicating the company's contribution to society and in managing relationships with a broad range of stakeholders including governments and non-governmental organizations, investors and the wider public (including through media engagement). As a key partner to the business, Corporate Affairs helps build the capabilities of Syngenta's team members to effectively partner with stakeholders and to align the company's key relationships with its business strategy. Partnerships also provide opportunity for improvement and innovation that creates new value for the organization.

### An outline of the corporate social responsibility policy

Syngenta is committed to promote and maintain high standards of corporate responsibility worldwide in an industry that is essential to global agriculture and food production. The company's long-standing Corporate Responsibility Policy formalizes the principles that guide it in all its business activities. Syngenta continuously engages with stakeholders around the world to shape its understanding of the corporate responsibility (CR) issues that it must address in its everyday business. The company listens to its stakeholders, tries to respond to their concerns, and reports on environmental and social performance annually in its Annual Review. Syngenta's CR approach is overseen and guided by a Board-level Corporate Responsibility Committee. It advises on overall CR priorities, policies and issues, external reporting, and monitors the implementation of the company's internal policies.

*(Continued)*

Recognizing the importance of independent oversight and benchmarking, Syngenta reports according to the Global Reporting Initiative (GRI) A+ standard as well as the UN Global Compact Principles. Under the GRI, the company is required to undertake a materiality assessment to determine material issues that are important to both Syngenta and its stakeholders. The company's reporting is tailored to ensure the transparent and rigorous tracking of its performance on these material issues.

### An assessment of stakeholders and stakeholder attributes

With operations in more than ninety countries, Syngenta interacts with a diverse array of stakeholders. The company's major stakeholders include growers, customers (distributors), industry organizations, non-governmental organizations and international agencies, investors, governments, politicians, officials, regulators, the food chain and its employees. There is growing recognition of the need to sustainably intensify agriculture to meet the global food security challenge, and Syngenta is constructively engaging with a wide variety of stakeholders who share its deep commitment to supporting growers in realizing this goal. Many of these stakeholders are actively and directly involved in initiatives under the *Good Growth Plan* in support of this critical goal.

Syngenta also closely engages with stakeholders who share the goal of improving global food and nutrition security, but who have reservations over the role of agricultural technologies in increasing productivity or the influence of large global corporations in the global food system. The company recognizes the importance of actively engaging with these stakeholders to understand their concerns and to build confidence in its technologies and trust in its operations. Syngenta holds the view that this trust can only be built through open and genuine engagement, listening to concerns and providing real examples of how the company's technologies are being responsibly integrated into sustainable farming systems.

As the World Bank has noted, with more people now living in cities than in rural areas, more than half the population is now completely removed from the origins of their food. The availability and affordability of nutritious food in many developed nations conceals the underlying global imperative to improve the productivity and efficiency of our food system. The need to address food security does not seem urgent to many urban-based people of the developed world. To achieve the change required, Syngenta has recognized the need to engage with these influential urban communities to raise awareness of the pressing challenge the world faces in ensuring food and nutrition security, and of how new technologies can be safely and sustainably harnessed to increase the productivity of farming.

Syngenta also encounters stakeholders who have a fundamentally different view on the role that technology should play in modern agriculture. Some of these stakeholders actively campaign against the company's products and directly question its legitimacy and existence. These stakeholders' views are often based on ideology and a more fundamental opposition to technology in agriculture, multinational companies and globalization. While these individuals and organizations often state their commitment to sustainable agriculture and addressing food security, their positions and proposals often belie the realities we face as a global community in addressing the future food and nutrition challenge.

## Stakeholder engagement

One of the most interesting and exciting collaborations Syngenta has forged under the *Good Growth Plan* is with the Open Data Institute (ODI). The ODI is an independent, non-profit open data expert, which works with organizations to create economic, environmental and social value from open data. In partnership with the ODI, Syngenta has made performance data from the *Good Growth Plan* searchable, useable and shareable over the Internet. This includes the baseline information for agricultural efficiency indicators collected on 3600 farms in 41 countries across the world. It is the first time information at a crop level – including resource efficiency – has been made public in this way by a commercial organization. Through making this comprehensive dataset public Syngenta is inviting and enabling people to make their own assessments of the progress it is making under the *Good Growth Plan*. The company's open-data strategy and the partnership-driven approach that underpins the *Good Growth Plan* are blurring the traditional roles of business, government and NGOs by highlighting the collective responsibility we face in addressing acute global challenges. Through the *Good Growth Plan*, Syngenta in partnership with key stakeholders is demonstrating and measuring the contribution that modern sustainable agricultural solutions can make in increasing productivity and efficiency on farms around the world.

## Social licence to operate

The future of the plant science industry, and Syngenta as a company within it, is highly dependent on maintaining a social licence to operate. The *Good Growth Plan* and Syngenta's wider corporate responsibility initiatives are essential in building societal trust and acceptance of the company and its technologies. The *Good Growth Plan* provides a way to demonstrate the value of Syngenta's business beyond the immediate benefit to the farmer. This value is reflected in a range of social and environmental impact assessments that are shared openly with society.

Syngenta is also implementing more targeted initiatives focused on securing its social licence to operate, including specific projects focused on lowering the barriers to acceptance of products of agricultural technology.

## Syngenta in Switzerland

Syngenta has a global focus, but is strongly anchored in Switzerland. The company is headquartered in Basel, and has significant research and development, and manufacturing facilities at different Swiss locations. Switzerland offers an internationally competitive regulatory framework for multinationals which supports business and research. Syngenta continues to work with Swiss decision makers and stakeholders to preserve and improve structures that foster innovation and investment. This includes working closely with federal, cantonal and municipal authorities, civil society, industry organizations, companies, academia and researchers across Switzerland, including on initiatives focused on improving sustainable productive agriculture in Switzerland and around the world.

*(Continued)*

## Conclusion

Syngenta is committed to playing a leading role in helping to achieve a worldwide step-change in farm productivity, and through doing so helping to address the global food security imperative. The *Good Growth Plan* is demonstrating the company's steadfast determination to make a real contribution, and to forge new partnerships with stakeholders to work together to increase the sustainability of agriculture. Society's trust in, and acceptance of, modern agricultural technology and companies like Syngenta, will be essential in order to enable farmers to access the modern tools and technologies they will depend upon to sustainably increase the productivity of food production around the world.

Through open, transparent and genuine engagement with its stakeholders – including wider society – Syngenta is committed to helping to create an operating environment that enables and supports growers to succeed in overcoming one of the biggest challenges of our time.

# 7

# THE RELEVANCE OF MAYHEW'S RHETORICAL PRACTICES

This chapter argues the importance of Leon Mayhew's theories of a *New Public* in which professional communicators influence social policy (Mayhew, 1997). It analyses Mayhew's rhetorical practices as they apply to corporate strategic communication. It develops an argument that places Mayhewian theory as a central tenet of future corporate strategic communication. While Mayhew's theory and his rhetorical practices were derived from political observations, we have reworked and adapted them for the corporate sphere. They are particularly relevant given that the western political sphere has in recent years shifted more into alignment with societal mores while the corporate sphere has drifted almost to the point of uncoupling from society.

It concludes by arguing the relevance of adopting Mayhewian argument within the corporate structure so that successful corporate strategic communication is aligned seamlessly within an ever-changing societal framework.

American sociologist Leon Mayhew made an important contribution to how we might understand the ways corporations fit into society. His theory pivoted around his empirical observation of a political event – a US presidential election – but it was not constrained by the event. Mayhew saw that western society was being persuaded and influenced by professional communicators working on behalf of governments and corporations. He lamented the overpowering nature of the rhetorical practices that pervaded society. In all places and spaces he saw persuasive actions that were disempowering, unrewarding and non-negotiable. His theory was simple: professional communicators acting as agents dominated public opinion. The public sphere, which had once been a place for objective discussion, had become subjected to systematic mass persuasion. The processes of mass persuasion, using the rhetoric of presentation developed and garnished within the advertising and marketing sectors, dominated public communication. (We have seen in earlier chapters how annual reports and other corporate artefacts use the rhetoric of presentation to embed their images in the minds of stakeholders.)

The rhetorical practices Mayhew was most concerned with he described as:

1  A lack of meaningful policy issues on the public agenda;
2  Appeals to attitudes that do not tap structures of solidarity that could support effective responses to sociopolitical problems;
3  One-sided communication that fails to provide opportunities for demands that claims be redeemed in discourse; and
4  Strategic responses that attempt to 'spin' rhetorical descriptions rather than to supply straightforward answers to queries and objections within the wider community.

He argued these four practices were the primary sources of *the inflation of influence* and that they clearly 'dissociated public deliberation from the structure of social life' (Mayhew, 1996, p. 236). While it is important to keep in mind that Mayhew was framing his theory against a political event it is equally important to grasp the relevance of his theory when we locate corporate activity in society. All four of the practices that he identified form and shape the communication strategies of the corporation.

While the first of his four practices may seem less salient to a study of corporate strategic communication, it is in fact deeply relevant. Policy issues are not framed by governments in isolation; they are built in government but their status is derived from the power of the stakeholders who surround government. The most important stakeholder group in the formulation of public policy is global corporations. The British government, for example, frames its energy policy only after deep off-the-record discussions with BP, Royal Dutch Shell and Rio Tinto, among others. Its own communication service identifies the importance of stakeholders in policy-making and delivery. Paradoxically, it adopts Freeman's (1984) observation about stakeholders – a limited managerial view from which owners were perceived to be paramount. It provides a list of stakeholders that includes other government departments, charities, media and regulators but it fails to identify the most persuasive and influential of British government stakeholders – corporations. As Mayhew attests, governments are the originators of the four rhetorical practices that have come to overpower public discourse. And they do not wish to amplify the persuasive and influential nature of their relationships with global corporate activity.

Before we begin our discussion of the four practices embedded in Mayhew's theory and before we attempt to apply them to corporate activity we need to understand a little more about the vocabulary adopted by Mayhew in his hunt for answers. And we need to understand the basis of his theory.

Mayhew's argument about the public, what it does and doesn't know, provides a paradoxical contrast between the idea that the public is unable to understand the degree to which it is persuaded and influenced and the idea that, deep down, it knows precisely what is going on. Mayhew attacked professional communicators for their role in casting a veil over accessibility. The communicators most reviled by Mayhew were public relationists, advertisers and marketers, all representing client-based communication as consumable product and seeking immunity from any *redemption of tokens* most often associated with *solidarity* between client and consumer. But what did he mean by redemption of tokens and solidarity between client and consumer? And why consumer rather than customer or another manifestation of stakeholder? By imagining historical mass publics in a particular way, Mayhew was at once able to inject professional communicators into the public sphere and demonize them while constructing his New Public in which mass opinion was cogniscent of the aims and goals of professionals and refusing thus to be persuaded and influenced. On the one hand he demonized public relationists for acting as agents of persuasion and influence, shielding the truth and reality of their clients' actions and strategies, while on the other he presented an argument that citizens were sufficiently informed to see through these strategies. Mayhew's argument was built upon the idea that professional communicators dominate public opinion, displacing the free public of the Enlightenment with a New Public subject to systematic persuasion and influence. Mayhew's New Public was therefore a *refeudalized* public sphere, imagined by German philosopher Jürgen Habermas (1989), in which the processes of rationalization of persuasion developed in advertising and market research dominate public communication and thus dominate sociopolitical policies and processes through the rhetoric of presentation. Mayhew imagined his New Public as hybrid, emerging from Habermas's generalist public sphere. He concluded somewhat strangely that the mass public of the late twentieth century, while unable to provide inputs to policy, was sufficiently informed to develop sound opinions and make rational decisions. He arrived at this conclusion by an unusually circuitous route. He concluded there was a need for 'serious rhetorical forums not given over to commerce in rhetorical tokens' (Mayhew, 1997 p. 286). He investigated what he referred to as *rhetorical tokens* and the *redemption of influence*. Mayhew was interested in how rhetoric was applied to promises made by political candidates and how citizens might redeem such commitments. Rather than seeing rhetorical tokens as instrumental, he attempted to present them as a way for a variety of stakeholder publics to insinuate themselves into public policy debates and therefore into the public sphere. In this, and its associated idea of the capacity for publics to redeem rhetorical tokens promised by others, lies its significance. The prospect of redemption (setting aside the religious overtones), however, has no basis in truth. Mayhew himself expressed a desire that 'to redeem a rhetorical claim is to respond to demands for clarification, specification and evidence' (Mayhew, 1997, p. 13). Some of his ideas for the redemption of rhetorical tokens included deliberative forums such as direct debate, third-party, diffuse citizen forums in which competing material was placed in the same medium. On balance his contribution was an appeal for fluid mechanisms to ameliorate the redemption of rhetorical tokens, rather than in the provision of soluble forums.

For Mayhew, the community was the legitimate bearer of public opinion, which in turn was the creator of public policy and thus the source of legitimate governing power. To recap, Mayhew argued that persuasion and influence through public relations dominated public communication, displacing Habermas's free public of the Enlightenment, and setting up a New Public which was subject to systematic mass persuasion. While there was no clear evidence that such an ideal public sphere ever existed the importance of the possibility of there having been such a sphere was vital to Mayhew's argument. He believed that an enormous transfer of power occurred from the public to professionals whose primary objective was the manipulation of the opinions of the public within. The rhetoric of presentation was such that *the display of symbols outweighed discursive argument*. He expanded this point to argue that professional communicators produced anti-discursive models which were filled with dangerously high levels of useless information. He argued that it was standard practice to advocate a positive position for an issue or event without specifying exactly how promised benefits from that position might materialize. Such syllogistic techniques are evident in the annual reports, media statements and briefing notes of most publicly listed corporations. They can be thought of as part of our second strategy – incentive and reward – where rhetorical devices attempt to overwhelm the detail of how promised benefits will materialize. There is a 'trust us we know what we're doing' mantra attached to the rhetoric. At first blush, Mayhew appeared to be suggesting that members of his New Public were unable to grasp the nature of the artifice in this type of persuasion, eager as they were to buy products and services and to elect political candidates on the basis of implication and the perceived redemption of a candidate's promised tokens in the same way as if they had bought a Blu-ray disc or a packet of crisps.

These tokens were frequently based on narrow or ill-defined *reputational capital* rather than any substantive future action. In following Jürgen Habermas, Mayhew imagined that true public discourse meant communicative action of discursive contests on public policy functioning specifically to allow citizens the opportunity to understand and formulate opinion without 'perceived' rhetorical influence. Habermas argued that persuasion and influence, transferred from the 'honorific avocation' of the politician to the paid professional, brought about the structural transformation of his public sphere. Similarly it has been argued by others that an inescapable promotional dynamic lies at the heart of contemporary sociopolitical culture (see, for example, Schlesinger, 1994). Within this culture marketers rely on the identification of *aggregates of preferences* in determining the potential sales of goods and services. They create frameworks in which these aggregates are measured against the supply of goods and services from industry. Habermas (1989) aligned the modernist idea of advertising with eighteenth-century European dramatic spectacle. These spectacles, however, Habermas thought of as far removed from authentic public dialogue of that earlier period. Habermas's public sphere was defined as a meeting place or public forum – a mediating environment – between citizens and the state in which information about relevant issues was discussed openly and objectively. We will return to the Habermasian concept of the public sphere in Chapter 8 when we discuss community as stakeholder.

## THE VOCABULARY OF THE NEW PUBLIC

Leon Mayhew gave us a number of applicative terms and phrases with which to construct an image of the corporation as it exists in society. He began by looking for meaning in the word 'public'. He also chose to peel away the layers from historical rhetoric. He cited *Cato's Letters*, collections of newspaper articles written by John Trenchard and Thomas Gordon in the 1720s which attempted to unmask the corrupt activities of the South Sea Corporation (Mayhew, 1997, p. 173). The letters were in fact essays written by Trenchard and Gordon, published in the *London Journal* and the *British Journal* arguing for free speech. The collected essays were believed to have later influenced the ideology of the American revolutionaries. They were arguably as popular at the time as John Locke's treatise on civil government. The public sphere, Mayhew argued, was not a realm of consensus. It embraced conflict and debate which was often indecisive. It frequently failed to 'produce consensual and effective answers to integrative questions' (Mayhew, 1997, p. 5). Rather than 'applying norms to the resolution of conflict by acts of deduction that are accepted by acclamation' the public preferred to engage in contesting and creating meaning. The public, he argued, was the 'ultimate source of legitimate governing power' (Mayhew, 1997, p. 137). If we take this phrase, *the ultimate source of legitimate governing power*, we can see that Mayhew was looking to the historical theory of democracy as a starting place. We also know that it is in itself a historically rhetorical device. The legitimacy of the public holding governing power has been eroded so that even the franchise, the vote we can apply to elect or 'unelect' governments every few years, is subjected to persuasive rhetorical influences.

If we take Mayhew's phrase out of the political sphere and place it in the corporate sphere we have the same application with reference to voting for a board of directors. If we exchange 'public' for 'shareholders' we could argue that *shareholders are the ultimate source of legitimate governing power*. But we know that this is no longer an accurate reflection of shareholder power, given the diffuse nature of other stakeholders.

### The rhetoric of presentation

Rhetoric of presentation is not new. An environment in which the display of symbols outweighs discursive argument occurs at all levels of society. A bag of salad displayed in the cool store of the local market does not provide discursive argument of its nutritional value.

It presents images of fresh clipped beetroot combined with leftover broccoli stalks as being representative of a healthy and nutritious accompaniment to lunch.

A child in primary school with a competing pitch to become the next school captain displays symbols evocative of strength or beauty, athleticism or popularity rather than a discourse on childhood values and parenthood. Of greatest importance in our understanding of the rhetoric of presentation in the corporate sense is Mayhew's inference that a new rhetoric of presentation has been framed in which discursive techniques have been devalued to the point of appearing to be dangerous and confusing. His inference is well supported. We might look to analyse any speech by any contemporary prime minister or president of any country and we will find nothing more than sound bites. Sound bites and talking points. We will find the same in the speeches of the presidents and chief executives of global corporations. And the candidates for primary school captain.

To an extent Mayhew defends the original rhetoric by invoking Aristotle's principles of speaker (ethos), argument (logos) and emotive stakeholders (pathos). With its emphasis on enthymeme, even the most rational rhetoric suggested by Aristotle employs tokens or symbols. Enthymemes are based on probabilities. They are rhetorical syllogisms that require only the first of three parts of an argument to be explicated. In contemporary corporate rhetoric and use of language, enthymeme is the preferred exponent. All corporate logos for example and accompanying catchlines are enthymemes – they are so simple they do not require explanatory assertions as the other two parts that go to make up a syllogism. (A syllogism is a logical argument that applies deduction. It has two or more premises that support a conclusion.)

Mayhew argued the rhetoric of presentation implied *rhetorical tokens* were self-contained, needing no 'redemption' or detailed explanation. 'Images speak for themselves' (Mayhew, 1997, p. 274); slogans and logos require no additional subtext.

## The rhetoric of spectacle

Much of the meaning surrounding political and advocacy campaigns in many African states is derived from street theatre. With large populations of illiterate or semi-literate adults, information campaigns must be represented in the least ambiguous way. Street theatre is an accepted and historical part of African culture so it is a logical technique for the dissemination of all types of information from health campaign messages to safety awareness.

Habermas's concept of medieval events as spectacle, including public beheadings, is recast by Mayhew as a refeudalization that has become attractive in modern communication campaigns. It has in fact become so widespread that a whole genre of television programmes has been built upon refeudalizing the public sphere, infusing it with home renovation, baking, singing and dancing, marrying farmers and snogging randoms. The reality genre of television is a refeudalized sphere in which individuals and collectives attempt to appear stupider than it seems possible while presenting a rhetoric of spectacle that rivals the medieval public and popular sports of hanging, disemboweling, emasculating, beheading and quartering. All in one rhetorical flourish.

Less gory social order spectacles included parades, ceremonies and tournaments to which the public were invited so they could see the relative power and importance of the powerful. Similar contemporary spectacles are enacted in every town and suburb. Many are underpinned financially by corporate donors. The corporation has taken the place of the lord and lady of the manor.

## Differentiation of rhetoric across rhetorical forums

What becomes important for corporations in the identification of rhetoric as a device for gaining positive position is how it is differentiated within different spaces and places – or across rhetorical forums. Differentiation applies to the idea of 'reasonable rhetoric' or rhetoric that 'gives primacy to persuasive appeals deemed reasonable according to cultural conceptions of reason in public discourse' (Mayhew, 1997, p. 41). This means the concept of reason, or rational argument, needs to be accepted by the individual or group on the receiving end of the rhetoric. It must be contextualized so that it can be rebutted or accepted. We will investigate in the following chapter the notion of *social licence to operate* which is another way of saying corporations gain legislative approvals for the activities but they also need society's approval so they need to match their rhetoric with society's expectations and context. They must also decide the relevance of the forums in which they are intending to engage. Once in a forum there is no way out. There are rules and guidelines and the corporation must contextualize or be rebutted. Mayhew refers to these forums as institutionalized – spaces where the speaker is 'constrained to employ reasonable argument and to keep other appeals within fixed bounds' (Mayhew, 1997, p. 41). The institutionalized forums must have guidelines and normative standards if they are to function appropriately and effectively. The most obvious such forum in the western world is the institution of parliament. It is important here to mention briefly the idea formulated by Jürgen Habermas that there is a difference between *communicative action* and another type of action which he termed *purposive-rational action*. Corporations have difficulty finding a balance between purposive-rational action and communicative action and tend to overbalance in favour of the former. Purposive-rational action is action which is identified by means and ends. It seeks to persuade at the edge, where persuasion becomes coercion. Unlike communicative action it does not seek any form of consensus.

## Structures of solidarity

Corporations communicate their actions in a number of ways. Most often they do so through a lead actor, as we have seen – a chief executive, chairman or president. The actor will use rhetorical devices to present the corporate narrative over the longer term or to explain events and circumstances that contribute in the short term to the longer term narrative. They communicate in arenas where there is a contest for meaning and for interpretations of meaning. And they attempt to create structures of solidarity. This means they look to use communication to forge bonds between and among people, bonds that were once unspoken but existing in a time and space where human association was valued in its own right. In German the words *Gemeinschaft* and *Gesellschaft* are used to distinguish community and society where community is said to be a natural state and society a fabricated state. Western urbanization is said to have contributed to the breakdown of communities. Similar breakdowns are occurring in Asia: as China urbanizes, millions of people are dislocated from rural communities and disengaged from traditional associations and structures of solidarities. But Mayhew argues that an assumption of solidarity grounded in 'fixed ties and obligations' fails to consider an associational model that has informed ideas of community for three hundred years (Mayhew, 1997, p. 15). Unsurprisingly he calls for a renewed form of solidarity to replace old kinships, clans and local communities: a 'differentiated solidarity consist(ing) in processes of communication' (Mayhew, 1997, p. 16). It is no coincidence that corporations, governments and other financially fit entities do exactly that: they use differentiated solidarities consist of processes of communication. They include Facebook, Twitter, LinkedIn and Instagram. All these rhetorical devices were heralded by Mayhew as the structures on which differentiated solidarities would be communicated and built. Community now has a new meaning. Facebook is a community. Twitter is a community. LinkedIn is a community.

Mayhew makes an additional crucial point about the relationship between solidarity and influence. Rhetoric will be seen to go in a positive direction when it is represented by trust, by leaders of 'solidary groups' who can be identified as having common goals and objectives – people who are seen as 'trustworthy representatives of solidary groups which possess generalized resources of persuasion, that is influence' (Mayhew, 1997, p. 125). 'Accordingly the structure of influence in [a] society parallels the structure of solidarity, which has a crucial consequence: the independence of the system of influence is grounded on a complex matrix of solidarities' (Mayhew, 1997, p. 125).

The eternal quest of the corporation is to build structures of solidarity that have as their spokesperson the head of the corporation itself. If the corporation can interpret the complex matrices of solidarities found among stakeholders and align stakeholder goals and objectives with those of the corporation, they have been successful in their influence.

## Rhetoric as the discourse of solidarity

The argument put by Kenneth Burke (1966) fifty years ago exemplifies the present relationship of rhetoric to the solidarity required by groups within society. Burke argues that common ground on either side of a position can be made using rhetoric. Rhetoric classifies and identifies oppositional modes of communication. It applies symbols and logic to arguments so that they can be seen clearly. It is reductive. It distils argument so that the symbols of solidarity do not appear to be as forthright as they may have seemed before the rhetorical turn was applied to them. *Climate change*. Two words that invoke different opinions and arguments from disparate groups and individuals. *Global warming*. A phrase that has been set aside in favour of the rhetoric of climate change. Global warming created rhetoric that was difficult to align with the discourse of solidarity. It was too easy for it to be demonstrated that large parts of the earth's surface were not warming but cooling. Climate change reset the discourse and provided solidarity for a wider number of groups to enter into the conversation and to thus build the narrative.

Burke's prescience is valuable when we consider the strategic communication of the corporation and the various communication instruments now available. Burke argues that language itself is inherently rhetorical. We can see from any Twitter feed that there is little room for reason in the Twittersphere. It is a place where the rhetorical flourish assists in setting the dominant discourse on any topic or event. The more outrageous the rhetoric, the more dominant the discourse. The idea that rhetoric is embedded in language goes to the core of the strategy of corporate communication. Corporations use rhetoric in language in the same way as individuals. The embedding allows the corporate narrative to play out alongside other socioeconomic narratives. So rather than being viewed as a nasty instrument of influence and persuasion, corporations employ rhetoric for the same purposes as other organizations within a society: for the positive position persuasion and influence provide.

## The solidarity of groups

Group solidarity or voluntary association is an aspect of corporate existence in society that has an impact on the activities of the corporate entity. When it manifests as oppositional activist solidarity it is capable of altering corporate behaviour. Collective action occurs when stakeholders perceive a problem with corporate activity.

People volunteer to join group activities for any number of different reasons. Some are isolated within their own society and seek common acknowledgement of their plight. Others are actively seeking redemption from an ideological perspective; they have negative sentiments about all corporate activity and they take satisfaction from joining others with similar feelings. They may never involve themselves in violence or other antisocial behaviour. They act by boycotting certain corporate institutions such as supermarkets. They buy their groceries from smaller 'independent' suppliers and they travel longer distances to do so. While buying their organic celeriac they wear their rockabilly fashion statements.

## Normative appeals to solidarity

The rhetorical process, Mayhew imagined, contained *normative components* that motivated conduct within society. Both those attempting to persuade and those being subjected to persuasion were imbued with norms. These norms did not coincide; if they had there would have been no place for rhetoric. What they did, however, was allow those attempting to persuade to use rhetoric to connect to the norms of the stakeholders being persuaded. Their predisposition to those norms meant they would be more likely to accept the persuasion because they fitted nicely with how they thought.

We have values and opinions that allow us to accept or reject even the most persuasive arguments. Our values and norms may not lie within a dominant culture; we may be part of a subculture – a music culture which has within it its own fringe genres – protometal, rockabilly, emo and dolewave are examples. The irony of advertising in western society is that it attempts to locate its rhetoric within subcultures or fringe genres with the object that products and services advertised are meant to have associated values and norms. Corporations identify these values and norms and pitch to them. One can invest heavily in outfits associated with rockabilly for example – clothing, hairstyles, spectacles, shoes – in exactly the same way that investments were made in the twentieth century in jazz, bebop, beat and hippy subcultures. It will come as no surprise that corporations frequently identify and build subcultures. Some emerge as free agents, such as the dolewave subculture that originated in Australia and New Zealand. Dolewave is hard to characterize but it appears to live outside the standard framework of music fringe genres that embrace class struggle at the same time as they project fashion (see for example The Twerps, *Back To You*, YouTube). Corporations attempt to redefine a fringe genre so that it becomes a consumer counter-culture with dedicated fashion and 'attitude'. Sony, a Japanese music and technology company, is very good at identifying music genres and applying normative appeals to solidarity. For music corporations the frame of reference is to create the attitude based on normative behaviours so that its stakeholders will feel a need for 'fitting in'.

## Rhetorical appeals to solidarity

If normative appeals to solidarity seek to understand values and opinions that exist in individuals and to locate rhetoric within the individual, rhetorical appeals seek to persuade using a slightly different technique. Rhetorical appeals locate the persuader and the stakeholder in the same frame. While normative appeals seek to persuade there is no obligation on the part of the stakeholder – assuming there is no associated coercion – to accept the normative appeal. It is not until the persuader locates themselves within the frame already occupied by the stakeholder that the appeal to solidarity alters from normative to rhetorical. The persuader presents an image which infers the results of the persuasion have the same impact on the persuader as on the stakeholder. Corporations use this type of appeal to solidarity when attempting to influence specific stakeholders such as employees. The alignment of persuader and stakeholder so that rhetorical appeals will resonate is not difficult. In this the media is complicit. Corporations and governments use the media as an agent of persuasion. Western news media falls under the ownership of corporations and governments. Changes in the use of language from exclusive to inclusive have provided a subtle shift in the way media supports corporate and government rhetoric. One example is the shift in use of the object and subject when identifying geographical and other physical elements. News bulletins no longer identify 'the' Midlands. It has become 'our' Midlands. It is a subtle shift but it assists in the rhetorical appeal to solidarity.

Mayhew argued that 'confidence in the credit instruments of the public debt institutionalized public opinion as a new form of solidarity. Fundamentalist attitudes that were overcome in the economic sphere by stable monetary systems continued to distrust solidarities not based on close-knit communities but this social fundamentalism was undermined by the emergence of confidence that opinion can function as a stabilizing force, rather than a source of disarray' (Mayhew, 1997, p. 181).

## Warrants of solidarity

Common interest or commonality of purpose underpins the idea of solidarity. *Warrants of solidarity* is a term coined by Leon Mayhew. He used it to identify an additional component of common interest and the ways in which persuaders orient their communicative actions. Common interest among individuals infers similarity in values and opinion but it also assumes truth in the values and opinions. Or at least truth as it has meaning for those with common interests. It may be a variation of the truth or it may not be true but for the sake of the solidarity of the group it is their truth. Scientific evidence or evidence-based information plays into the behaviour of solidary groups.

Activists opposed to corporate behaviour engage with scientific evidence to support common interest claims. It is hard to be in oppositional mode to scientific evidence that fossil fuel is responsible for changing weather patterns and the negative impact of climate change. Yet there are those who remain opposed to the assertions that surface from the scientific evidence. Mayhew suggested the importance of the addition of a warrant that *an argument has its basis in identifiable shared interests*. It did not need to be undifferentiated nor without an element of conflict. But it did need to have a common cause basis. He suggested a warrant of solidarity was an agreement that there was some validity in a rhetorical claim – that the claim could be redeemed if called upon and that it would be redeemed by further discourse. Of great importance to our thinking about corporate rhetoric, and how it might provide warrants of solidarity, was Mayhew's contention that *warrants of solidarity* combine with the freedom to redeem *tokens of solidarity* to create symmetrical communication. Corporations attempt to create solidarities that appear to have their basis in community. They use rhetorical devices rather than reasoned argument although the rhetoric is represented in such a way that it appears to be reasonable argument. Numerous instrumental devices are used as agents of the rhetoric that appear to be reasoned rather than rhetorical. Corporations establish other organizations to act as agents of rhetoric. Mining companies, for example, as we will see in Chapter 10, create foundations for education on the basis of shared equity.

## Rhetorical tokens

Rhetorical tokens are tied to power and persuasion. They are symbolic gestures that have been reduced to sound bites. Rhetorical argument is constrained by time and space. We are no longer willing to invest hours listening to or watching political debates that seek to use logic or reason and we do not have an opportunity to listen to or watch corporate leaders speaking endlessly about their products or services because they are fully aware of the negative consequences of such actions. What we have, Aristotle identified, is the problem of truth associated with rhetoric. This was expanded by Mayhew who argued that persuaders do not need to provide definitive arguments. They need only to provide symbolic tokens in the understanding that they will expand the argument if called upon to do so. But this rarely occurs. The rhetorical token becomes the reality. Mayhew concludes 'tokens allow for strategic rhetoric that delivers suggestive cues but avoids confrontations that would require redeeming these tokens with more extensive arguments' (Mayhew, 1997, p. 48). Corporations rely on the diffuse acceptance by stakeholders of a variety of tokens. The tokens are handed out in the knowledge that there will rarely be a requirement for them to be redeemed in more detailed discourse. Acceptance of the tokens means corporations can expand their corporate narrative within a societal context without fear of analysis or investigation by the society in which they are located other than by force majeure.

## Rhetorical forms of contested influence

While Mayhew moved slowly towards the idea that rhetoric was an acceptable form of communication within contemporary society and that there were opportunities for symmetrical communication to ensue, he was more concerned with the contests that could avert such possibilities. The problem was the 'asymmetrical distribution of information' (Mayhew, 1997, p. 151). Public opinion, or more precisely for our purposes, stakeholder opinion, was based upon rhetorical tokens. Competing interests presented competing tokens and competing forums. Unless all competing interests represented the same information as accurate then it was difficult to develop an informed opinion.

The competing interests of supermarkets in western societies is an example. As we have seen in Chapter 2 global corporations compete to sell food and groceries. The strategic communication they use includes elements of rhetoric such as reputation and brand. They compete for price and they compete for value. They offer in-house products at lower prices than branded products. In doing so they have an expectation that customers and consumers will accept one or other of their rhetorical tokens, and warrants of solidarity – that they will form an opinion about a competing product based upon the level of information received and interpreted.

## The differentiation of influence

Corporate chief executives, presidents and chairmen have power. They exercise power and they have influence. But this does not mean that they reflect the opinions of stakeholders nor that they are accepted as leaders. It does not mean that they are capable of using rhetoric effectively. Managers also have power and influence but they, too, do not necessarily have the ability to persuade. Their persuasive capacity is most often limited to the capture, as Mayhew argues, of 'free floating disposable loyalties' (Mayhew, 1997, p. 126). Influence is the capacity to speak on behalf of the solidarities of groups bound by common interests. Real persuaders, the people Mayhew refers to as 'prolocutors', are those who emerge rather than stand before. They are not appointed to represent groups; they are not persuasive because of their prestige or position. They may claim to represent solidarities or common interests but they do not do so until the stakeholders they seek to persuade allow them to claim that status.

The meaning of the differentiation of influence lies in the traditional view that persuasion and influence were a part of a societal structure, an accepted hierarchy. In non-western societies, particularly Asian and Middle Eastern societies, a hierarchy of influence remains institutionalized. In contemporary western society as Mayhew asserts, 'influence becomes differentiated from the general status order as it comes to be based on resources that must be created by rhetorical bids to speak for particular, often new or emergent, groups and alliances of people who can be brought together under a banner of common interest' (Mayhew, 1997, p. 126). In corporate terms, this means the status of the corporation is based upon the resources that it is capable of applying to its strategic communication to achieve its objectives.

## The inflation of influence and its sources

We have an innate understanding that the structure of a society, particularly in the west, is made up of a variety of public opinions which are based upon freedom of speech and freedom of expression. Persuasion and influence are parts of the structure. As we have seen above, communication within a society can be normative or rhetorical. Mayhew argues that *normative communication* has given way to *rhetorical communication* and that all communication has measurable objectives that can be reached using rhetorical devices. Influence is inflated when these devices are triggered so that all rational or reasoned argument is subsumed by rhetoric or persuasive argument. This is similar to the meaning we have applied to strategic communication where strategic denotes a competing position and the need to obtain a profitable result.

The art of rhetoric, as it was called by Aristotle, is now practiced across all sectors of society and as Mayhew contends, it dissociates real issues. The rhetoric applied to superfluous events and issues – which country spends the most on New Year's Eve fireworks; which country's football team will be the best in the world – overpowers by spectacle and theatre the underlying socioeconomic issues on which a society lives or dies. Mayhew, as we have noted, identified four rhetorical practices that disengage publics from the structure of the western societies in which they live. He was concerned with the practices from political and governmental perspectives but they are able to be re-imagined for our purposes as four practices that are used widely by corporations. Our empirical observations of the practices can be applied to the case studies in this book to give them credibility.

In our identification of these four practices we might also like to seek some flexibility given that a generation has passed by since Mayhew framed them. Let's set them out again then think about their meanings and about how they might have altered in shape and content. Then we will analyse them in the context of their use by global corporations.

The first was a lack of meaningful policy issues on the public agenda. The second was the use of appeals to attitudes that do not tap structures of solidarity that could support effective responses to sociopolitical problems. The third was the existence of one-sided communication that fails to provide opportunities for demands that claims be redeemed in discourse. The fourth was the use of strategic responses that attempt to 'spin' rhetorical descriptions rather than to supply straightforward answers to queries and objections within the wider community.

## Lack of meaningful policy issues

What does Mayhew mean by meaningful? An issue that may resonate with one stakeholder may be meaningless to another. Climate change has been called the most important global environmental threat of our time yet there are diffuse opinions about such a claim. Governments ramp up their rhetoric while corporations involved in fossil fuel extraction play it down. Global environmental agencies publish millions of words on it. High-profile conferences and government forums aim to create unified policies on it. Presidents and prime ministers agree that it is the most serious man-made threat the planet has ever faced. It is therefore a meaningful policy issue and it is on the public agenda. It is so high on the public agenda that in most western countries it has become the dominant narrative. But while it is at the top of the agenda, very little appears to be happening to reduce the threat that it creates. Western governments agree then disagree to create 'targets' for reducing their countries' carbon emissions but then point to China as one of the world's largest atmosphere polluters, claiming that without China's involvement it is pointless to seek to reduce other carbon emissions. Is it possible that the contested ground – the competing narratives that frame climate change – is so unstable because the source of the inflation of influence reduces the issue to emotional responses rather than reasoned discourse? It is here that the resources applied by those who wish to influence the debate are brought to bear. Environmental policy that privileges climate change has the potential to alter the profitability of a large number of the world's leading corporations. Is it possible for corporations with an interest in maintaining the status quo to use rhetoric to exert influence so that an issue as important as climate change is reduced in status and becomes less meaningful? A variety of other meaningful associated issues are allocated public space because they have direct or indirect links to climate change. Security of water supply and quality; the effect of drought on agriculture and farming; and healthcare in rural communities are some. What about issues not related to climate change?

Terrorism is another issue on the public policy agenda. Is it meaningful? How much influence is applied to discursive politics by corporations with an interest in military technology and hardware? News media and governments work to keep terrorism alive as a meaningful issue in western countries using a grim portrait of fundamentalism as the backdrop. In corporate terms the question is who benefits if the issue remains in the public sphere? Significant and meaningful issues were once the province of the front page of the world's important newspapers and the lead items in nightly television news bulletins. A massive technological shift in news content production and delivery occurred in the early years of the twenty-first century that altered inexorably the shape of the news media. (Two previous shifts had the same effect: the invention of moveable type and the invention of the Macintosh computer.) So it was no longer a matter of picking up a copy of *The Guardian* or the *New York Times* to find out which issues were significant. As the news media adopted new technology and made every individual with a smartphone a roving 'citizen reporter' issues that may have once been considered marginal began to be privileged. The transformation of the mundane and insignificant meant stakeholders had to work harder to discover which issue was more meaningful and therefore worth more thinking time. The privileging of issues did not make them meaningful. But it did provide them with more voice than they may have had under the old regime.

Another change in new media added to the difficulty of identifying meaning. As corporate media owners sought increased profit margins the resources employed to produce news were being reduced. Fewer employees were required to source and produce more content that would have greater impact in a 24-hour news cycle. Newspapers that may have historically published one or two editions a day with thousands of staff were required to produce a 24-hourly cycle of news and features with vastly fewer employees. Subeditors were dispatched and news was uploaded and published directly from the reporter. As online publishing and broadcasting were embraced and shifted from fringe to populist, more stories were published in a truncated format so that some were no more than headlines and lead paragraphs. But more stories did not change the number of issues. What this did was allow more stories on a specific issue to be published, more angles and a wider frame, but the issues remained the same. The perception, however, from the perspective of the stakeholder attempting to make sense of the issues, was to be more confused than ever. The wide range of angles were all superficial. There was no time available for reporters to research. No luxury of investigation. The new media landscape meant editors required reporters who may have filed one story every few days to now file six or seven pieces. Facts and proofreading were cast out.

This shift in focus of the news media was beneficial for corporations and governments. A rolling 24-hour news cycle meant less scrutiny of their activities as time was of the essence and new stories were being sought to satisfy the appetite of the voracious news-hungry stakeholder. Issues only remained in the cycle for more than a day or two if they were considered disastrous. An ocean oil spill, a nuclear meltdown or an airline crash topped the bulletin and stayed in focus longer than other issues. The issues of almost equal importance in the western news media at the beginning of the twenty-first century were natural disasters, large-scale terrorism and a sequence of national financial crises. This is not to suggest that corporations and governments were involved in activities that required greater scrutiny. It does though imply that the role of the news media as a brake on rampant behaviour that may not have been in the public interest has been removed. Checks and balances must be evident if corporations and governments are to persuade stakeholders of their value in society.

## Appeals to attitudes that do not tap structures of solidarity

When Mayhew imagined institutions using rhetoric to appeal to stakeholders outside the framework of common interest and community, he was referring to the isolation of the individual in society. Much had been and continues to be written about isolation in large-scale societies – in cities where millions of people go about their daily lives in relative anonymity. Nisbet (1950) and Putnam (2000) spanned fifty years of investment in such research. Apple, one of the world's largest corporations, also identified the issue of isolation and turned it into a marketing opportunity: the results were the iPod, iPhone, ipad and iWatch. The names speak for themselves. Apple made the appeal to the attitude that did not tap a structure of solidarity – the desire for self-worth and its associated self-absorption. It could be argued that Apple in fact created an effective response to the sociopolitical problem of isolation and in so doing turned the Mayhewian notion on its head. But Apple is itself an isolated example. As mentioned above, Sony and other music and entertainment-based corporate entities such as US-owned Warner and French-owned Universal apply rhetoric to stakeholders strategically with the objective of isolating attitudes and behaviour rather than seeking to tap structures of solidarity.

## The existence of one-sided communication

We have seen evidence that corporations communicate asymmetrically with a variety of stakeholders. One-sided communication allows an information provider to create a narrative with a specific angle or focus whether or not the narrative has its basis in fact or truth. Mayhew claimed that one-sided communication itself was the problem because it did not seek to be questioned about its validity. By its nature one-sided communication is not discursive practice – the opportunity for engagement, for questions, or for amplification of an issue or action. So one-sided communication cannot of itself provide opportunities for demands to be redeemed in discourse. As soon as it became part of a discourse it would no longer be one-sided. What Mayhew may have been offering was the prospect that one-sided communication, once it had been logged in the public sphere, was reticent about scrutiny. Claims made against an issue or event, demands for additional information, clarification or amplification were lost because they were unsupported at levels equal to or greater than those of the information provider.

An example might be a large housing development proposal. A corporate development company has identified an opportunity to build a large-scale housing project. It makes an approach to the relevant local authority to seek approval. A number of existing residents of the town, village or city are opposed to the development. But they are opposed on planning grounds, not ideological grounds. They are not nimbys (not in my back yard); they wish to obtain factual information about how the development will proceed and how the local authority will work to offset the external problems the development will create – additional traffic congestion, waste management and security. The development corporation provides some slick marketing brochures and says it will hold public meetings to discuss the concerns of the residents. It convenes a meeting at which a spokesman for the corporation points out the investment opportunities and the local authority spokeswoman points out the contribution from the corporation for additional green space and playgrounds. Residents ask questions about the three significant issues: traffic, waste and security, but no acceptable answers are forthcoming. The local newspapers report the meeting with a photograph of a hand-painted banner at the back of the meeting room which states its opposition to all development. The discourse was limited and the one-sided communication by the corporate developer was reported as fact in the newspapers.

## Strategic responses that attempt to 'spin' rhetorical descriptions

Our example above of the developer corporation building large-scale high-rise housing resonates with Mayhew's fourth premise. Community meetings, whether they are set up by corporations, governments or a combined effort, generally look to provide a strategic response to community interest or concern. Rhetorical descriptors outweigh discursive responses. A strategic response includes 'throwing' a question or objection between spokespeople – from developer to local authority then back to developer so that no answer is provided to even the most straightforward questions or objections.

The fourth rhetorical practice seems self-evident. Strategic responses assume stakeholders are going to be in oppositional mode to the activity of the entity being questioned. The corporation or government conceptualizes a response based on the assumption. It may be a correct response or it may not. In Mayhewian terms a strategic response develops rhetorical descriptors that fit the aims and objectives of the corporate actor. The action is *purposive-rational* rather than communicative. It adopts an asymmetrical position so there is no space for it to ever become a communicative action. In other words, community groups or other oppositional stakeholders – activists, unions, or the media – will feel the full force of the resources the corporation can apply to overcome objections and questions without ever attempting to reach a consensus. For Mayhew this was the nadir of communication in his new public. Any action proposed by oppositional forces was doomed.

## WHAT MAYHEW DID NOT DO

Leon Mayhew did not go far enough. He set forth to carve meaning from his inferences and in so doing came up with a substantial framework to counter the four rhetorical practices he had identified. He conceptualized within the Habermasian public sphere deliberative forums for communicative redemption (Mayhew, 1997, p. 255). These forums, he argued, required legitimacy, publicity, representation, integrated participation and access to leaders. He was imagining these forums as spaces in which reason or logical argument would be applied to public policy. What he neglected was to examine closely the interweaving of the corporation into the fabric of society and thus into public policy: he opined for deliberative forums that were free from subjectivity. Fortunately, the irony of such forums was not lost on him. He invented a 'national forum for citizens' which he imagined could be founded and sponsored by a further imagined group he called 'citizens for democratic deliberation'.

In conclusion, Mayhew's plea was for societal integration to be founded on solidarity that was itself based upon *communities of discourse*. New identities and new solidarities were the positives he took from the fragmentation of earlier societies. Public discourse, he said, can create a new community or society but it needs to come about in a public sphere where 'people in search of new selves and new values can find serious rhetorical forums not entirely given over to commerce in rhetorical tokens' (Mayhew, 1997, p. 286).

We will see in the following chapter, that corporate entities have gone quite some way towards integrating themselves into Mayhew's new public and that not all serious rhetorical forums are given over to commerce in rhetorical tokens.

## CONCLUSION

The identification of rhetoric as a device for gaining positive position must be differentiated within different spaces and places across rhetorical forums.

Reason or rational argument as rhetoric needs to be accepted by individuals or groups. It must be contextualized so that it can be rebutted or accepted.

Normative appeals to solidarity seek to understand values and opinions that exist in individuals and to locate rhetoric within the individual. Rhetorical appeals seek to persuade using different techniques.

Corporations build structures of solidarity that have the head of the corporation as spokesperson. Corporations are influential communicators when they interpret complex matrices of solidarities and align stakeholder goals and objectives with those of the corporation.

Communities are bearers of opinion which creates policy, so they are the source of legitimate governing power. While shareholders were once the legitimate source of governing power of the corporation the diffuse nature of other shareholders has changed the balance.

Corporations attempt to create structures of solidarity in arenas where meaning is contested. Facebook, LinkedIn, Twitter and Instagram are examples of differentiated solidarities. The structure of influence in a society runs parallel to the structure of solidarity.

Group solidarity has impact and influence on corporate activity. Rhetorical appeals to solidarity locate the persuader and the stakeholder in the same frame. Corporations and governments use the media as agents of rhetorical persuasion.

Common interest underpins solidarity. It assumes truth in value and opinion. Warrants of solidarity are those which assume an issue or argument has its basis in shared interests.

 **DISCUSSION QUESTIONS**

1 What are the four sources of the inflation of influence and why are they important to corporate communication?
2 How might corporations weave themselves into the fabric of a society?
3 When communities of discourse are created, who are the legitimate owners?

# CORPORATE SOCIAL RESPONSIBILITY

This chapter explains the notion of corporate responsibility, contextualizing it socioeconomically and socioculturally. It presents evidence of existing corporate responsibility models and argues that most operate without recourse to a balanced engagement with stakeholders. It provides an outline for a new corporate responsibility through strategic stakeholder communication.

It examines the notion of *social licence to operate* exerted upon corporations by community groups. Activists do not respect the boundaries constructed by corporations and governments; activists trample boundaries and must therefore be engaged using equally effective communication strategies and tactics. This chapter explains the social licence to operate model. It provides an analysis of its relevance to corporate activity and offers suggestions for how a corporate entity might best engage in order to ameliorate real and future problems and hurdles created by activists and community groups.

## WHAT IS COMMUNITY AND WHY DOES IT MATTER TO CORPORATE STRATEGIC COMMUNICATION?

Before we set out to identify and define community we need to revisit for a moment the concept of solidarity. We need to do this because the meaning of solidarity for Leon Mayhew (1997) and his focus on stakeholders who were outside government and corporate entities was exactly the same as the meaning of solidarity from within the corporation or a government. Solidarity for a community or stakeholders opposed to corporate activity means banding together for a common purpose. It is different to sociability. Most often, when the common goal or purpose is achieved, the solidarity dissipates. For some stakeholders, solidarity is a cause, even though the members comprising the solidary action are different to each other. Unions are an example. Unions are what UK experts Gofee and Jones call high-solidarity communities. Two of the hallmarks of high solidarity, they suggest, are 'ruthlessness and piercing focus' (Gofee and Jones, 1998, p. 28).

Gofee and Jones provide interesting examples from a corporate perspective of solidarity within the corporation. Shareholders and customers look for solidarity – the completion of shared tasks, mutual interests and clearly understood shared goals that benefit all parties – in the corporate dynamic. Gofee and Jones represent solidarity within the corporation as an alternative to sociability. Solidarity represents goals and competitive strategies. Sociability as an alternative corporate culture is less about goals and objectives and more about consensus in the working environment. Sociability is derived from the normative relationships that occur with families and friends. Solidarity can also exist at family and friend level as an additional relationship layer. It is human nature to seek to build *solidary* rather than *solitary* relationships. Gofee and Jones conceptualized a model of corporate culture in the shape of a cube. The cube was subdivided into quadrants. One quadrant – communal culture – identified a characteristic of corporate existence that has been played out by some of the world's leading corporate entities. Gofee and Jones drilled into communal culture and identified both solidarity and sociability as contributing factors to the success of corporations that identify with communal culture. In this they inferred that the notion of family played out strongly.

## DEFINING COMMUNITY FOR CORPORATE STRATEGIC COMMUNICATION

'Community' is a difficult word. It is applied inappropriately to a range of human and non-human intersections. It can also be applied to a corporation. The word 'corporation' is synonymous with community. Typical dictionary definitions of the word suggest it is a social 'unit' that shares common values. But a solidarity is also a unit with shared common values though it may not be social in the sense of sociability. Community is hard to define. Governments delight in applying it to all their activities. Corporations are a little more conservative in applying it to stakeholders. A variety of oppositional groups refer to themselves as communities in an attempt to create an image of sociability and solidarity.

In the middle of the last century Columbia University sociologist Robert Nisbet explained why community was such a powerful word. He believed that every period of modern human history was marked by key words 'which by their repetitive use and redefinition mark the distinctive channels of faith and thought' (Nisbet, 1953, p. 1). The symbolic value of certain words, he said, 'exert great influence' on the way society thinks and acts. Nisbet was concerned with the alienation of the individual in society, with the erosion of families, neighbourhoods and civic associations in the face of the emergence of control by government.

The *OED* defines community as a body of individuals; an organized political or social body; a body of people living in the same locality; a body of people having religion or professionalism in common; a body of nations unified by common interests; a group of animals living or acting together; or a group of interdependent plants or animals growing or living together in natural conditions. It may seem to be labouring the point to include all these defining features but, as we will see, the use of other words with community serves to identify it more clearly for the purposes of corporate understanding. The word 'body', for example, is applied to community when it is human-related. For animals and plants it becomes a group or grouping. The *OED* provides additional layers which assist in defining community in relation to corporate entities. Community is the state of being shared or held in common. It is joint ownership or liability. It is life in association with others; society; the social state.

We can see that some of the aspects of Mayhew's solidarity flow into the definition of community – shared or held in common – and that the definition can be as easily applied to corporate entities as to activists or other oppositional stakeholders. The annual reports of corporations invariably include the word 'community' relative to some aspect of their existence. Yet oppositional stakeholder groups appear to have captured the word, applying it effectively so that it has become aligned with them and allowed their issue to become the dominant narrative. This is less complicated than it sounds. As Nisbet pointed out words get used repetitively in one context so that they fail to take on meaning in another. In western societies communities struggle against the might of governments and corporations. The power of the word 'community' is attached to bodies of people such as those opposed to mining or logging but it is less powerful when applied by governments and corporations.

## THE MANY MEANINGS OF COMMUNITY

Community became a subject of popular interest in the second half of the twentieth century. The word itself is derived from the Latin *communitas* which means having commonality. Community is tied to society. It extends beyond family and kinships to embrace relationships which form around objects or ideas. But in more recent times it has become a catchword for all types of actions or events. Local government authorities publish community calendars of events; schools and hospitals employ community managers; and football teams talk about supporters as their community. Most of these community applications are rhetorical devices designed to make the proposing organization appear to be warm and friendly. Common purpose or social capital arising from them is non-existent. They are fabricated as part of a wider public relations and marketing strategy.

Let's look at the *triangulation of society* and see how community is used in each. It appears in civil society, in government and in the corporate sphere. In all three, community is used differently with the same objective: to influence behaviour and persuade stakeholders to alter or retain attitudes and opinions.

## THE TRIANGULATION OF SOCIETY

### Civil society communities

Societies throw up a vast array of communities. They have two sides: communities that form for the mutual intellectual and emotional needs of individuals; and those which form in opposition to actions and events they don't like. The latter usually form with intent and then disband when the intent is resolved. Both types are founded on principles and beliefs that are shared among the body of individuals who make up the community. One way to describe civil society communities is that they are *communities of need or identity* or *communities of place*. These communities include town, suburban or neighbourhood associations. Examples include quilting and sewing in which individuals meet at a location and go about making things collectively. Such bodies may or may not be offshoots of religious or other faith-based organizations. Clubs and teams should not be included under the rubric of community, though we tend towards the idea that both have offshoots which they term community for the purposes of gaining some influence with individual stakeholders.

Identifying community groups that lie outside government and corporate sponsorship is difficult. They do not publicly advertise their existence but they have influence because they seek commonality in their actions and activities. Commonality reinforces their political and social will and translates into action when they vote and when they invest in products and services. There appear to be fewer male community bodies in western civil society and more mixed or female. This definition does not include sporting teams or other organized communities such as clubs and societies which are codified.

## Government-sponsored communities

Governments have embraced the idea of community with overzealous enthusiasm. Communities sponsored by governments are rampant. They are conceptualized, resourced and operationalized at every level of government. In every government in the western world and in many non-western countries there is a department of community or a department that is concerned with its communities. In the United Kingdom the Department of Communities and Local Government was set up to 'create great places to live and work, and to give more power to local people to shape what happens in their area'. The irony of this statement is most likely lost on the community. The Department is what is called a ministerial department supported by ten agencies and what are known as public bodies which includes Homes and Communities Agency, the Ebbsfleet Development Corporation and the Planning Inspectorate.

The French government combines sport, youth and popular education with community life to form a ministry which has as its focus the objectives of a national policy on sport. Community appears to be an appendix.

The government of India has community embedded in a vast number of departments and agencies, though they are less specific about the use of the word.

The Republic of the Philippines hosts a Department of Social Welfare and Development which provides initiatives that 'mobilize and utilize the family and community to respond to a problem, need or issue or concern of children, youth, women, persons with disabilities, older persons and families who are in need and at risk' (Philippines Government, 2016).

The Serbian government used community to frame Serbians who live in Kosovo-Metohija when it stated that the 'main priority of the Ministry for Kosovo-Metohija will be safeguarding the Serbian community [...] and its economic strengthening' (Serbian Government, 2016). Other statements from the Serbian government referred to the international community, the Jewish community, the Islamic community and the European community (Serbian Government, 2016).

The government of the Republic of Slovenia uses community to refer to a range of issues and bodies most notably the Roma community, the Slovenian community, the German-speaking community and the Slovenian national community (Slovenian Government, 2016).

More frequently, community is found at levels below federal government, such as state and local government.

The provincial government of Ontario hosts a Department of Community and Social Services which provides programmes that 'help to build communities that are resilient, inclusive and sustained' (Ontario Government, 2016).

The state government of New South Wales hosts a Department of Family and Community Services which under the subheading Community Services states it is 'promoting the safety and well being of children and young people [and] working to build stronger families and communities'. It further states that it 'works closely with other government departments, NGOs and the community' (NSW Government, 2016).

## Corporate communities: fabricated or real?

As much as stakeholders invest in corporations, corporations also invest in stakeholders. Corporate investment in communities is tied to the idea of corporate social responsibility.

Corporations attempt to identify and invest in events and activities that will enhance their reputation, image and brand. They invest in professional international sporting fixtures – tennis, golf, football, rugby, swimming – where their stakeholders are most likely to be persuaded of their social good. They invest in intellectual pursuits – music, art and drama; they sponsor orchestras and they provide resources such as airline travel, instruments, accommodation and sustenance. But the amount of money invested does not always match the expectation of the corporation that there will be a concomitant degree of acceptance of reputation, image and brand.

In 2007 the Australian government came up with a scheme to get Australian businesses to become more involved in Australian society. It called it Corporate Community Investment in Australia and it identified issues that had increased corporate investment in other societies that needed to be implemented in Australia. The report concluded that there were rising community expectations that companies would make a wider contribution to community well-being and that corporate responses to a poor image or lack of trust in the community affected their legitimacy and capacity to perform. By 2014 the Australian government was backing away from the original inflated rhetoric that launched the programme. It blamed an 'economic downturn' suggesting Australian corporates had 'budget pressures' and 'financial pressure'. It said some companies were 'adjusting their priorities'. It said companies were seeking a return on investment and 'choices of engagement' that were aligned with business issues and 'corporate competencies'. In 2015 the Department of Social Services made a new commitment to the programme but it was reticent regarding the inflated rhetoric of 2007. It continued the deflationary tone of the year before.

Corporations have a variety of views about how they ought to go about creating relationships with communities. Barclays, a bank based in England, states it 'plays a broader role in the communities in which we live and work beyond what we deliver through our core business activities. We do this through community investment programmes and the direct efforts of our employees' (Barclays, 2016). It claims to offer such programmes in five locations: Africa, the Americas, Asia Pacific, Europe and the United Kingdom. In South Africa, for example, it runs three programmes: South African Institute of Entrepreneurship, Junior Achievement South Africa and Technoserve, a £330,000 programme that promotes the small–medium enterprise sector with agribusiness. The word 'community' appeared 270 times on the Barclays home website in the United Kingdom when accessed in January 2016. It was used to complete a number of phrases – 'Barclays community', 'isolated community', 'business in the community', 'local community', 'community cycling', 'global community' and 'remote community'.

Similarly, PwC, the consulting firm, considers that it is responsible not only for its £2.8 billion in UK revenue in 2014, and its clients and its employees, but to 'broader society'. It states its vision 'of doing the right thing for our clients, our people and our communities is […] about giving something back through sharing our talent' (PwC, 2016). It claims to have a community programme that will make an impact on behalf of 'significant community stakeholders'. It runs its community programmes from a registered charitable company, the PwC Foundation, which focuses on fundraising.

BP, the large energy company, has a specific strategy for investment in Canadian communities. It states that 'BP Canada's community investment programme focuses on three key areas – education, environment and community. Our goal is to play an active, dedicated role in the communities we operate within' (BP, 2016). It claims to be focused on 'supporting initiatives that help strengthen the community. The value of our community investment is magnified by providing opportunities for our employees to be engaged in the community'. To achieve its goal in this it matches funds raised by employees through personal donations and volunteer time.

The world's largest producer of alcoholic spirits, Diageo, offers community support that it claims extends backwards through history to its roots in Guinness. Diageo, headquartered in England, says:

> Our stakeholders expect global companies like Diageo to contribute to socioeconomic development in the communities in which they operate. At Diageo giving back to our communities has been a part of our history dating back to the founders of our predecessor companies. Diageo claims socioeconomic strategies – local wealth creation; community investment; and advocacy and awareness. Its community investment is designed to 'empower individuals and communities. (Diageo, 2016)

It outlines four elements of its community investment – responsible drinking; access to clean water; empowerment through skills, education and enterprise; and supporting local interests and infrastructure. Two examples it provides are improved sanitation in Cambodia and access to clean water in Tanzania. It invested £50,000 in Cambodia and £52,000 in Tanzania (Diageo, 2016).

In New Zealand the ANZ Bank, one of that country's largest corporations, says it has 'a proud commitment to enhancing the well-being and prosperity of all New Zealanders. Our focus is on developing programs to strengthen our connection with the communities in which our people work and live' (ANZ, 2016). The main focus for the company's community role is through employees volunteering their skills and time. Staff volunteering accounts for 15,000 hours a year.

## THE RELEVANCE OF COMMUNITY IN CORPORATE STRATEGY

For corporations and governments, 'community' is a word they use to keep them ahead of the curve. They use it to enhance their rhetorical communication with a variety of stakeholders. Governments apply it to constituent stakeholders, those who are eligible to vote sometime in the future. Corporations like to use it for employee stakeholders to give them a sense of empowerment. Corporations seek to acquire relevance within the boundaries of their operations. They may be headquartered in England, as we have seen above with Diageo. They choose to act outside their constitutional boundaries for good reason. Western societies continue to play a patriarchal financial support role for developing countries. These countries, once referred to as Third World, receive financial support from the governments of developed countries through the IMF and World Bank. They also look increasingly to corporate contributions as corporations seek to strengthen their image in their major markets by acts of patriarchal kindness. Thus Diageo invests in Cambodia and Tanzania.

Corporations take their lead from the concept of community drawn by Robert Nisbet as we saw above. Nisbet identified a problem within western societies that continues today. His observations were of a society in which the individual was isolated (solitary) and insecure. He concluded that the original instruments of isolation, those pursued by progressive intellectuals – big government and the welfare state – were becoming the focus for conservative intellectuals. The vocabulary built around the conservative notion of community included integration, status, membership, hierarchy and identification (Nisbet, 1953, p. 19). Conservative governments in co-operation with business represented the opportunity for individuals to become empowered, to become masters of the universe.

It took some time, though, for corporations to understand their true responsibility to society. Conservative governments were not blameless. They allowed corporate entities to undertake activities that were often environmentally or socially irresponsible. And the corporations acted because there were limited checks and balances. If a government provided a flexible legislative framework, the corporation could hardly be blamed for taking advantage of it if it meant greater profitability.

Flexibility in government and the extent to which corporations could act with impunity reached its tipping point in the late 1990s. It had been rampant for the previous twenty years. With the final five years of the century in view, corporations began to see the limits of their irresponsibility – profits were not rising as expected, employees were becoming more disgruntled and governments were beginning to impose sanctions that had previously been thought unlikely if not impossible. Corporations began to think about the concept of operating within their societies rather than operating despite them. Within a short time the idea of being socially responsible had surfaced and a new theory was set out: corporate social responsibility.

## LOCATIVE CORPORATIONS AND SOCIAL RESPONSIBILITY

This book is about corporate strategic communication. But embedded within is the principle that corporations function most effectively when they embrace the societies in which they are located. The essence of the embedding can be found in Latin. *Locus* in Latin means place and locative case is a grammatical term meaning location. Locative has been applied to technology so we have locative media which means location-based communications media which is established at a specific place. Cloud computing is an example of locative media.

The locative corporation is one which has a sense of place and identifies with it by establishing its presence. It will headquarter its operations in a city or town of its choosing – a place that has a locative element that allows it to invest in the community first then the wider society where it chooses to be. Corporations with a sense of locus are normatively societally responsible. Some take their responsibility a step further and locate outside major cities. Historically, this was standard practice. Corporations would headquarter on top of their raw material or manufacturing. British industry was spread across the Midlands; American manufacturing across the east and as far west as Illinois where Caterpillar Tractor Company is still located today. Contemporary corporate awareness is less about location at the site of raw material and more about location at the site of societal responsibility. Examples might include Bank of America headquartered in Charlotte, North Carolina; Toyota, headquartered at the eponymously named Toyota, Aichi Prefecture; Microsoft headquartered in Redmond, Washington; and Airbus headquartered in Blagnac, Haute-Garonne. Corporations located within the United States are more likely to headquarter in regional towns and cities than their counterparts in the rest of the western world. Australia and New Zealand have no substantial locative presence outside their major cities. In the

United Kingdom there is a trend towards technology companies locating outside London but major corporations continue to locate their headquarters in the world's financial capital.

A corporate headquarter is the site of the overall responsibility of the entity. It is where policy is conceptualized, where strategy is formulated and from where the company's corporate governance is directed. And it has a direct bearing on the relationship of the corporation to the community and society in which it operates. Relative prestige is drawn from the *locus* of a headquarters. The establishment of a corporate headquarters has the potential to draw other businesses to a location. It is not necessary for it to link its headquarters to the sites of its operations; most manufacturing, for example, is now undertaken in China. It would be a nonsense for English, American and European manufacturers to locate their headquarters in China at the site of their manufacturing facilities. Equally, energy and other corporations with a focus on raw materials shift their operations to the sites where the raw materials are discovered. A headquarters in their place of national registration is normative. What becomes important is the measurement of the success of the relationship between the corporation and its society. A government will offer diffuse incentives to win the prestige associated with the location of the headquarters of a global corporate. Of most interest to the residents of a corporate headquarters is the existence of the facilities they expect to be provided by the community for their continued high-level lifestyles. These include medical, educational and retail facilities. Of most interest to the residents of a town or city being considered by the corporation is not what already exists but what the location of the headquarters will bring. And residents are not always persuaded by the rhetoric of prestige or the tokens of solidarity that are offered. The siting of a corporate headquarters in a town or small city might mean the influx of 2000–5000 additional residents, a prospect that has short- and long-term ramifications.

## Is corporate social responsibility redundant?

Corporations, whether they are locative or not, create rhetorical images of their societal responsibility. Some of these images are rational while others are irrational. The question is whether corporate social responsibility is a redundancy. It is an addition to a business model that ought to exist without being stated. Corporations operate within a legislative environment. There is no requirement for them to act outside the legislative framework of the sovereign nation in which they are located. Since the end of the twenty-first century, however, a body of work on the theory of corporate social responsibility (CSR) has surfaced and dominated the corporate narrative. CSR emerged from the similarly popular idea of triple bottom line accountability. Triple bottom line accountability infers that corporations ought to look to two additional elements of their operations as well as financial profit and loss: social and environmental accountability. The problem with the populist phrases *triple bottom line accountability* and *corporate social responsibility* lies in their origins and in the adoption of the phrases by corporations.

The transformation of the principles of societal responsibility for corporations from an activist movement arguing for corporations to be more narrowly regulated to a corporate business model is well documented (see, for example, Shamir, 2011). CSR is self-regulating. Corporations define and apply meaning to their operations within several contexts, most notably the financial and economic outcomes they can achieve. They are constrained by legislation. Until recently they were unconstrained by environment and society. Corporations report regularly on their environmental and societal responsibilities. They provide evidence of their actions by way of the rhetoric of spectacle and the rhetoric of presentation. But the evidence is most often related, as we have seen above, to a philanthropic function rather than a true investment in meaningful policy issues. Locative corporations such as Toyota state in their annual reports:

> Basic Corporate Social Responsibility (CSR) policy is to contribute to the sustainable development of society. This phrase embodies the spirit of the Toyota guiding principles, and clarifies our CSR stance for our stakeholders, both within and outside the Company. Toyota subsidiaries and suppliers share this CSR policy, and we expect them to adhere to the spirit of the policy in their operations.
>
> (Toyota, 2014)

Bank of America claims its corporate social responsibility,

> plays a critical role in our business strategy of responsible growth and connects us to our core purpose of making people's financial lives better around the world. We focus on driving our strategy of growing responsibly, managing our risk, and deepening our relationships and engagement with customers, clients, communities and other stakeholders. We support local, national and global efforts to fulfil our purpose of making financial lives better, recognizing that we only succeed when others are thriving.
>
> (Bank of America, 2014)

Airbus represents its CSR as active corporate citizenship in which it 'works with key stakeholders and local communities to build and maintain long term relationships across three primary areas: humanitarian assistance, youth development and research support' (Airbus, 2014). Airbus identifies four additional elements of CSR: strengthening governance; fostering innovation; developing and engaging people; and building supplier partnerships. As part of its active citizenship focus it provides humanitarian relief flights of food and medical supplies to 'disaster zones' and support for poverty alleviation in China where it has assisted in building schools and hospitals (Airbus, 2014).

Microsoft says it 'has an enduring commitment working to fulfil our public responsibilities and to serving the needs of people in communities worldwide. Fundamental to this commitment is the role we serve as a responsible global corporate citizen' (Microsoft, 2014). Microsoft chief executive Satya Nadella said 'our customers and society expect us to maximize the value of technology while also preserving the values that are timeless. Microsoft's commitments to corporate citizenship help us to meet these expectations' (Microsoft, 2014). In 2014 Microsoft donated $119 million in cash and $948.6 million in 'kind' to NFPs and other charitable funds.

## HOW AND WHY COMMUNITIES WORK EFFECTIVELY TO STOP CORPORATE ACTIVITY

Despite their best efforts and promises that rhetorical tokens will be able to be redeemed through the self-regulation of CSR or corporate citizenship, corporations continue to fall foul of the communities they claim to support. Global activism against corporate entities is not new. But unlike the old-school days of hand-painted banners and street marches that ended at pubs and bistros it is now sophisticated, slick and strategic. There are a number of ways of looking at anti-corporate activism. The first is from the standpoint of the anti-globalization movement. The second is from the local community standpoint.

## Anti-globalization and the corporation

The anti-globalization movement owes its existence to an ideology opposed to corporate capitalism. Stakeholders argue limited regulatory powers allow corporations to act in ways that are not in the best interests of societies. Deregulated markets and bilateral trade agreements frame the movement. 'Fair trade', 'human rights' and 'sustainable development' are the phrases used to offset their arguments. For the anti-globalizers, the primary institutions that provoke their outrage are the WTO and the IMF. There is some conjecture surrounding the term anti-globalization. From our perspective it appears to be opposed to corporate globalization rather than an ideology that might include cross-border migration and justice, among others. Nobel laureate Joseph Stiglitz concluded that 'for many people, multinational corporations have come to symbolize what is wrong with globalization; many would say they are a primary cause of its problems' (Stiglitz, 2006, p. 187). Some of these companies, he added, were richer than most developing countries. But he was supportive of the corporate global presence. It had assisted in raising living standards by taking developing world production to developed world markets; acting as agents in technology transfer to developing countries; and providing foreign direct investment (Stiglitz, 2006, p. 188). Then again, he argued, without government regulation and civil society pressure, there would be no incentive for corporations to protect the environment. It was cheaper to refine oil and generate energy at higher pollutant levels.

With specific reference to CSR Stiglitz identified an aspect of it which was self-interested. Corporations had concluded that doing good in communities was normative while doing bad created an image problem. Blame for events that occur a long way from headquarters have 'led to a number of voluntary initiatives by companies to improve the lot of their workers and the communities where they do business' (Stiglitz, 2006, p. 198). Most importantly, Stiglitz identified the real problem of CSR. Corporations, he concluded, 'are becoming adept at image manipulation, and have learned to speak in favour of social responsibility even while they continue to evade it' (Stiglitz, 2006, p. 199). It is this damning indictment that motivates activists to create global solidarities in opposition to corporate activity.

## Local communities and the corporation

It is the surfacing and sustenance of local community activist stakeholders that are of most interest to us. To understand corporate strategic communication we need to grasp the significance of localized community opposition to it. The reverse engineering process is designed to assist stakeholders to interpret corporate strategic communication (rhetorical action) and to apply counter-measures as purposive-rational action. Anti-globalization movements have worked hard to develop effective counter-communication strategies that have a direct impact on the work of governments and corporations. They have adopted competitive communication tactics so that they have come to dominate the global narrative. News media stakeholders will turn first to the anti-global angle rather than to seek the corporate angle when telling the story of global capitalism. Part of the reason for the rise and effectiveness of local activist community bodies can be attributed to their opposition to small government conservatism. Conservatism was historically aligned with the empowerment of the individual citizen. Contemporary conservative governments, which resurfaced strongly in the United States and Britain in the mid 1970s, offered individuals empowerment. This was oppositional to progressive liberal large governments who wanted to provide greater welfare. Widespread welfare equalled greater control. Activists work against corporate activity that is aligned with small government.

Local community activists use corporate and political campaign strategies and tactics. They adapt tactics to suit different campaigns but essentially they are taken from the same playbook. What began as the voice of local residents opposed to a residential tower block in their single-storey neighbourhood has become the voice of activists opposed to all development, all extractive industries and all fishing and forestry. From this blanket opposition to corporate activity arose the problem of 'protest fatigue'. Constant protests, which did not always identify specific sites of activity, became lost in a binary competition between the activists and the corporations. Unfortunately for the activists, corporations were resourced to invest in advertising and marketing campaigns that drew attention away from the protest. Government referees were unable to differentiate between genuine local community protests and general protests based on ideology. So any potential support from that quarter was distilled. Activist local community groups around the world have benefited considerably from the accessibility and diffusion of Internet technologies. Local community activism has historically been reactive. More recently governments have begun to include community bodies in their planning processes. The objective is to divert potential protest and to absorb community interest into planning policy but it is also seen as a way to fragment protests. The emergence of Internet technologies as tactical instruments has created a deep reservoir of data and information that is accessible to activist bodies fighting against different issues or the same issue in different locations.

## What the frack?: A meaningful issue

Coal seam gas, or coal bed methane, is a meaningful issue on the policy agenda. But it was not on the agenda before local community opposition put it there. Coal bed methane, coal seam gas and coal mine methane are different names for the same natural gas. It is a source of energy with significant reserves in the United States, Australia, Canada, the United Kingdom, India and in any country where there has been large-scale coal mining activity. The coal bed methane (CBM) issue is complex and political. As a gas for use in electricity generation it has half the greenhouse effect of coal-fired power generation. And its extraction before the mining process itself is viewed in the energy industry as a valuable way to reduce methane emissions from coal mining. But it draws large volumes of water from subsurface aquifers. Water that comes to the surface as a by-product may contain salt, chemicals and heavy metals. Additionally, the process of extraction has become the focus of debate. Hydraulic fracturing is the process of injection of water or other pressurized liquid into rock through bores so that natural gas will flow freely from them. It is a technical process that was invented in 1947 and used extensively since 1950. It is used for methane as well as oil extraction.

For local communities opposed to the development of CBM, hydraulic fracturing provided the answer to their oppositional prayers. Campaigns to stop the spread of CBM extraction have been underpinned by one vitally important and emotive word: fracking. It is not a nice sounding word. Its employment is based upon an argument that it has an environmental impact beyond its economic value. Environmental effects of fracking are considered by those opposed to CBM to be the contamination of surface water and ground water, noise and air pollution and the potential for it to cause earthquakes. Proponents argue that their have been more than 2.5 million hydraulic fractures performed around the world in the past sixty years, with limited side effects. The potential for seismic activity as a result of hydraulic fracturing, however, has caused the EU to consider regulating it while in some countries it has been banned and in others placed on hold. The question is whether the issue is economic, political, geographic or, indeed, technical. We may set aside the technical. We may assume that hydraulic fracturing is the least expensive method of extraction. If it were not, corporate energy companies would abandon it. We might also be less interested in the geographic. The world is awash with coal reserves. The most accessible will be the most profitable. If those reserves happen to be sitting under a major city such as Paris or London, then so be it. This leaves us with the economic and the political. It is no secret that energy companies work closely with governments to frame legislation that favours their proposed activities. And there is nothing complicit or illegal in this. A corporation that intends to undertake economic activity within a country must know the legislative requirements in advance. Let's look at the case of CBM in two very different countries: France and Australia.

## Energy in France and Australia

Coal constitutes less than 4 per cent of France's energy supply. Most of its energy comes from nuclear power. It closed its last coal mine in 2004. So the issue of CBM is an interesting one given that there are reserves of more than 30 billion square metres in the Lorraine Basin. French government policy is opposed to the exploration and development of CBM for political and environmental reasons but energy corporations claimed ten years' worth of gas consumption is contained within the Lorraine Basin. Française de l'Energie, an energy corporation, invested €40 million in the Basin and anticipated being able to supply gas to French energy corporations Total and Solvay by 2016. But in 2011 the French government favoured the persuasive arguments of activists groups opposed to CBM exploration and mining over those of the corporate energy providers. Part of the community stakeholder argument focused on the government's lack of consultation prior to allowing exploration and mining. Claims emerged that the government had undertaken limited environmental and economic research. Detailed analysis, community stakeholders argued, would have thrown up the prospect of potential damage to the water table from the effects of 'fracking' chemicals leeching into subsurface aquifers. The French government was keen to create a domestic market for energy to stabilize prices. Imported energy was expensive. It was less keen, though, to lose votes and the persuasive arguments against CBM were being pressed by Greens from within the European Parliament. The French Union of Petroleum Industries (UFIP), a trade association, works on behalf of French energy companies in exploration and production of oil and natural gas, including refining and marketing of those products. Its mission was to keep the French oil industry competitive and to engage in what it called a 'social dialogue'. Its stakeholders, which it called interlocutors, included public authorities or governments, unions, consumers, environmental bodies, the media and the 'general public'. In 2013 then president of UFIP Jean-Louis Schilansky remarked that 'natural gas will play a decisive role in energy transformation especially for the generation of electricity by limiting $CO_2$ emissions'. He added 'our most fervent wish is that the reflection of all participants remains guided and animated by the desire to listen and by the spirit of reality and common sense that our country exercises in similar situations' (UFIP, 2015). In 2015 UFIP demonstrated there would be an increased demand for gas and other hydrocarbon products including oil between 2015 and 2040. The data used to determine the 2014 position was derived from research undertaken by Exxon Mobil. The Exxon Mobil report 'The Outlook For Energy: A View to 2040' begins by asking a question: why energy? It answers with a rhetorical flourish:

*A house. A car. Lights at night and heat in the winter. A refrigerator to keep food fresh and a stove for cooking. A better education and a good job. Modern health care. Wireless communications. Technology and innovation. The freedom to focus one's daily activities on something more than mere subsistence. These are among the many benefits of modern energy.*

*(Exxon Mobil, 2014)*

As Mayhewian as this appears – rhetorical tokens that appear unable to be redeemed in discourse – the report forecast that by 2014 'natural gas, nuclear and renewables are expected to deliver more than seventy percent of the world's electricity'. Unsurprisingly, the report acknowledged the importance of 'unconventional' natural gas for future energy use and points to the safety of its extraction for more than sixty years. North American unconventional gas production grew by more than 30 per cent between 2010 and 2013, it said. And by 2020 it was expected to surpass Russia as the world's largest gas-producing region. Exxon Mobil was not a member company of UFIP.

In Australia, on the other side of the world from France and the EU, the CBM issue was on the policy agenda at all three levels of government. The oil and gas industry was represented by the Australian Petroleum Production and Exploration Association (APPEA). It claimed its members accounted for more than 98 per cent of Australian petroleum production. Its members were made up of international corporations including BP, Chevron, ConocoPhillips, Exxon Mobil, Mitsubishi, Mitsui, Petronas, Santos, Royal Dutch Shell, Total and Vermillon. APPEA appeared before a Senate inquiry in mid 2015. The inquiry was set up to review the rights of landholders to refuse corporations entry to their land to explore for gas. In some states, most notably the more populated of Victoria and New South Wales, provincial governments succumbed to pressure from community stakeholders concerned with the effects of fracking. As in France, community stakeholders employed a combination of emotive rhetoric and scientific evidence to the issue. They claimed water and prime farming land would be destroyed by gas extraction using hydraulic fracturing. Australia has no nuclear power. Its main energy source is coal-fired power. Gas exploration is focused on future domestic use but it is mainly about exports to the large Asian market. The Senate inquiry was an initiative put forward by Greens politicians. It was a bill introduced to give landholders rights of entry refusal but it was also part of a Greens' agenda to ban fracking in Australia. Some states had already put in place a limited-time ban on fracking. Unsurprisingly, an APPEA submission to the inquiry supported CBM stating that,

*the current phase of investment in the gas industry has seen the re-invigoration of many rural towns and communities across Australia with the building and funding of vital infrastructure. Whether it be through the expansion of airline services to remote communities, the funding of roads and emergency services, or the supply of energy – the industry has bought many benefits to everyday Australians.*

*(APPEA, 2015)*

It added that it did not see any justification for the federal government to 'over-ride' the existing powers of provincial governments to regulate access to resources.

In New South Wales, the most populous Australian province, the government created legislation in 2015 which it called 'NSW Gas Plan: Protecting What's Valuable, Securing Our Future'. The plan stated: 'We have been listening to communities and land holders across NSW about their environmental and social concerns. We also recognize the need to secure our future gas supply needs in NSW.' It added: 'More than a million households rely on gas each day for cooking and heating.' And further: 'NSW could face gas shortages in the next five years if things do not change. To put downward pressure on energy prices and secure supply, we need the growth of viable gas projects. It's that simple' (NSW Government, 2016).

# THE EMERGENCE OF THE CONCEPT OF SOCIAL LICENCE TO OPERATE

As we have seen above, corporations submit proposals to governments for approval to operate their activities across all sectors of economies. Corporations work within the legislative frameworks of sovereign nations. They also operate within the legislative frameworks of foreign countries. The internationalization of corporations allows them to establish their operations so long as they do so within legal limits. The complexity of the contemporary corporate entity is unprecedented. It is a multi-layered, multi-faceted entity with its own complex legal and policy framework. So it is not surprising that the role of government in regulating corporate activity has become difficult to sustain. Corporations are professional – they build around expertise and core competences. They create solidarities of meaning. Governments, on the other hand, are comprised of elected representatives of disparate and often low levels of expertise. They are comprised of elected representatives and they seek advice from the permanent departments which function within the financial capacity of tax receipts. While corporations attract and employ resources at the forefront of their expertise, governments function as social administrators.

The surfacing of civil society influence as a check and balance on corporate activity was a natural evolutionary process. With governments unable to deflect the power and influence of the corporation, the transference of authority to other sources, such as civil society, was inevitable. Within western societies the image emerged of governments unable to cope with the complexity of corporate activity by way of legislation alone. Legislative licences were frameworks in which economic activity could be carried out. Societies, however, towards the end of the twentieth century, determined that these were insufficient to provide the balance needed between the pursuit of economic activity and how that activity fitted in with societal aims and goals. The emergence of the concept of social licence to operate was meant to provide a buttress against unfettered corporate activity. It was, however, as Australian researcher Sara Bice points out, 'a metaphor to encapsulate values, activities and ideals which companies must espouse within society to ensure successful operations and not a literal licencing arrangement' (Bice, 2014, p. 63).

Social licence to operate is different to CSR. One is derived by communities; the other by corporations. There is some cross-over. Social licence to operate has its origins in the mining sector. Local towns and communities, particularly in America, Australia and Canada, became unsatisfied with what Prno and Slocombe call 'conventional approaches to mineral development' (Prno and Slocombe, 2012, p. 346). Local communities demanded a greater share of the perceived benefits of mining and a larger share in the decision-making processes. For Prno and Slocombe 'these trends have been spurred by the growth of the sustainable development paradigm and governance shifts that have increasingly transferred governing authority towards non-state actors' (Prno and Slocombe, 2012, p. 346). A social licence to operate is the consequence of this activism. It is now widely regarded that mining companies need one if they are to avoid conflict that could be financially costly or societally risky.

It is no coincidence that western societal opposition to coal bed methane has created financial and societal problems for corporate energy companies. Oppositional stakeholders, as we have seen above, are the leading actors. They include environmental activists, media, farmers and local townspeople. Townspeople are not historically aligned with environmental activists. Nor are farmers; but in many countries in Europe, plus the United Kingdom, Canada and Australia, the old oppositions have become the new alignments. In their opposition to unconventional gas exploration these new alignments have opened up new lines of communication and sharing of resources. Many of the strategies and tactics have their basis in traditional political campaigns. But the underlying reality is that at some point in the evolution of an issue, stakeholders are going to seek to redeem the rhetorical tokens from one side of the issue or the other. The problem for the newly aligned communities lies in their ability to fulfil their promises: to have their tokens redeemed. Their solidarity is based on the idea that corporate gas exploration will destroy the planet. As energy corporations provide more information, there is potential that publics on both sides are seeking to influence, to reassess trust in the newly aligned communities.

A non-mining exemplification of the notion of social licence to operate is the Canadian agricultural sector. Historically, Canadians had a direct connection to land through agrarian pursuits. With the shift from a rural to an urban population came a dissociation from rural life. Food production became an imagined issue. But the reliance on trust remained; it was crucial to be able to trust farmers to grow food without constant checks and balances which imposed additional economic costs on production. Agriculture's social licence to operate is exactly the same as that inferred by mining and other industries. When public trust is eroded a social licence becomes more proscriptive. It may still exist but it requires increased checks and balances against activity. The head of the Ontario Federation of Agriculture, Don McCabe, offered an important perspective on the social licence to operate. If it was defined as a privilege to operate with minimal restrictions by maintaining the public's trust for doing what was right,

> there are challenges being raised about agriculture's social licence because it is easy for anyone to publicize information. The opportunity for a disconnect between farmers and consumers, or misinformation about food and farming, is greater than ever. Information masquerading as science creates confusion and fuels growing mistrust of some of the science and technology used to produce food. When public mistrust grows, whether it is based on fact or emotion, we are at risk of losing the licence to operate with minimal restrictions. And that's when new regulations get imposed.
>
> (OFA, 2016)

For community stakeholders, social licence to operate is gifted when trust in corporate activity is high. For corporations, social licence to operate is carefully crafted communication of the societal impact of their activities. Both sides are equally empowered.

## CONCLUSION

Symbolic value in words and phrases exerts influence upon the way a society thinks and acts. Community is a word that exerts influence due to the erosion of other power words such as family and neighbourhood.

Corporations use the word community in their narrative arc. In western societies communities struggle against the influence and power of governments and corporations.

Corporate investment in communities is also know as corporate social responsibility. Corporations invest in community events and activities to enhance their reputation, image and brand. Corporations have different standpoints on creating relationships with communities. They use the word community to enhance rhetorical communication especially with employees to provide them with a sense of empowerment.

Corporations use community as a locative mechanism. The locative corporation has a sense of place and identifies by establishing a presence.

Corporations draw prestige and power from the location of their headquarters and the communities that surround them.

Despite their best efforts corporations are not always loved by their communities. The anti-globalization movement, for example, is ideological and opposed to corporate activity.

Corporations engage with communities by way of a social licence to operate. They engage with governments by way of a legislative licence to operate.

Civil society as a check and balance against corporate activity evolved in response to fewer government regulations.

 **DISCUSSION QUESTIONS**

1  How did communities become more relevant to corporations than a lot of other stakeholders?
2  Why are communities important to the future of corporations?
3  What are some of the ways corporations invest in communities as stakeholders?

 **CASE STUDY: Bci**

### We are different

*Daniela Silva Rodighiero, CSR Lecturer, Universidad Finis Terrae, Chile.*

Bci – formerly known as Banco de Crédito e Inversiones[1] – was founded in 1937 by a group of Palestinian, Spanish and Italian immigrants (the most important of the group was the Palestinian family, Yarur). These immigrants worked hard and grew healthy businesses in Chile but they lacked access to the financial system. Bci was created with the objective of supporting family businesses and entrepreneurship.

Nowadays Bci is the third most important Chilean bank (Ch\$15.77 trillion total loans, 13.08 per cent market share and 10,511 employees) and it is the only bank in the country still owned by its founders. With *We are different* as its slogan, Bci's vision aims to be the regional leader in innovation, customer closeness and experience, and to be renowned as the best company to work for. 'Being different has made us leaders of customer experience, innovation and CSR, which upholds our dream of making a contribution to Chile' states the 2014 Sustainability Report. That dream goes even further when the bank states that its purpose is 'To make dreams come true with trusting relations throughout our customers' lives' (Bci, 2014), a purpose fulfilled with integrity, respect and excellence as its core values.

---

[1] The bank shortened its name and changed its marketing strategy and brand image in 1992.

Bci claims that innovation is present in its DNA because it is always seeking new solutions for products, services, models, channels and processes (Bci, 2014). Loyal to its roots, and linking innovation with its aim to help people make their dreams come true, the bank has developed a competitive advantage financing entrepreneurs through its Nace and Renace programmes. They are the core of Bci's shared value strategy and have grown into a new and profitable business line.

### Bci corporate communication strategy aims and objectives

Bci has been well known for strategically communicating its vision within Chilean banking and developing a strong reputation, image and brand. With a clear understanding of its stakeholder interests and needs, and focusing on fostering a strong relationship with them, Bci was recognized in 2014 as the *Most Responsible Company in Chile* by leading CSR Foundation PROhumana. It also received the *Most Sustainable Bank in Chile* award from the World Finance Banking Awards; MERCO's *Most Responsible Company with the Best Corporate Governance*; and Pro Calidad's *National Customer Satisfaction Awards – Large Bank Category* and *Most Transparent Company in Chile*.

Bci conceives its strategic corporate communication in a dialogical manner. It has built a broad and strong stakeholder engagement strategy around symmetrical relationship and information flow, actively seeking feedback by means of a series of channels and dialogue platforms. This effective communication strategy aims to 'feed and align corporate management with specific stakeholder needs as quickly and efficiently as possible' (Bci, 2014). It is operationalized through three levels of engagement for each stakeholder: mass information channels, segmented information channels and participative information channels[2]. In recent years, Bci has extensively used digital media and social networks to pro-actively enhance dialogue with stakeholders. For example there is Bci Connected, which works through Facebook and has more than 111,000 followers, providing a platform for company/stakeholder dialogue and offering products and services for its customers.

### Where the communication strategy sits within the corporate structure

Corporate communications and corporate social responsibility are under the responsibility of one manager, located at senior management level. This reveals that Bci understands the strategic importance of closely linking its corporate social responsibility strategy with its corporate communications strategy and stakeholder engagement. Bci has assigned such weight to these areas that the Sustainability and CSR Committee is one of the five existent Board Committees, which is attended by five directors of the bank and is chaired by Bci's Chairman.

For Paola Alvano, Bci's Corporate Communications and CSR Manager, this view of sustainability as a top hierarchy issue has prompted a more integral view of sustainability and corporate social responsibility within the bank. It has driven the company to see itself in a different way and to be able to convey in the best way the amplitude of view required for sustainability in the company (RSE Extremadura, 2015).

---

[2] More information on page 13 of Bci's 2014 Sustainability Report.

(Continued)

### An outline of Bci's corporate social responsibility policy

Even though Bci has always had a social focus as a part of its strategy, it was just in 2005 that it started using the concept of corporate social responsibility. However, moving at a fast pace, in a decade it has built a strong and successful strategy of sustainability, which is not only located at the top of the hierarchy but embraced throughout the company. This strategy is embedded in its DNA and strongly linked with corporate communications and stakeholder engagement strategy. All of this is reflected in the many important recognitions awarded to the bank in past years. Bci's sustainability model has a strategic focus because all the company's actions in this area must be linked to its core business. Therefore it looks to create shared value and 'seeks to enhance the economic, social and environmental well-being of all the people related to its business' (Bci, 2014). Eugenio Von Chrismar, Bci's CEO, reinforced this perspective when receiving the PROhumana's Most Responsible Company award: 'This way of doing business has prepared us to respond effectively and timely to the increasing demands of society for greater transparency, trust, participation and innovation, as it has also allowed us to strengthen our virtuous equation: happy employees create happy customers, and this in turn allows shareholders to be happy.'

It is one of the targets set by the organization in its balanced scorecard and sets goals for each stakeholder, evaluating the company's performance on social, economic and environmental areas, thus considering its triple bottom line (Bci, 2014).

### Bci's sustainability strategy model

Bci's sustainability is underpinned by four pillars: transparency and trust, community commitment, employee experience and sustainable customers.

*Transparency and trust*: transparency is one of the main values of Bci. The bank aims to provide complete, clear and timely information, as the basis of trusting and long-term customer relations. It is also an issue that has gained attention from the government and public opinion. Bci addresses these issues at corporate level through three areas – Information, Education and Advice – that comprise different initiatives. For example, Bci has a mini website for the bank's transparency policies. It also offers an online financial education platform (www.conletragrande.cl) that explains banking services for people to familiarize themselves with. These are complemented with a spot and educational publications on Chilean newspapers. The bank has also an Ethics Code and Ethics Committee operating since 1996.

*Community commitment*: Bci engages in initiatives that create value for communities, thus enhancing corporate reputation and fostering engagement and trust with its stakeholders. These include a partnership with Enseña Chile to help with education issues, Bci's corporate volunteer programme, the promotion of artistic creativity and donations to social, educational and cultural activities. In 2014 Bci organized its first Consultative Sustainability Council, which contemplated round tables with leaders from the academic, social, private and governmental realms. Its conclusions on topics such as customer experience, shared value, customer accessibility, communication and advertising, corporate transparency, labour inclusion for groups discriminated against, how to make Bci an attractive place to work and environmental sustainability are integrated into the bank's sustainability master plan (Bci, 2014). In terms of its environmental strategy, Bci is progressing on more sustainable operations, with initiatives of energy efficiency, sustainable construction and reduction of electricity, water and paper consumption. Regarding its products and services it is working on developing financing lines for environmental investment projects and it is raising awareness about sustainability among its main stakeholders. In relations to its suppliers, Bci seeks to incorporate products and services with a high social value that lead to a real improvement in quality of life. Thus, Bci is enhancing its supplier engagement channels, socializing good management practices and rewarding excellence in supply.

*Employee experience*: Bci aims to 'offer a dignified quality of life and stable work with possibilities of personal, professional and family development' (Bci, 2014). Consequently it has designed an employee experience based on its core values: integrity, respect and excellence that translate into principles of respect for the dignity of people, non-discrimination and meritocracy as the key to professional development. In this area, Bci offers employee benefits such as school for Bci parents, co-financing selected team-developed initiatives, flexible working programmes, a talent management programme, a comprehensive training and coaching system, an employee recognition model and a work inclusion programme targeted at people with disabilities and also retired seniors, among others. It also has a selection and recruitment self-managed model based on closeness, transparency and agility.

*Sustainable customers*: driven by the motto 'What is not good for the customer is not good for Bci' (Bci, 2014), the bank has focused on customer experience strategy since 2012. The concept is to provide a service focused on giving customers a unique and memorable experience, exceeding their expectations and building emotional ties that harvest a long-term, mutually beneficial and trust-based relationship with them. This tactic aims to differentiate Bci from its competitors. It is framed around Nace and Renace programmes as flagship initiatives launched in 2007. Nace – the only value proposal of its kind in Chile that supports entrepreneurs from their earliest stage of development (Bci, 2014) – involves financing entrepreneurs who have no access to banking, thus creating unique credit assessment criteria focused on business plan quality, commitment and perseverance. Furthermore, Nace's customers obtain access to Bci's networks and support plans. Bci grouped together around 1800 new Santiago Nace customers in the First Enterprise Centre in Latin America, run by ten specialized executives and two assistant managers. Nace is complemented by the Renace programme, which allows business recovery to former customers who were financially responsible but unsuccessful in their business attempt.

## Stakeholder engagement

In Chile more than 2 million people live with some kind of disability. They are stakeholders whose needs have been overlooked by banking. Bci has a work inclusion programme targeted at people with disabilities, but aims to make it friendlier to customers with disabilities. 'If we would like to be a company which drives social change we can't cover our eyes and not see there are people who face barriers, who we have decided to throw away', said Ignacio Yarur, one of Yarur's heirs and Retail Banking Manager.

*(Continued)*

Led by top management, Bci worked for a year alongside employees with disabilities and clients with accessibility problems discussing problems found in its services and solutions that would provide an excellent customer experience for them. The result of this dialogue was *Bci Accesible*, a $US 7 million programme, which was launched by Bci in 2015. Within two years Bci will have 80 branches and 82 per cent contact points adapted to accessibility international standards, with specially trained staff, braille contracts and sign language video conferences. The plan has been widely highlighted by Chilean media and supported by government. Bci's focus on stakeholder engagement, its vision of permanently creating new products and services that meet their needs, and its shared value creation vision have given the company a competitive advantage in the market and have built a strong reputation and good image. Bci has therefore obtained and maintained a *social licence to operate* among its stakeholders. This is even more important nowadays, when banking is suffering a reputation/trust crisis due to corruption and conflict of interest cases.

### References

Bci Con Letra Grande, https://www.conletragrande.cl/

Bci Investor Relations, https://ww3.bci.cl/investor-relations-eng

Bci Sustentainability, http://www.bci.cl/accionistas/rse/index.html

Bci, '2014 Sustainability Report' http://www.bci.cl/medios/2012/investor/dectos/rse/Bci_Informe_de_Sustentabilidad_2014_Ingles.pdf

Bci, '73 años de compromiso con el desarrollo de Chile', *Ediciones Especiales El Mercurio*, http://www.edicionesespeciales.elmercurio.com/hoy/detalle/index.asp?idnoticia=20100915496647&idcuerpo=905

Canessa, M. (2012). *Empresas Familiares: Familia YARUR y el BCI (Chile)*, 16 April, http://mrcanessa.blogspot.cl/2012/04/empresas—familiares—familia—yarur—y—el.html

Corresponsables (2014). 'La RSE debe generar progreso para todos nuestros grupos de interés'. *In Actualidad Chile Corresponsables*. Retrieved from http://chile.corresponsables.com/actualidad/la-rse-debe-generar-progreso-para-todos-nuestros-grupos-de-interes

EMB (2014). 'En sustentabilidad se busca el valor compartido'. *In HSEC*, http://goo.gl/ZJ4Hvk

FSG. *Banking on Shared Value*. Retrieved from http://sharedvalue.org/sites/default/files/resource-files/FSG_Banking%20on%20Shared%20Value_0.pdf

FSG. *BCI Supports Entrepreneurs from the Beginning*. Retrieved from https://sharedvalue.org/groups/bci-supports-entrepreneurs-beginning

Grupo Yarur, http://www.poderopedia.org/cl/organizaciones/Grupo_Yarur#tab_perfil

Observatorio de Responsabilidad Social de Extremadura (2015). Los comités de sostenibilidad en la empresa de hoy. *In Noticias Junta de Extremadura*. Retrieved from http://www.rsextremadura.es/index.php?modulo=noticias&pagina=noticia.php&id_noticia=7999

Mendoza, L. (2015), 'Ignacio Yarur, el heredero del BCI, hace su estreno en sociedad', *La Segunda*, 12 June, http://www.nexchannel.cl/Nex/noticias/noticia_pescrita.php?nota=12584268

PROhumana (2015). 'Bci y el retorno de la sustentabilidad en el negocio', *In Noticias PROhumana*, http://prohumana.cl/2015/09/te-presentamos-las-mejores-practicas-de-bci-ganador-del-ranking-de-sustentabilidad-empresarial-prohumana-2015/

Ruiz, M. (2015). 'Clienta del Bci: "Por fin puedo cobrar un cheque directamente"', *Las Últimas Noticias*, 3 June, http://www.nexchannel.cl/Nex/noticias/noticia_pescrita.php?nota=12587050

# STRUCTURING REPORTING MECHANISMS AND THE FUNCTIONS OF CORPORATE COMMUNICATION

This chapter looks closely at corporate accountability in relation to regulators in different countries. It explains the various regulatory frameworks that operate and how they function. It explains the value in parliamentary committees such as the Leveson Inquiry in Britain. It links regulatory frameworks to the case study country chapters. It also presents the various functions of strategic corporate communication that are linked to other forms of communication. In this it expands on the linkages between employee relations, media relations and investor relations – all internal and external communications.

## CORPORATE ACCOUNTABILITY

Corporations are accountable to themselves and to their stakeholders. They operate within legislative frameworks and they are regulated by governments. As we have seen in Chapter 8 they are also regulated by society. Corporations create communication campaigns and strategies that are pitched at their accountabilities. They identify their accountabilities then frame their communication accordingly. Strategies include different tactics for different stakeholder accountabilities. One might assume this to be a given but it can work only in situations where stakeholders are identified clearly and where accountabilities are spelt out. What, then, is an accountability? When applied to leadership, accountability is defined as responsibility for policies. If a president or chairman is ultimately responsibility for the actions of a corporation then it can be inferred that the communication associated with those actions would also come from the top. A corporation succeeds when accountability is taken seriously by its leadership. Corporate accountability is not the same as political accountability, although shareholders as voters may think it is. Let's look at corporate stakeholders and see how they might be imagined by corporations in terms of whether or not they have accountable value.

Accountable value is the value ascribed to stakeholders by corporations. It varies in degree of worth relative to the corporate share price and the standpoint of the corporation. Accountability is sometimes linked to the idea of sustainability which is a nice touch – sustain + account = ability. But it is nothing more than another rhetorical device if it is not linked to objectives.

### Shareholder accountability

Despite all the literature and all the rhetoric, corporations exist to provide value to their shareholders. They do this in two ways – by increasing the value of the shareholders' capital investment in the corporation and by offering dividends. Corporations communicate with shareholders using the medium of money. According to Chartered Secretaries Australia, an advisory firm, accountability at shareholder level is important. A cascading accountability sees shareholders checking the decisions of the board and the board reviewing the actions of the chief executive and management:

> Accountability mechanisms exist to constrain management power and strengthen shareholder controls, with key strategies being the clarification in law of legal duties imposed upon directors and senior management, the requirement of shareholder approval for a wider range of corporate transactions, and the disclosure of governance frameworks and processes in the annual report.
>
> (Chartered Secretaries Australia, 2011)

The annual report is the most important communication instrument applied to shareholders. It is a one-way asymmetrical communication. It is partly factual and partly rhetorical. Factual financial data is analysed by shareholders who make decisions on the figures presented. Along with the financial data, corporations provide shareholders with reports from the chairman and the chief executive. These reports, or letters or messages, contained with the annual report direct shareholders to the past, present and future position of the company. The corporate message must align with shareholders' expectations for future earnings. At the very least it must present an image that is in alignment with the expectations of the shareholder over the short, medium and longer terms.

In 2015 one of the world's largest global resources companies, BHP Billiton, set out to 'demerge' some of its assets. In its 2014 annual report it claimed its purpose was to 'create long-term shareholder value through the discovery, acquisition, development and marketing of natural resources' (BHPbilliton, 2014a, p. i). In the chairman's review, Jac Nasser AO flagged a new direction for the 130-year-old company, proposing a demerger of some of its aluminium, coal, manganese, nickel and silver assets. A demerger is the dissolution of a merger between companies. Mr Nasser stated that the demerger would 'allow BHP Billiton to improve the productivity of our largest businesses more quickly and create a new global metals and mining company specifically designed to enhance the performance of the demerged assets' (BHPbilliton, 2014a, p. 8). The relevance of stakeholder accountability then came into play. Mr Nasser added,

> all BHP Billiton shareholders would retain the existing shares in BHP Billiton and receive shares in the new company pro-rata with your BHP Billiton shareholding. Following the demerger, BHP Billiton would seek to steadily increase or at least maintain its dividend per share in US dollar terms – implying a higher payout ratio. Subject to final Board approval to proceed, shareholder approval and the receipt of satisfactory third party approvals, the demerger is expected to be completed in the first half of the 2015 calendar year.
>
> (BHP billiton, 2014a, p. 8)

The demerger was finalized in May 2015 with a new company, South32, surfacing. As expected, the board voted to approve the demerger. As did the shareholders. Shareholders received a 196-page document entitled 'BHP Billiton, Resourcing the Future: Shareholder Circular' (BHPbilliton, 2014b). It was a high-quality glossy production, the contents of which included a letter from the chairman Mr Nasser, a summary, expected timetable, advantages and disadvantages and risks, implementation, tax implications, an independent accountants report and an independent expert's report. It also contained consolidated income and cash flow for BHP Billiton and South32. The letter from Mr Nasser to shareholders pointed out that the company encouraged 'you to make your own decision on the merits of the demerger proposal. However, your Board considers the demerger to be in the best interests of BHP Billiton shareholders as a whole and accordingly recommends you vote in favour of the demerger resolution'.

The object of the demerger was to reduce BHP Billiton's assets from forty-one to twenty-nine and to assist in achieving its ambition of holding nineteen assets across the 'four pillars' of petroleum, copper, iron ore and coal with a potential for a fifth pillar of potash. Its petroleum assets were in the Gulf of Mexico, onshore USA and offshore Australia. Potash was located in Canada, copper in Chile, Peru and Australia, iron ore in Australia and Brazil, and coal in Australia and Columbia. Seventeen consenting parties were required to frame the demerger proposal. They included Goldman Sachs as lead financial adviser, UBS as joint financial adviser for the Johannesburg Stock Exchange listing, KPMG as independent accountant and auditors, Grant Samuel as independent expert, Herbert Smith Freehills as Australian legal adviser, Slaughter and May as UK legal and tax adviser, and Ernst & Young as South African tax adviser. The demerged company, South32, was listed on the Australian Stock Exchange and was therefore subject to Australian law. BHP Billiton PLC was subject to its articles of association, UKLA listing rules, the City Code on Takeovers and Mergers, and English law.

## Legal accountability

Corporations must behave within the legal framework of the sovereign nations in which they transact business. They are accountable within the laws that govern their activities. Some countries enact federal laws that govern corporate activity while others are constrained with state or provincial laws. In the United States corporations respond to state law but the trading of securities in publicly listed companies is federally-based. Government regulations or laws differ from country to country. In the United Kingdom corporations work within the Companies Act 2006 while in Australia it is the Corporations Act 2001 which governs activity.

Legal frameworks are not rigid. They alter or are amended to reflect changes in societies and changes in structures. Corporations persuade legislators and influence legislation. The popular method of influence is lobbying. Lobbying is a private activity not subject to the scrutiny of the media or other stakeholders. Its name originated from the presence of agents who waited in the 'lobby' of parliament for parliamentarians to emerge from chambers so they could present their case. Governments are voted out of office in western societies by popular vote in general elections. It is not uncommon for political parties seeking election to promise to 'reform' legislation. Progressive or liberal governments tend to tighten laws that govern corporate activity while conservative governments offer more freedom.

In Singapore in 2007 the Ministry of Finance argued the need for reform of the Companies Act which had been enshrined in legislation in 1967. The result was the Companies (Amendment) Act 2015 which was designed to reflect Singapore's growth as a global business hub. The new legislation was conceptualized by the Ministry of Finance and Accounting and Corporate Regulatory Authority (ACRA). Part of its review of the existing act was to invite public comment on the proposal. The review panel recommended that the new act should contain core company law while providing specific legislation to deal with foreign companies. As part of its review the government presented issues papers to business and other stakeholders and held seventeen focus group meetings. Public comment on such an important legislative change was a tactic that embraced two-way symmetrical communication; the public (including corporations whom the legislation was aimed at) was included in the process. It was incumbent upon the corporate entities interested in the legislation to provide written and oral responses. The Singapore government published a summary of the comments and submissions but it did not disclose the identities of the respondents. A discourse analysis of the summary, however, revealed that respondents appeared to agree generally with the proposed alterations and amendments as might be expected. The respondents most likely to submit feedback would be those corporations which were operating under existing foreign company law.

If we return to the BHP Billiton example, we can see that the persuasive tone of the demerger document pitched to shareholders was not the only communication of interest. The document's alignment was fixed precisely on the regulatory provisions of the countries in which the entities intended to operate. Legal accountability was spread amongst the advisers as well as the board of directors and management. Under the subheading 'Preparation of and responsibility for this document', KPMG, Grant Samuel and BHP Billiton accepted legal responsibility for various aspects of it. Presentation of financial information was also subject to legal accounting standards required in Australia, the EU and International Financial Reporting Standards required by the International Accounting Standards Board.

## THE REGULATORY FRAMEWORK

Corporations in all western societies are regulated by governments. Regulation is the direction applied to the corporation by way of guiding principles, rules, laws or a combination of all three. Regulators have legal powers and authority to impose sanctions on corporations that do not abide by the rules, the law or the principles set out by regulators on behalf of government. Regulators look to boards of directors to be accountable for the actions of the corporation. Throughout corporate history directors have done remarkably well in getting themselves sent to prison for not obeying the regulators. Corporate crime is activity committed by agents of a corporation, most often management and directors, with the express purpose of benefiting shareholders. It is activity that lies outside the regulatory framework.

Despite the presence of strong regulators corporate crime persists. In 2001 US company Enron declared itself bankrupt. Its chief executive Ken Lay and its chief operating officer Jeffrey Skilling were convicted of fraud. The United States is relatively lenient with corporate criminals. Fines and compliance reform promises usually outweigh prison as alternatives. The Deepwater oil spill in the Gulf of Mexico in 2010 was a turning point. BP was charged and fined for its involvement. The financial settlement for the largest oil spill in US history was a record $18.7 billion. A number of BP employees along with partner agencies Halliburton and Transocean were charged with federal crimes. Kurt Mix, a BP engineer, was charged with obstructing justice. Site managers Donald Vidrine and Robert Kaluza were charged with manslaughter. David Rainey, former vice president for exploration, was charged with obstructing congress. Even at the worst of times, as in the case of BP, a corporation will continue to attempt to 'spin' the narrative in its favour. Its communication strategy was to segment its stakeholders. In doing so it was able to identify the points at which it ought to apply the most influence.

The regulatory framework is more resistant to persuasion and influence than other corporate stakeholders. Regulators exist for the purpose of regulating corporate activity, applying checks and balances so that disasters such as Deepwater and fraud such as Enron are, if not eliminated, at least limited in scope. Let's look at some of the more robust regulators.

## Securities and Exchange Commission (USA)

The mission of the US Securities and Exchange Commission (SEC) is to protect investors; maintain fair, orderly and efficient markets; and facilitate capital formation. The laws and rules that govern the securities industry in the United States derive from a simple and straightforward concept: all investors, whether large institutions or private individuals, should have access to certain basic facts about an investment prior to buying it and as long as they hold it. To achieve this the SEC requires public companies to disclose meaningful financial and other information to stakeholders. This provides a common pool of knowledge for all investors to use to judge for themselves whether to buy, sell or hold a particular security. The result of this information flow, SEC claims, 'is a more active, efficient, and transparent capital market that facilitates capital formation. The SEC works with all major market participants, including especially the investors in our securities markets, to listen to their concerns and to learn from their experience'.

The SEC oversees the key participants in the securities world, including securities exchanges, securities brokers and dealers, investment advisors and mutual funds. Here the SEC is concerned primarily with promoting the disclosure of important market-related information, maintaining fair dealing and protecting against fraud. Though it is the primary overseer and regulator of the US securities markets, the SEC works closely with many other institutions, including Congress, other federal departments and agencies, self-regulatory organizations (the stock exchanges), state securities regulators and various private sector organizations. In particular, the Chairman of the SEC, together with the Chairman of the Federal Reserve, the Secretary of the Treasury and the Chairman of the Commodity Futures Trading Commission, serve as a member of the President's Working group on Financial Markets.

When the US stock market crashed in 1929 public confidence and trust evaporated. Investors large and small, as well as the banks who had lent to them, lost vast sums of money in the ensuing Great Depression. There was a consensus that for the economy to recover the public's faith in the capital markets needed to be restored. Congress held hearings to identify the problems and find solutions. Based on the findings of the hearings Congress – during the peak year of the Depression – passed the Securities Act 1933. Together with the Securities Exchange Act of 1934, which created the SEC, this was designed to restore investor confidence in capital markets by providing investors and the markets with more reliable information and clear rules of honest dealing. The main purposes of the laws can be reduced to two common-sense notions:

- Companies publicly offering securities for investment dollars must tell the public the truth about their businesses, the securities they are selling and the risks involved in investing.
- People who sell and trade securities – brokers, dealers and exchanges – must treat investors fairly and honestly, putting investors' interests first.

Conduct that led to SEC investigations included:

- Misrepresentation or omission of important information about securities
- Manipulating the market prices of securities
- Stealing customer funds or securities
- Violating broker-dealers' responsibility to treat customers fairly
- Insider trading (violating a trust relationship by trading while in possession of material, non-public information about a security)
- Selling unregistered securities.

## Australian Securities and Investment Commission

The Australian Securities and Investment Commission (ASIC) is Australia's corporate markets and financial services regulator. It claims to contribute to Australia's economic reputation and well-being by ensuring that financial markets are fair and transparent and supported by confident and informed investors and consumers. It is an independent Commonwealth government body. It was established by the Australian Securities and Investments Commission Act 2001. It functions under the Corporations Act 2001.

ASIC's brief is to:

- Maintain, facilitate and improve the performance of the financial system and entities in it
- Promote confident and informed participation by investors and consumers in the financial system
- Administer the law effectively and with minimal procedural requirements;
- Enforce and give effect to the law
- Make available to stakeholders information about companies and other bodies.

ASIC administers legislation and relevant regulations including:

- Australian Securities and Investments Commission Act 2001
- Corporations Act 2001
- Business Names Registration Act 2011
- Business Names Registration (Transitional and Consequential Provisions) Act 2011
- Insurance Contracts Act 1984
- Superannuation (Resolution of Complaints) Act 1993
- Superannuation Industry (Supervision) Act 1993
- Retirement Savings Accounts Act 1997
- Life Insurance Act 1995
- National Consumer Credit Protection Act 2009
- Medical Indemnity (Prudential Supervision and Product Standards) Act 2003.

ASIC regulates Australian companies, financial markets, financial services organizations and professionals who deal in investments, superannuation, insurance, deposit-taking and credit. As the consumer credit regulator, it licenses and regulates people and businesses engaging in consumer credit activities (including banks, credit unions, finance companies, and mortgage and finance brokers). It claims to ensure that licensees meet the standards – including their responsibilities to consumers – that are set out in the National Consumer Credit Protection Act 2009.

As the market regulator, ASIC assesses how effectively authorized financial markets are complying with their legal obligations to operate fair, orderly and transparent markets.

As the financial services regulator, ASIC licenses and monitors financial services businesses to ensure they operate efficiently, honestly and fairly. These businesses typically deal in superannuation, managed funds, shares and company securities, derivatives and insurance.

The laws ASIC administers provide facilitative, regulatory and enforcement powers. They include the power to:

- Register companies and managed investment schemes
- Grant Australian financial services licences and Australian credit licences
- Register auditors and liquidators
- Maintain publicly accessible registers of information about companies, financial services licensees and credit licensees
- Make rules aimed at ensuring the integrity of financial markets
- Investigate suspected breaches of the law
- Issue infringement notices in relation to breaches of laws
- Seek civil penalties from the courts
- Commence prosecutions.

## Financial Services Agency (Japan)

The Financial Services Agency (FSA) in Japan claims responsibility for ensuring the stability of Japan's financial system, protection of depositors, insurance policyholders and securities investors, and smooth finance through such measures as planning and policymaking concerning the financial system, inspection and supervision of private sector financial institutions, and surveillance of securities transactions. The FSA role for the sound development of the national economy includes administration and authority for:

- Planning and policymaking within the financial system
- Inspection and supervision of private sector financial institutions including banks and insurance companies
- Establishment of rules for market trading
- Establishment of business accounting standards for corporate finance
- Supervision of certified public accountants and auditing firms
- Surveillance of compliance of market rules.

Financial regulation and supervision have three major policy objectives:

- Establishment of a stable financial system
- Establishment of fair and transparent financial markets
- Protection of users and improvement in user convenience.

The FSA says finance is a function that can be established only when trust or reliability exists. Without trust, users of financial services cannot comfortably conduct the transactions of financial instruments or supply funds. However, there are limitations to the ability of users of financial services to sufficiently comprehend by themselves the business conditions of financial institutions or the risks relevant to financial instruments. The FSA claims it is improving rules for the protection of users as well as appropriate implementation of rules for inspections and supervision. It argues that regulatory authorities of many other nations have shared these policies for a long time without any essential changes, but the environment surrounding the financial world, including technological innovation and globalization of the financial system, is changing continuously. The FSA believes its major task is to strive for qualitative improvement of financial regulation and supervision by adjusting the measures to these changes. Within the FSA lies the Japanese 'market watchdog' – the Securities and Exchange Surveillance Commission (SESC). Its mission is to ensure the integrity of capital markets and the protection of investors. An executive bureau established with the SESC has authority for market oversight, inspections of financial instruments, market misconduct and inspection of disclosure documents. In the event of criminal activity the SESC files formal complaints with the public prosecutor. It is also responsible for the legislative framework and proposes legislative amendments directly to the prime minister or the finance minister.

## Securities and Exchange Board of India

The Securities and Exchange Board of India (SEBI) was enacted in 1992 in accordance with the provisions of the Securities and Exchange Board of India Act, 1992. Its mission is to protect the interests of investors in securities and to promote the development of and regulation of the securities market.

It is entrusted with:

- Regulating the business in stock exchanges and any other securities markets
- Registering and regulating the working of stock brokers, sub-brokers, share transfer agents, bankers to an issue, trustees of trust deeds, registrars to an issue, merchant bankers, underwriters, portfolio managers, investment advisers and such other intermediaries who may be associated with securities markets in any manner
- Registering and regulating the working of the depositories, custodians of securities, foreign institutional investors and credit rating agencies
- Registering and regulating the working of venture capital funds and collective investment schemes, including mutual funds
- Promoting and regulating self-regulatory organizations
- Prohibiting fraudulent and unfair trade practices relating to securities markets;
- Promoting investors' education and training of intermediaries in securities markets
- Prohibiting insider trading in securities
- Regulating substantial acquisition of shares and takeover of companies
- Calling for information from, undertaking inspection, conducting inquiries and audits of the stock exchanges, mutual funds, other persons associated with the securities market intermediaries and self-regulatory organizations in the securities market.

It has the power to suspend the trading of any security in a recognized stock exchange and can:

- Restrain persons from accessing the securities market and prohibit any person associated with securities market to buy, sell or deal in securities
- Suspend any office-bearer of any stock exchange or self-regulatory organization from holding such position
- Impound and retain the proceeds or securities in respect of any transaction which is under investigation.

In 2014 SEBI embarked upon a number of policy reforms designed to continue its standpoint of keeping the Indian securities market integrated within the global regulatory regime. Reforms were made to the primary securities market, the secondary securities market, mutual funds, intermediaries associated with securities markets, and foreign institutional investors.

## Autorité des Marchés Financiers (France)

The Autorité des Marchés Financiers (AMF) was established in 2003. It has a board and an enforcement committee empowered to impose disciplinary sanctions and fines. The AMF has a staff of around 450 and is financially independent. It regulates participants and products in France's financial markets. It regulates, authorizes, monitors and, where necessary, conducts investigations and issues sanctions. It ensures investors receive relevant information and provides mediation to assist them in disputes.

The AMF's tasks are to regulate, inform and protect. It is an independent public body with a remit to safeguard investments in financial products, ensure investors receive relevant information and maintain orderly financial markets. It regulates participants and products on French financial markets, including financial markets and market infrastructures, listed companies, financial intermediaries authorized to provide investment services and financial investment advice (credit institutions authorized to provide investment services, investment firms, investment management companies, financial investment advisers, direct marketers), and collective investment products invested in financial instruments.

The powers and responsibilities of the AMF include:

- Setting rules
- Authorizing participants, approving disclosures relating to corporate finance transactions and authorizing collective investment products
- Monitoring the participants and savings products under its supervision
- Conducting investigations and inspections
- Enforcement powers.

The AMF coordinates its activities with other French regulators, especially in the banking and insurance sectors, and co-operates actively with its European and international counterparts. The AMF is empowered to set the rules that apply to the participants and products falling within its jurisdiction including financial markets, listed companies, financial intermediaries and collective investment products. As part of this, it prepares the AMF General Regulation and disseminates policy to help participants apply the rules.

To ensure it properly fulfils its remit, the AMF publishes a General Regulation that sets rules and procedures to enforce legislation. The General Regulation is amended regularly to reflect the findings of working groups set up by the AMF, as well as domestic law and European directives. The AMF also plays an active part in many European and international initiatives aimed at ensuring better regulation of financial markets. Whenever an amendment is drafted, the General Regulation is put to public consultation before being adopted by the board and then submitted to the Minister for the Economy, who ratifies the change through an executive order published in the Official Journal of the French Republic.

AMF policy includes instructions, positions, recommendations and other publications that define and detail the manner in which the laws and regulations for listed companies, investment products and financial market participants are applied in practice. Before publishing a new policy document the AMF consults with financial intermediaries, professional organizations, investor advocacy groups and other stakeholders before submitting the final document to its board for approval.

The AMF approves the rules applicable to financial markets and market infrastructures, approves the corporate finance transactions of listed companies and authorizes financial services professionals and the collective investment products under its supervision. The AMF checks the regulatory compliance of the disclosures that listed companies and securities issuers prepare during corporate finance transactions such as initial public offerings, rights issues and takeover bids. It makes sure that advertising messages linked to a corporate finance transaction are clearly identifiable and do not contain information that could mislead the public.

It claims to maintain orderly financial markets through:

- Approving the rules for regulated markets, including equity, bond, as well as markets such as Alternext that are considered to be unregulated but organized because they are covered by rules prepared by the market operator
- Approving the operating rules of market infrastructures, including clearing houses, settlement system operators and central securities depositories
- Issuing professional licences to the people within market infrastructures who are responsible for monitoring trading and supervising members and compliance.

## Financial Conduct Authority (UK)

The Financial Services Act 2012 set out a new system for regulating financial services in order to protect and improve the United Kingdom's economy. Its purpose was to ensure markets work so that consumers received a 'fair deal'.

The mission of the Financial Conduct Authority (FCA) is to maintain and ensure the integrity of the market; regulate financial services firms so that they give consumers a fair deal; and to control the financial services market so that it is competitive. In 2014 the FCA claimed to have made a commitment to take a more strategic approach to risk, as well as developing a common view of markets and key sectors. It claimed it would take a more market-focused approach to tackle risks, while focusing on specific issues within firms.

It claims to play a key role in the UK along with the Treasury, the Bank of England and the Prudential Regulation Authority in implementing domestic and European legislation as well as international policy. Much of its domestic regulation originates in the EU. Active engagement with Europe is an important part of the FCA strategy. It claims to have a strong international focus.

It argues there is risk that market reputation will weaken if consumers and investors lack confidence in their fairness and transparency. If realized, the FCA says, it may lead investors to move capital away from UK markets which would have a negative impact on the UK economy. It says increased transparency across a wider range of asset classes and greater regulation of trading venues has been recognized in the revisions being made to the Markets in Financial Instruments Directive (MiFID).

The strategic objective of the FCA is to ensure the relevant financial markets function well. The strategy emphasises sector and market-wide analysis. Changes to intelligence and data-analysis processes created a more consistent, collective view of markets and sectors.

To support its strategic objective FCA has three operational objectives:

- To secure an appropriate degree of protection for consumers
- To protect and enhance the integrity of the UK financial system
- To promote effective competition in the interests of consumers.

It examines corporations as they apply to be authorized. FCA is interested in the corporations' internal culture, business models and how they treat customers.

## China Securities Regulatory Commission

China Securities Regulatory Commission (CSRC) is a ministerial-level public institution responsible to the Chinese State Council. It has a unified regulatory function over the securities and futures market according to relevant laws and regulations, and with the authority of the State Council. It maintains securities and futures market order and controls the legal operation of the capital market.

The CSRC is located in Beijing. It has a chairman, four vice chairmen and a secretary of the Disciplinary Inspection Commission (at vice-ministerial level). CSRC has eighteen functional departments, one inspection division and three centres. In accordance with Article 14 of the Securities Law of the People's Republic of China, CSRC has set up a public offering review committee comprised of professionals of CSRC and invited experts. It has established thirty-six securities regulatory bureaus in provinces, autonomous regions and municipalities directly under the central government.

The CSRC performs specific duties in the supervision and administration of the securities market:

- Study and formulate policies and development plans for the securities and futures markets; draft the relevant laws and regulations for securities and futures markets as well as put forward suggestions for formulation or modification of laws and regulations; and create relevant rules, regulations and measures for the securities and futures markets.
- Exercise a vertical administration over the domestic securities and futures regulatory institutions and supervise the securities and futures markets; perform a regulatory supervision over the management and the managerial officials of the relevant securities companies.
- Supervise the issuance, listing, trading, custody and settlement of stocks, convertible bonds, bonds of securities companies and bonds and other securities under the charge of CSRC as assigned by the State Council; supervise securities investment bonds; approve the listing of corporate bonds; and supervise the trading of listed treasury bonds and corporate bonds.
- Supervise securities market behaviour of listed companies and their shareholders.
- Supervise the listing, trading and settlement of domestic contract-based futures; monitor the overseas futures business of domestic institutions in accordance with relevant regulations.
- Supervise securities and futures exchanges as well as their senior managerial personnel in accordance with relevant regulations; supervise securities and futures associations in the capacity of a competent authority.
- Supervise securities and futures business institutions, securities investment fund management companies, securities depository and clearing corporations, futures

clearing institutions, securities and futures investment consulting institutions, and securities credit rating institutions; examine and approve the qualifications of fund custodian institutions, and supervise their fund custody businesses; formulate and implement measures on the qualifications of senior management for relevant institutions; and guide the Securities Association of China and the Futures Associations of China in the administration of the qualifications of personnel engaged in securities and futures businesses.

- Supervise the direct or indirect issuance and listing of shares overseas by domestic enterprises as well as the listing of convertible bonds by companies listed overseas; supervise the establishment of securities and futures institutions overseas by domestic securities and futures business institutions; and supervise the establishment of securities and futures institutions in China by overseas institutions for securities and futures businesses.
- Supervise the communication of securities and futures information; take charge of the management of the statistics and information resources for securities and futures markets.
- Work with relevant authorities in the examination and approval of the qualifications of the accounting firms, the asset evaluation institutions and their personnel for securities and futures intermediary businesses; supervise law firms, lawyers and eligible accounting firms, asset appraisal institutions and their personnel in their securities and futures business activities.
- Investigate and penalize the activities in violation of the relevant securities and futures laws and regulations.
- Administer foreign exchanges and international cooperation affairs of the securities and futures sector.

## Bundesanstalt für Finanzdienstleistungsaufsicht (Germany)

The Bundesanstalt für Finanzdienstleistungsaufsicht (BaFin), the Federal Financial Supervisory Authority of Germany, has a primary objective to ensure the proper functioning, stability and integrity of the German financial system. Bank customers, insurance policyholders and investors ought to be able to trust the financial system.

Under its solvency supervision, BaFin helps ensure the ability of banks, financial services institutions and insurance undertakings to meet their payment obligations. Through its market supervision, BaFin also enforces standards of professional conduct which preserve investors' trust in the financial markets. As part of its investor protection, BaFin also seeks to prevent unauthorized financial business. BaFin is a public-law institution with legal capacity. It is funded by fees and contributions from the institutions and businesses that it supervises and is thus independent of the Federal budget.

BaFin supervises 1850 banks, 680 financial services institutions, 590 insurance companies and 30 pension funds as well as 6100 German funds and 77 asset management companies. With its solvency supervision, it contributes to ensuring that credit institutions, insurance companies and financial services providers are able to meet their payment obligations. Through its market supervision BaFin enforces fair and transparent conditions on the markets. It is dedicated to the promotion of investor protection. On its helpline, BaFin answers around 22,000 questions from consumers a year. In addition, it deals with around 18,000 enquiries and complaints about banks, insurance undertakings and financial services providers. To the extent possible, BaFin helps consumers – for example, by exercising its influence on a company to correct errors or by explaining the legal situation to the complainant.

BaFin is represented and involved in numerous European bodies to create a single European financial market. It argues it is important for a smoothly functioning securities trading that all market participants can rely on fair and transparent market conditions.

In cases of suspected market manipulation or insider trading, BaFin monitors listed companies and their shareholders for compliance with their publication requirements. Among other things, companies must publish ad hoc announcements, directors' dealings and financial reports. Shareholders are obliged to report if they hold significant percentages of the voting rights in a listed company. Anyone who holds at least 30 per cent of the voting rights must make an offer to the other shareholders to buy their shares. In addition, securities supervision monitors financial service providers, asset management companies and investment funds set up by them. BaFin examines prospectuses, including listing prospectuses, and checks whether they contain the minimum information required. Together with the Financial Reporting Enforcement Panel (FREP), BaFin examines the accounting of publicly traded companies (around 830 companies are subject to supervision). BaFin is subject to the legal and technical oversight of the Federal Ministry of Finance, within the framework of which the legality and fitness for purpose of BaFin's administrative actions are monitored.

Banking Supervision, Insurance Supervision and Securities Supervision/Asset Management are the different organizational units within BaFin – the so-called Directorates. There are fourteen departments within which specialist sections supervise credit institutions, insurance undertakings, financial services institutions and asset management companies (*Kapitalanlagegesellschaften*), and investigate and prosecute market abuse. Issues of fundamental importance for supervisory law are dealt with in basic issues sections.

BaFin's international activities are pooled in the International Policy/Affairs department, which directly reports to the President. This department represents the German interests in the EU and other international bodies. Functions that extend beyond individual sectors are carried out by the departments of the Regulatory Services/Human Resources Directorate. These departments are responsible, among other things, for prosecuting enterprises that conduct financial business without authorization and for dealing with complaints. There is a department that deals exclusively with money laundering and terrorist financing.

## Bank of Russia

The Bank of Russia is the regulator of corporate activity in that country. It performs its functions in compliance with the Constitution of the Russian Federation and other federal laws. According to Article 75 of the Constitution of the Russian Federation the principal function of the bank is to protect the ruble and ensure its stability. The bank is the sole issuer of currency. It has power and authority over all aspects of the financial and monetary systems of Russia. In collaboration with the federal government it elaborates and implements a single state monetary policy. It designs and implements policy towards developing the financial market of the Russian Federation and ensuring its stability. It is the sole issuer of cash and organizer of cash circulation. It is creditor of last resort for credit institutions and it organizes the credit institution refinance system. It exercises supervision and oversight of the national payment system. In addition it:

- Sets the rules for conducting banking operations
- Services budget accounts of all levels of the Russian budget system, unless the federal laws stipulate otherwise, by effecting settlements at the instruction of the authorized

bodies of executive power and government extra-budgetary funds, which are assigned the task of organising the execution of and executing the budgets
- Manages the Bank of Russia international reserves
- Makes the decision on the state registration of credit institutions, issues banking licences to credit institutions and suspends and revokes them
- Makes decisions on the state registration of non-governmental pension funds;
- Supervises the activities of credit institutions and banking groups
- Exercises regulation, control and supervision over the activities of non-credit financial institutions in compliance with federal laws
- Registers securities issues and prospectuses and registers reports on the results of securities issues
- Exercises control and supervision over the compliance by issuers with the requirements of federal legislation on joint-stock companies and securities
- Exercises regulation, control and supervision over corporate governance in joint-stock companies
- Conducts independently or at the instruction of the Russian Government all types of banking operations and other transactions necessary for the performance of Bank of Russia functions
- Organizes and exercises foreign exchange regulation and foreign exchange control pursuant to federal legislation
- Sets the procedure for effecting settlements with international organizations, foreign states and legal entities and private individuals
- Approves industry accounting standards for credit institutions, the Bank of Russia and non-credit financial institutions; the chart of accounts for credit institutions and the procedure for its application; the chart of accounts for the Bank of Russia; and the procedure for its application
- Sets and publishes official exchange rates of foreign currencies against the ruble
- Takes part in the compiling of Russia's balance of payments forecast and organises the compiling of Russia's balance of payments
- Takes part in the development of the methodology for compiling Russia's financial account within the national account system and organizes the compiling of Russia's financial account
- Keeps official statistical records of direct investments to and from Russia in compliance with federal legislation
- Establishes independently the statistical methodology of direct investments to and from Russia, the list of respondents, and approves the procedure for their submitting of primary statistical data on direct investments, including the methods of federal statistical review
- Analyses and makes forecasts for the situation in the Russian economy and publishes the corresponding materials and statistical data
- Pays compensation for household deposits with bankrupt banks uncovered by the compulsory deposit insurance system in the cases and according to the procedure established by the federal law
- Is the depository of the IMF funds in the Russian currency and conducts operations and transactions provided by the Articles of Agreement of the IMF and the agreements with the IMF
- Exercises control over the compliance with the requirements of federal legislation on countering the illegal use of insider information and market manipulation

- Protects the rights and legitimate interests of shareholders and investors in the financial markets, insurers, insured persons, and beneficiaries recognized as such in accordance with the insurance legislation, and also insured persons in the system of compulsory pension insurance, depositors and participants of a non-governmental pension fund in the system of non-governmental pension insurance.

## CORPORATIONS AND GOVERNMENTS: PARLIAMENTARY COMMITTEES AND COMMISSIONS

Corporations communicate directly with governments. They set out the course of their actions so that they will receive approval to operate. International trade is one of the world's most vibrant and important activities. Corporations trade with each other and with the world's 196 countries every hour of every day. The WTO is the arbiter of global trade. It works on behalf of governments who, in turn, work on behalf of the corporations within their sovereign borders. But it is not capable of overseeing each and every action undertaken by corporations and governments. So governments and other supranational bodies are required to keep their own watch on corporate activity. They do this most often by referring activity to their own parliaments. Committees of inquiry or commissions of inquiry are set up to investigate and analyse all manner of corporate activity. The Leveson Inquiry in Britain in 2011 was an example of government investigating the actions of a newspaper which was owned by one of the world's largest corporations: Newscorp.

In Australia in 2006 the government established a more specific committee – the Parliamentary Joint Committee on Corporations and Financial Services – to examine Australian corporate responsibility and how it managed risk and created value. This committee examined the activities of ASIC, the Australian corporate 'watchdog'. It examined the relevant legislation and also the annual report published by ASIC. In doing so it was keen to discover whether Australian corporations were looking out for the interests of stakeholders and what it described as broader community or whether they were simply focused on shareholders. The inquiry was established by a progressive Labour Party government.

In Britain the Leveson Inquiry was established as a judicial public inquiry into the 'culture, practices and ethics' of the British press following a revelation that a newspaper reporter had intercepted telephone messages and that others had 'hacked' the message bank of a murder victim. The inquiry, set up under the Inquiries Act 2005, recommended the establishment of an independent body subject to new laws to regulate the British media. It also recommended criminal action against a number of people.

In the United States both houses of congress establish committees of investigation. There are standing committees, select committee and joint committees. Select committees are those set up to investigate issues and activities that lie outside the framework of the standing committees. They can also be permanent committees. There were two permanent select committees on ethics and intelligence in 2015. Similarly, in the UK, select committees are set up to examine issues of national importance.

Western governments are generally wary of the establishment of committees of inquiry into corporate activity for fear that they might drive companies towards alternative prospects. Parliamentary committees are more likely to appear to be examining other activity while tangentially focusing on the specifics of the corporation. Such was the initial setup of the Leveson Inquiry. British committees that look at corporations but appear to be looking elsewhere include the Business Innovation and Skills Select Committee; Energy and Climate Change Select Committee; Environment, Food and Rural Affairs Committee; and the Arms Export Control Committees.

## The European Commission

The establishment of the EU created a need for an examining body that was larger than an individual country member of the Union. The European Commission (EC) represents the interests of the EU as a whole. It proposes new legislation to the European Parliament and the Council of the European Union, and it ensures that EU law is correctly applied by member countries. The EC investigates and examines proposed corporate mergers, acquisitions and takeovers.

In 2002 the EC commissioned a report on corporate governance within the EU. It was published by Weil, Gotshal and Manges, a law firm, as 'Comparative Matrix of Corporate Governance Codes Relevant to the European Union and its Member States'. A senior partner at the firm, Ira Millstein, defined corporate governance as 'that blend of law, regulation, and appropriate voluntary private-sector practices which enables the corporation to attract financial and human capital, perform efficiently, and thereby perpetuate itself by generating long-term economic value for its shareholders, while respecting the interests of stakeholders and society as a whole' (Millstein, 2002).

The report defined corporate governance as 'the internal means by which corporations are operated and controlled. While governments play a central role in shaping the legal, institutional and regulatory climate within which individual corporate governance systems are developed, the main responsibility lies with the private sector' (Weil, Gotshal and Manges, 2002, p. 11). It compared corporate governance codes of countries within the EU.

The report outlined the role of stakeholders. It stated that the corporate governance framework should recognize the rights of stakeholders as established by law and encourage active co-operation between corporations and stakeholders in creating wealth, jobs and the sustainability of financially sound enterprises. Specifically it noted that:

- The corporate governance framework should assure that the rights of stakeholders that are protected by law are respected.
- Where stakeholder interests are protected by law, stakeholders should have the opportunity to obtain effective redress for violation of their rights.
- The corporate governance framework should permit performance-enhancing mechanisms for stakeholder participation.
- Where stakeholders participate in the corporate governance process, they should have access to relevant information.

In constructing the matrix the report drew from a number of national committees and reports into corporate activity in those countries.

It drew from the Dual Code of the Belgian BXS that:

*Transparency is the basis on which trust between the company and its stakeholders is built, notwithstanding the constraints imposed on the company by its competitive environment. Transparency is conducive to the company's effectiveness because it allows the board of directors to act promptly when necessary. (Weil, Gotshal and Manges, 2002, p. 32)*

From the Nørby Report in Denmark it concluded that:

*It is decisive for a company's prosperity and future possibilities that the company has a good relationship with its stakeholders. Stakeholders are everyone who is directly affected by the company's decisions and business. It is desirable that the company's management runs and develops the company with due consideration of its stakeholders.*

*(Weil, Gotshal and Manges, 2002, p. 33)*

From the Berlin Initiative Code in Germany it found that

*Company management must sensibly balance the interests of the various stakeholders of the company. Among those with an interest in the public corporation are principally the owners (stockholders), but also employees, customers, loan creditors and suppliers, as well as the public at large. Particular significance attaches to stockholders as the providers of risk capital. Distinctive of the constitution of German companies is the inclusion of employees by means of various forms of participation (co-determination).*

*(Weil, Gotshal and Manges, 2002, p. 35)*

Sweden's Shareholder Association Policy stated:

*All stakeholders need information so they can form an opinion of the company's financial standing and development, thereby giving them a basis for a true evaluation of the company's stock. This information must therefore be open, correct, relevant and current, and its contents must be clear, true and fair.*

*(Weil, Gotshal and Manges, 2002, p. 38)*

In Italy, the Preda Report identified,

*the maximization of shareholder value as the primary objective of good corporate governance, considering that, in the longer term, the pursuit of this goal can give rise to a virtuous circle in terms of efficiency and company integrity, with beneficial effects for other stakeholders – such as customers, creditors, consumers, suppliers, employees, local communities and the environment – whose interests are already protected in the Italian legal system.*

*(Weil, Gotshal and Manges, 2002, p. 36)*

In the United Kingdom the Hampel Report noted different types of companies would have different relationships, and directors could meet their legal duties to shareholders and pursue the objective of long-term shareholder value successfully only by developing and sustaining these stakeholder relationships:

*We believe that shareholders recognize that it is in their interests for companies to do this and increasingly to have regard to the broader public acceptability of their conduct.*

*(Weil, Gotshal and Manges, 2002, p. 39)*

An example of EC investigating capacity was that of its probing of a US-based firm's proposed takeover of a Dutch company where the merger may have placed constraints on competition. In 2015 the commission began an investigation into a proposal by Fedex to buy Dutch company TNT Express. The Commission was concerned that the merger would diminish competition in the package delivery market in which there would be two other competitors, UPS and DHL, the latter of which was owned by Deutsche Post. The Commission's investigation indicated that the other 'integrators' would be the only significant competitive constraint on the merged entity for most international express services with a destination within or without the European Economic Area (EEA). As the proposed transaction would have reduced the number of integrators competing in the EEA from four to three, the competitive constraint on the merged entity would be significantly reduced, leading to a concentrated market in several member states for international express delivery services to a destination within or outside the EEA. The Commission was concerned that the increase in e-commerce created a proportionate increase in package delivery which needed to remain competitively priced.

Other investigations were made into the merger between two Danish telecommunication companies to make sure the joint venture was within EU merger regulations; the merger of two telecommunications companies in Spain; and a joint venture between coffee manufacturers D.E. Master Blender (DEMB), parent company of Douwe Egbert, of the Netherlands and Mondelēz International of the United States. The Commission approved the merger of the coffee manufacturers. It was initially concerned that the joint venture could lead to higher prices and less innovation by bringing together DEMB's Senseo single-serve system and Mondelēz's Tassimo single-serve system. Although the Senseo and Tassimo single-serve machines were sold by Philips and Bosch respectively, DEMB and Mondelēz could have influenced the price paid for these machines by consumers by offering cash-backs and coupons. Coffee companies had an incentive to do this because market penetration of these coffee machines would increase their sales of compatible capsules, pads or pods. The Commission concluded the joint venture would compete against its strong rival Nestlé, which owned the other two single-serve systems – Dolce Gusto and Nespresso. In fact, Nestlé's Dolce Gusto competed particularly closely with Tassimo as they both responded to similar consumer needs by offering a variety of hot drinks (spiced coffees, milky coffees, tea and hot chocolate). The Commission also found the joint venture would continue to have incentives to support sales of Tassimo and Senseo coffee machines in a similar manner, because only by maintaining a high level of sales of these single-serve machines could the joint venture ensure a sufficient level of profitability on its sales of the corresponding filter pads and T-discs (ec.europa.eu).

## CONCLUSION

Corporations operate within legislative frameworks created by governments. Corporate strategic communication is framed with the operation of relevant legislation. Stakeholders are identified by their accountable value. An annual report is the most important communication instrument applied to stakeholders.

Legislation governing corporations is flexible and alters with changes in societies and economies. But regulators are not as easily persuaded as other stakeholders because they exist to control and regulate corporate activity.

 **DISCUSSION QUESTIONS**

1 What type of regulation governs corporate activity?
2 When is it relevant for a regulator to act at a global or supranational level?
3 How do corporate regulators function in different countries?

**CASE STUDY: Fiducian Group Ltd**

*Philippa Yelland, Head of Marketing and Communications*

### Overview and place in Australia

Fiducian Group Ltd (ASX: FID) has a unique place in Australia's compulsory superannuation (pension) system because the publicly listed company is one of the country's very few successful end-to-end financial services businesses in a fiercely competitive sector where larger players struggle to achieve this end-to-end goal.

Compulsory superannuation began in 1992 with employers contributing 3 per cent of employees' earnings. The system now covers almost all working Australians with 9.5 per cent of their earnings flowing into various types of funds: retail, industry, corporate, public sector, self-managed (SMSF) and small Australian Prudential Regulation Authority (APRA) funds. The total amount of money in all these funds is now estimated at A\$2.6 trillion (http://www.abs.gov.au/ausstats/abs@.nsf/mf/5655.0).

Through the vision of founding managing director, Indy Singh, the company listed in 2000 as Fiducian Portfolio Services Ltd on the Australian Securities Exchange and, after a restructure in early 2015, is now listed as Fiducian Group Ltd. With Funds Under Management Advice and Administration of A\$4.386 billion, the company is a specialist financial services organization providing:

1 Funds management and investment, including wrap platforms and client portfolio administration (Fiducian Investment Management Services Ltd)
2 Financial planning and wealth management (Fiducian Financial Services PL)
3 Superannuation (Fiducian Portfolio Services Ltd)
4 Technology solutions for financial planners and their clients (Fiducian Services PL)
5 Accounting/resourcing and SMSF administration (Fiducian Business Services PL).

### Aims of Fiducian corporate strategic communication

Fiducian aims to deliver high-quality and ethical financial planning to as many people as possible. This is reflected in the company's name, Fiducian, which derives from the Latin *fiducia*. People of high integrity, in positions of responsibility, who command trust and respect for their knowledge and expertise, are described as exercising their duties in a fiduciary capacity.

This standpoint informs Indy Singh's emphasis on 'clients', not 'customers'. He explains that a 'customer' pays a price to buy goods or services, whereas a 'client' is one who is under the protection of another and who obtains it from a professional.

Accordingly, its corporate strategic communication positions Fiducian as the national network of financial planners who always have the clients' best interests as their goal. The other pillars – such as funds management, superannuation, technology solutions and business services – are also communicated as striving for the best outcomes for their clients.

*(Continued)*

### Objectives of Fiducian's corporate strategic communication

Communication of Fiducian's aims is to all 'clients', both external and internal, existing and potential.

The first objective has been to build a robust multi-asset, multi-manager investment platform that delivers consistently above-average returns with reduced risk to investors and superannuation clients. This is done through blended funds (using a Manage The Manager approach) and the strategy has proven itself since inception. Fiducian's funds continue to rank highly with Morningstar Research and Rainmaker's SelectingSuper.

The second objective was to build a national network of well-qualified financial planners who can advise on many areas: investments, children's school funding, savings plans, government benefits, and aged and estate planning, to name just a few.

The third objective is to craft a seamless social media dialogue with clients. This is done through YouTube, Facebook, Twitter, LinkedIn and Fiducian's own website.

### Communication strategy's place within our corporate structure

The corporate communication strategy is built into the warp and weft of Fiducian's structure because the Head of Marketing & Communications reports directly to Indy Singh. Indy talks almost daily with me about how best to communicate with external and internal clients, either existing or potential.

While each conversation is not framed with these exact words, Mr Singh's concern is to keep all clients informed – his metaphor is one of familial responsibility.

### Corporate social responsibility policy

Fiducian is dedicated to delivering outstanding performance for investors, customers and personnel. We aspire to continue our success while operating openly with honesty, integrity and responsibility, and maintaining a strong sense of corporate social responsibility. The group deals fairly and responsibly with clients. Personnel are expected to help deliver superior service to each client. Ethics, honesty and clear communication are cornerstones of the group's success in building lasting business relationships (see http://www.fiducian.com.au/linkref/FG_CodeofConduct.pdf).

In response to Australians' move to ethical investing, in 2015 Fiducian launched the Diversified Social Aspirations Fund. In common with all Fiducian funds, this fund uses various managers to lower financial risks for investors.

### Fiducian stakeholders and stakeholder attributes

#### The public

Fiducian is now one of the very few independent financial services companies that is not aligned with Australia's Big Four banks (ANZ, Commonwealth, NAB, Westpac) nor with AMP.

Various scandals have hit financial services in Australia in the past decade, with the result that some of the public are suspicious about financial planners. This is a continuing challenge for strategic corporate communications which Fiducian addresses by citing its unblemished record: no enforceable undertakings, no breaches with the regulators, and continuing education and assessment of planners.

## Financial planners

The main internal 'clients' (or stakeholders) are our financial planners because they are the public face of the company. They are called on to deliver unbiased financial advice that keeps the clients' best interests always to the fore. Planners also must address their clients' questions when Australian and overseas markets are disrupted and this has prompted Fiducian to publish economic and market updates that planners can send to their clients.

## Investors (superannuation members, direct investors in funds)

As Australia's population ages and lives longer, pressure is increasing on funds to deliver consistently high financial returns. During the year to December 2015, Fiducian's multi-asset, multi-style approach has delivered attractive returns: specialist funds include the Fiducian India Fund which returned 6.1 per cent, and the Fiducian Technology Fund at 21.8 per cent. Fiducian's diversified funds were a standout according to Morningstar Research:

- Ultra Growth Fund returned 15.1 per cent and ranked 2nd out of 121 funds
- Growth Fund returned 9.0 per cent and ranked 2nd out of 198 funds
- Balanced Fund returned 7.9 per cent and ranked 4th out of 198 funds
- Capital Stable Fund returned 4.6 per cent and ranked 2nd out of 127 funds.

The communication challenge here is to emphasise the Manage the Manager process to ensure the long-term returns – rather than focus on returns for the past year. This is a challenge for the entire Australian superannuation industry for a growing number of reasons. People are living longer and are chronically ill for longer, while at the same time the Australian government seeks to lower expenditure on aged care and health as well as encouraging people to become self-funding in retirement.

## Shareholders

In late August 2015, Fiducian Group Ltd (ASX: FID) delivered its results for the financial year 2014/15. Underlying net profit after tax rose 28 per cent, with all operating divisions contributing to the result. Highlights included:

- Up 28 per cent underlying NPAT to A$5.75 million
- Up 19 per cent underlying EBITDA to A$8.07 million
- Up 14 per cent funds under advice, management and administration to A$4.08 billion
- Up 11 per cent net operating cash flows to A$6.51 million.

A fully franked final dividend of 5.5 cents per share was declared and brought the total fully franked dividend declared for the 2015 financial year to 10 cents, an increase of 10 per cent (2014: 9.1 cents).

Public companies' results must be lodged with the Australian Securities Exchange (ASX) within a very tight timeframe. The benefit of this pressure is that the media, both general and trade, watch the ASX site for company results and so communication is with multiple stakeholders.

*(Continued)*

## Media – general and trade

Almost forty publications (online, TV, radio, print) in the general and trade media cover financial services in Australia. These publications range from the quality dailies in the Fairfax and News Ltd stables to highly focused online publications that cater for very narrow niche sections in the financial services sector.

Topics for coverage go in and out of fashion – in early 2015, the flavour of the month was self-managed superannuation. By late 2015, the media pack had moved on to robo-advice.

Corporate strategic communication is about seeing around corners and recognizing the next trend before it takes shape. Fiducian's response is to develop thought-disruption articles that identify the parameters of an issue, send those articles to selected journalists, and then be available for interviews.

The disruptor in the media is Apple's iOS9 which takes ad-blocking to a new level. Online publishers are privately very concerned about the spread of ad-blockers to mobile devices because advertisers, both existing and potential, are asking about the veracity of viewers' statistics. With this profound disruption of online media profitability, Fiducian is questioning the value of advertising and looking to new ways of communicating.

## Regulatory bodies ASIC, APRA, ASX

The Australian Securities & Investment Commission (ASIC) is the independent Australian Federal Government body that regulates company and financial services laws to protect consumers, investors and creditors. It began in 1991, replacing the National Companies and Securities Commission and the Corporate Affairs offices of the states and territories.

The Australian Prudential Regulation Authority (APRA) oversees banks, credit unions, building societies, general insurance and reinsurance companies, life insurance, private health insurance, friendly societies and most members of the superannuation industry. It was established in 1998. The difference between the two bodies is that ASIC is concerned with the provision of financial services to consumers while APRA is concerned with the viability and governance of financial institutions of selected industries, e.g. banks, insurance, superannuation.

As a public company, Fiducian Group Ltd (FGL) also reports to the Australian Securities Exchange (ASX). So in reporting to three bodies, the challenge is to walk the fine line between regulation and innovation.

## Engaging with stakeholders

Fiducian's approach to corporate communication is dynamic – clients (whether external or internal) advance and recede in importance, depending on complex economic, social and political events.

For example, in mid 2015, economic shocks hit Greece and then China. Fiducian's financial planners needed cogent analysis of the situations and their effect on investments.

Fiducian's head of business services, Jai Singh, and head of investment, Conrad Burge, produced numerous bulletins in a very short time for planners and their clients to explain the issues and also to assure them that the multi-manager system protected investors from being over-exposed to risky markets. These bulletins were also sent to media (both general and financial trade).

### A sense of Fiducian's attachment to Australia

Fiducian Group Ltd is twenty years old in 2016. In those two decades, the company has grown from Indy Singh's vision to a solid and ethical reality that adapts to the needs of its clients. Thus, the structure of its strategic communication is fluid, dynamic and proactive. Sometimes the emphasis is on communicating with planners' clients because of market events; at other times, the emphasis moves to media, both general and trade. In everything, the goal is the clients' best interests – whoever those clients may be.

# 10

# ASSESSMENTS AND CHALLENGES

This chapter assesses the communication theories, models and strategies that have been laid out in the previous chapters. It looks at the challenges corporations will face if they choose to adopt the theories, models and strategies. It recommends the development and application of a reverse engineering tool to reveal the core communication competences that drive the communication strategies of successful corporate entities. It recommends a general social and economic theory for corporate strategic communication based on a differential transmission of communication model. It concludes by arguing the relevance of adopting a new paradigm – a Mayhewian argument – within the corporate structure so that successful strategic corporate communication is aligned seamlessly within an ever-changing societal framework.

There is a new and different challenge confronting global corporations. It is not like any previous challenge. It does not involve individual issues that can be identified and dealt with quickly and painlessly. It is not about natural disasters or the challenge of climate change. It is not economic. It is societal. It is Malthusian in scale. It is not as simple as global population growth outstripping global agricultural production. But it is simple.

## THE CHALLENGE PRESENTED BY THE UPSTART UBERCORP

The challenge is *truth in communication*. In 1997 General Electric (GE) chief executive Jack Welch stood up in front of the annual GE conference of senior managers. He said he had bad news for them. The company's financial performance had been excellent so why was there bad news? The bad news, he said, was economic; deflation was looming – falling prices combined with production over-capacity. He predicted a collapse in the Asian economies. At the same time he said it was vital that GE maintain its integrity given its world-class reputation. He was not interested in excuses for falling prices and how they might be interpreted by customers and other stakeholders. He was more concerned with leadership and the empowerment of one of his most important stakeholders during the forthcoming challenge: employees.

Similar values – leadership and empowerment – are the new hallmarks of corporations that owe their existence to disruptive technologies. Disruptive technologies, or disruptive innovation, creates markets. Old markets give way to improved products and services that employ disruptive innovations. Disruptive innovations are different to sustainable innovations. Sustainable innovations improve existing technologies. Most of the corporations discussed and analysed in the preceding chapters can be described as innovators where sustaining existing markets for their products and services is paramount. Their existing products and services are altered over time by stakeholder expectation.

Disruptive innovation has thrown up opportunities for 'uber' corporations to create new markets. These ubercorps have adapted their communication strategies so that they are in approximate alignment with the theory of the new public proposed by Leon Mayhew. Let's look at some of them and compare their narratives with those of older industrialists. We might also put the ubercorps into the disruptive category while keeping the industrialists in a sustainable category.

In 2015 a listed company based in California – Box – published its code of business conduct and ethics. The language of the code reflected the narrative of the corporation. It was pitched at employees of the company and to its directors. It set out clearly and concisely the challenges that corporations faced if they failed to adequately communicate their intentions. It said: 'the Code represents our values, our integrity, and our fundamental approach to getting stuff done. Ultimately, this document boils down to how Box does business. When it comes to finding your ethical compass in any business situation, this Code is your guide' (Box, 2015).

In creating the code, Box chief executive Aaron Levie was reflecting on the challenges the company faced in communicating its intentions within a society that is changing far more rapidly than that which confronted Jack Welch almost twenty years earlier. But Levie used similar language to structure his corporate narrative. Just as Welch saw his message to his shareholders as one of his most important communications, so, too, Levie used his message to stockholders in the 2015 annual report to identify specific challenges and how they would be met. For Levie the emerging disruptor – the uber upstart – was the challenge for traditional enterprises:

*Most enterprises are grappling with how to compete with the current or future "Uber" of their industry – an emerging disruptor that competes through technology advantage. In every market, from retail to financial services, new technology players are emerging to provide digital experiences that are cheaper, faster, smarter, and smoother for consumers. These upstarts don't bring the same baggage or legacy approaches when attacking their respective industry, and they're building experiences for customers that were never before possible. To compete in this dynamic global landscape, traditional enterprises need to become digital enterprises.*

*(Box, 2015)*

Levie went further. He invoked the qualities found in traditional industries and how they are flexible enough to compete. He mentioned GE:

*A digital enterprise looks like GE, whose jet engines can be optimized to leverage data and predictive analytics to save airliners on fuel costs. It looks like Gap, which is bridging the worlds of physical and digital commerce to better serve its customers. And it looks like Eli Lilly, as it collaborates virtually on the latest drug discovery with partners around the world.*

*(Box, 2015)*

In structuring his corporation's narrative, Levie used a vocabulary that fitted seamlessly with the language of the society in which Box was located. In its code of conduct, in his corporate message, the language was unmistakably culturally relaxed but at the same time demonstrated corporate intent. Phrases such as 'outdated legacy investments', 'dynamic global landscape' and 'emerging disruptor that competes through technology advantage' communicated precisely where Box was as a locative corporation. Other phrases communicated its intent – 're-imagination of IT strategies', 'foundational pillar', 'transform the way people and organizations work' (Box, 2015).

In 1998 GE was awarded, by *Fortune* magazine, the title of most admired company in America. There was a strong field of contenders. GE was followed by Microsoft, Coca-Cola,

Intel, Hewlett-Packard, Southwest Airlines, Berkshire Hathaway, Disney, Johnson & Johnson and Merck. But back then the corporation's RIB – reputation, image and brand – remained rooted in the economy. Tom Stewart of *Fortune* said: 'In their variety, America's ten most admired companies resemble the economy. But as they stand above the rest of corporate America in reputation, so do they tower over it in performance' (Stewart, 1998. www. fortune.com). Fortune tried to define what it was that made these companies great. It picked leadership as the factor that differentiated the top ten from the rest.

By 2015 *Fortune* had adjusted to globalization. Its rankings altered in name from America's most admired to the world's most admired. And the top ten? Apple, Google, Berkshire Hathaway, Amazon, Starbucks, Disney, Southwest Airlines, American Express, GE and Coca-Cola. The attributes *Fortune* applied to its rankings were: innovation, people management, use of corporate assets, social responsibility, quality of management, financial soundness, long-term investment value, quality of products and services, and global competitiveness. When the attributes were identified individually they showed a different ranking. For community responsibility Walt Disney was first, followed by Whole Food Markets, Nestlé, Uniliver, Johnson & Johnson, Toyota, John Deere, Wells Fargo, US Bancorp, Nextra Energy and Cisco Systems. *Fortune* did not expand on what was meant by 'community responsibility' (www.fortune.com).

In 1998 Jack Welch credited GE's performance to the idea that change should not be feared; it was good. By 2014 the company mission was to 'invent the next industrial era, to build, move, power and cure the world'. The preface to its 2014 annual report stated:

> *GE imagines things others don't, builds things others can't and delivers outcomes that make the world work better. GE brings together the physical and digital worlds in ways no other company can. In its labs and factories and on the ground with customers, GE is inventing the next industrial era to move, power, build and cure the world.*

> *(GE, 2014)*

In the report's 'CEO letter' GE's chief executive, Jeffrey Immelt, used language that redefined the GE narrative of the last century. He described a 'volatile world', 'a volatile economy', and companies that 'defend the status quo' and 'manage momentum'. The new GE 'beliefs', he said, were: customers determine success; stay lean to go fast; learn and adapt to win; empower and inspire each other; and deliver results in an uncertain world. Of GE, he said: 'we lead the merger of machines and analytics through the industrial internet'; 'we are focused on delivering an important financial pivot'; 'we have a foundation of broad and deep competitive advantage'; and 'leadership in infrastructure requires breadth and depth' (GE, 2014). GE has been in existence for more than 130 years so it appears to have a bit of an idea about sustainability:

> *At GE, we define sustainability as aligning our business strategy to meet societal needs, while minimizing environmental impact and advancing social development. As one of the world's leading infrastructure companies, we embrace our unique potential to help solve some of the most difficult sustainability challenges. To identify our highest sustainability priorities we began by evaluating the world's needs with stakeholders and identifying the intersections of those needs with GE's business strategies. Our sustainability strategy and reporting process are also informed by external stakeholder feedback gathered through formal advisory panels and regular engagement with customers and peer companies, academics, industry associations, NGOs, sustainability strategists and other partners. We work regularly with hundreds of customers, regulators, non-governmental organizations, academics, government bodies and other partners to identify emerging issues and develop collaborative solutions.*

> *(GE, 2015)*

# UBERS RULE THE WORLD

Uber upstarts are not confined to the United States. In the United Kingdom they challenge the traditional standpoints of the industrials and the 'too big to fails'. The top ten most admired companies headquartered in the United Kingdom in 2015 were BP, Diageo, GlaxoSmithKline, HSBC, Intercontinental Hotels, International Airlines, Rio Tinto, Rolls-Royce, Royal Mail, Liberty Global and Vodafone. The list was a mix of industrials, telecoms, hospitality and pharmaceuticals. No uber upstarts in the list. But they were there being disruptive. They were a little harder to find than those in the United States but they were there. Appear Here, a company that put vacant retail spaces together with retailers looking for space, began life in 2012. Its narrative included 'the ambition to find empty space, share an idea and start a story'. Appear Here was not corporate in the sense that it was a listed company yet it had global potential. Its marketing included conceptualizing a blackout supermarket in which customers would be blindfolded before trying food by taste. Customers would not see what they had bought until they left the store. The company's marketer, Alice Ratcliffe, described the concept: 'it would be great to see how branding affects our perception of taste' (Appear Here, 2016).

But the disruptors have made the old school industrialists and techs more competitive. Their presence has provided the incentive to become more competitive and to seek different opportunities. And they have discovered how to communicate in the New Public and with a wider range of stakeholders. Rolls-Royce is an example of a company, like GE, that had already changed direction. It began life as an English luxury car maker for which engines were a major focus. It transformed itself into a global corporation that 'designs, develops, manufactures and services integrated power systems for use in the air, on land and at sea'. It has two divisions: aerospace and land and sea. It works across civil and defence aerospace, nuclear submarine power and conventional power systems. Its annual report for 2014 claimed:

> Our world is changing, the climate is altering and populations are increasing. We need more power but not at any cost to society. The world needs better power. Rolls-Royce is committed to research and technology in order to develop innovative and advanced power systems that can help. Our vision is to deliver better power for a changing world
>
> (Rolls-Royce, 2014)

Rolls-Royce engines power Airbus commercial aircraft, Gulfstream and Cessna private aircraft and Lockheed Martin military aircraft.

The Rolls-Royce report was instructive in its language. Chairman Ian Davis revealed that there had been challenges in creating profit for shareholders. While the company had plenty of orders for its products, government investment in defence was lower, and the oil and gas and construction and mining sectors encountered tough markets. Davis said the short-term challenges did not change the fundamental long-term growth of the company. He said shareholders, customers and employees would benefit from a focus on expansion in the 'highly attractive markets for power and propulsion' (Rolls-Royce, 2014). Corporate governance, Davis added, was the 'hallmark of excellent companies'. He said the company remained committed to being a leader in ethical behaviour and in environmental and social responsibility. But he added a caveat that a new code of conduct had been issued to employees following an inquiry into bribery and corruption allegations against the company that involved 'intermediaries in overseas markets'. Rolls-Royce was implicated in a multibillion dollar bribery scheme at Brazil's state-owned oil producer, Petrobras, in 2015. Rolls-Royce supplied gas turbines for Petrobras oil platforms. The company was also implicated in serious fraud allegations in China and Indonesia.

In Germany the top ten most admired companies were BMW, Allianz, Volkswagen, Robert Bosch, SAP, BASF, Bayer, Continental, Daimler and Deutsche Post. They included motor vehicle manufacturers, chemical manufacturers and technology companies. Again, no disruptors, and no ubers, even though the word was derived from German, meaning 'over' or 'above'. Again, they are there disrupting the German market.

In 2012 Sebastian Diemer and Alexander Graubner-Müller founded Kreditech, which began as a credit bureau to sell better scoring data to banks. It is now a lending business. Diemer and Graubner-Müller built a bank around the idea of a credit bureau. The corporate narrative predicted:

> Banking as we know it today is dead. Your banking branch won't exist ten years from now, and neither will cost intensive, manual banking processes. We believe algorithms and automated processes are the way to customer-friendly banking. That's why we offer individual products at individual prices to customers via their smartphones.
>
> (www.kreditech.com)

Kreditech is interested in those it calls 'the underscored' – 73 per cent of the world's population (i.e. 5 billion) who do not get scored by credit bureaus. Standard scoring uses five points such as repayment history and payment of utility bills. Kreditech uses a 20,000-point proprietary algorithm to identify and approve customers.

BMW, the most admired German company, is a motor vehicle manufacturer that has been in existence since 1916. In its 2014 annual report, chairman of the board of management, Norbert Reithofer, pointed to the fact that the company will be one hundred years old in 2016. Its time in existence was, he said, 'a testament to our value-based corporate philosophy, geared towards the long term and shaped by independent-minded decisions'. But he pointed to the challenges faced by the company, arguing that it was important to look to the future. Competition, market volatility, political uncertainty and 'new trends in our environment' were part of the 'daily business' of BMW. Shareholders, he said, could rely on the company to sustain its profitability. He pointed to the recent record number of sales of the three brands manufactured by the company, BMW, Mini and Rolls-Royce – 2 million worldwide. The annual report claims 'The BMW Group is one of the most successful makers of cars and motorcycles worldwide and among the largest industrial companies in Germany' (BMW, 2014). The report acknowledged the need for good corporate governance:

> Acting in accordance with the principles of responsible management aimed at increasing the value of the business on a sustainable basis – is an essential requirement for the BMW Group embracing all areas of the business. Corporate culture within the BMW Group is founded on transparent reporting and internal communication, a policy of corporate governance aimed at the interests of stakeholders, fair and open dealings between the Board of Management and the Supervisory Board as well as among employees and compliance with the law.
>
> (BMW, 2014)

## UBERCORPS MUST BE LOCATIVE

Investors and other stakeholders would be wary of corporations that did not have at least their headquarters tied down and secure. So in some sense the ubercorp disruptor – the upstart looking to divert the market – is itself a traditional corporation. To maintain an image that will be attractive to stakeholders, particularly investors, employees, customers and suppliers, it must be locative. This means the communication strategy of the uber-corp disruptor must be differentiated from the corporations with whom they choose to compete. Differentiation will allow the ubercorp narrative to play out as if it is aligned with the Mayhewian notion of truth in communication.

For ubercorps, there is also the requirement that they take a different approach to stake-holders and stakeholder attributes. Ubercorps need to identify stakeholder attributes, as they have been described in Chapter 4.

Many metaphors exist for our upstart ubercorp. Sport climbing is a good one. Sport climbing is a form of rock climbing that is enabled by the use of anchors such as ring bolts and 'carrot bolts'. Unlike traditional rock climbing where the climber places individual pieces of protection in natural formations such as cracks and fissures in the rock, sport climbers attach protective aids to anchors fixed in the rock. Sport climbing is generally on shorter routes of one pitch. Traditional or 'trad' climbing can be anywhere from one pitch to multi-pitches depending upon the scale of the rock. Dawn Wall, on Yosemite Valley's El Capitan, at three thousand feet, is the longest rock climb in the world. Sports climbs, like ubercorps, are most prolific in Europe and the United States. According to The Crag, a col-laborative online database, there are 176,767 climbs in Europe, 80,496 in the United States, 56,407 in Australia and 9339 in New Zealand. In Europe, the United Kingdom is home to more traditional rock climbs while sport climbs are more popular in Switzerland, France, Belgium and Germany (www.thecrag.com).

Ubercorps and sport climbs have both been the subject of attack from traditionalists. They have been framed by the way they engage with their environments and their societies. While traditional rock climbers have been environmentally conscious of their activities, sport climbers continue to endanger the environment by their actions in drilling bolts into rock. The traditional corporation argues the ubercorp is equally environmen-tally unfriendly, littering the planet with useless information that's supposed to fire the imagination. It is worth noting that traditional climbing began with a mix of fixed aid and natural protection. It was not until the late 1970s and early 1980s that climbers became more environmentally friendly. They began 'chopping' old bolts from climbs to 'free' them. The sustainability of the climbs, like the present rhetoric surrounding the sustainability of the corporation, became more important than the act of conquest.

## THE POPULARITY OF THE UBERCORP: PRESENTATION AND SPECTACLE

Like sport climbers, ubercorps have carved a space for themselves by applying early usage of the vocabulary of Mayhew's New Public. The display of symbols in the rhetoric of presentation offers a new language for old meaning. The refeudalization of the space in the rhetoric of spectacle offers new images of old actions. Sport climbing ramped up the grading applied to traditional climbs by reducing the risk – a display of symbols that enticed a generation of new climbers and created wealth for the owners of indoor climbing gyms. The refeudalization of outdoor sport climbs opened up previously high risk, or more dangerous climbs of shorter length, expanding the spectacle of climbing closer to stake-holders. Less accessible crags and cliffs in wilderness areas were no longer the only places the rhetoric of spectacle could be performed. Sport climbing popularized an old activity.

So, too, ubercorps have popularized an old activity – the creation of wealth from the creation of products and services. One of the important elements of the popularity of the ubercorp is its public listing. To be successful in attracting and sustaining investors, it must display the symbols of the rhetoric of presentation and differentiate itself by the use of the rhetoric of spectacle.

Ubercorps don't have to be technology-based but they need to demonstrate a degree of disruption. Technology assists that process. Mobile, Internet and cloud reduce the cost of entry to markets. New corporations that communicate strategically and grasp the significance of stakeholder engagement are most likely to succeed. There are no limits for ubercorps. There are, however, limits for upstarts that choose to begin operations in defined industries. A law firm, for example, cannot do something that ceases to define it by the proscriptive force that surrounds it. It cannot act outside the framework of the legislation of the sovereign country in which it operates. If it did, it would cease to be a law firm. Many firms that were once focused on law have altered their boundaries substantially. They are now involved in various activities that were not traditionally the province of the law firm. Full service law firms act in a variety of corporate areas including mergers and acquisitions, initial public offerings, and rescue and restructuring. Regulatory advice and litigation are also high on the legal agenda. Law firms can become publicly listed companies in the United Kingdom and in Australia. But they are rare. When they do, they tend to be similar in nature and attractive to investors because they have peculiar fee structures, use technology to advantage and are consolidated within the legal services supply chain (Riddell, 2015). Riddell claims a strategy based on four attributes – a redefined legal service business model, clear focus and market identity, scale, and technology investment – will make legal upstarts more common in the future. Let's look at the vocabulary, the presentation and the spectacle.

Slater and Gordon, a law firm with more than 5200 employees in Britain and Australia, was listed on the Australian stock exchange and became a public company in 2007. It began life in England in the 1920s as a traditional law firm. It referred to itself as a 'law company built on social justice values, so it's no surprise that giving back to the community is part of our business' (slatergordon.com.au). It claimed a commitment to the environment by being 'thoughtful about how we use our resources. It's one of our core values, and we're committed to playing our part in creating a more sustainable workplace' (slatergordon.com.au). The question is whether the narrative of the corporation allowed it to take its place within the sphere of ubercorps. For Slater and Gordon there was an additional stakeholder at the top of the list. The company code of conduct pointed out its obligations to clients, shareholders, employees, suppliers and to the 'court'. It aimed to be 'a good corporate citizen and comply with not only the letter, but with the spirit of the law, wherever we do business'. Under a heading 'Professional Obligations' the code of conduct stated 'if there is a conflict, the first duty is to the court over all duties, and then the duty to the client will prevail over the duty to the shareholders' (Slater and Gordon, 2014a). This took the focus from the shareholder and placed it firstly with a regulator as stakeholder, then with the customer, or client. For some other stakeholders the code provided clear direction:

> S&G has a long history of close links directly to the labour movement with the firm acting
> for a large number of trade unions in many jurisdictions in which it operates. Any use of
> S&G to provide endorsement, donations, material, gifts or benefits to any party or candi-
> date must be approved by the Board. You should not take part in a political event such

*as a fundraiser as a representative of S&G without the express permission of your direct manager. [...] S&G's communications with investors, the media and other stakeholders in relation to the operations (financial or non-financial) of S&G are conducted exclusively by the Managing Director, or as delegated by the Managing Director. Duly authorised employees may discuss with the media individual client matters (subject to the client's approval) or specific areas of law in which they practice and have expertise, provided that they comply with the S&G Practice Standards and any other applicable policy.*

*(Slater and Gordon, 2014a)*

The company's annual report for 2014 included an outside front cover tagline 'Brighter outcomes'. It added: 'we believe that by understanding our clients' needs and providing high quality legal services affordably and conveniently, we can guide our clients to brighter outcomes and deliver sustainable returns for our shareholders' (Slater and Gordon, 2014b).

Slater and Gordon redefined its legal business model by incorporating. It claimed it provided a clear focus with its claim to brighter outcomes. Its market identity was defined by its claim to provide the 'leading consolidation of the UK consumer legal services market'. It stated it had 'now achieved the scale required to compete effectively in the UK consumer law market. Over the next few years we will exploit this scale and continue to grow market share both organically and through acquisitions'. On technology investment the company claimed 'our highly developed work process design and technology expertise provides us with a unique competitive advantage' (Slater and Gordon, 2015). Its market identity was highlighted in the report of the managing director, Andrew Grech: 'A refreshed brand identity was created and recently launched. The evolved brand aims to better represent the contemporary Slater and Gordon as a trusted advisor which navigates clients through the legal process, and guides them to a brighter outcome' (Slater and Gordon, 2015).

## THE CHALLENGE OF MEANINGFUL POLICY ISSUES

Leon Mayhew argued meaningful policy issues were not on the public agenda. In the 1990s, the time of his analysis, there was a conscious change occurring in non-European countries that worked towards the merger of public policy with corporate policy. In Europe, corporatist activity had been in existence since the end of the Second World War. Corporatism had been the hallmark of western European nations such as Germany, Switzerland, the Netherlands and Italy. It might be described simply as the sociopolitical framework of society in which groups – corporations, business, military, agribusiness, unions for example – form around common societal interests. While it is outside the topic of this book it is interesting to note that Jürgen Habermas followed the work of Émile Durkheim, the first French sociologist who expanded a theory of corporatism which he called 'solidarism'. His theory was built on the idea that society is collective rather than individual and that community bodies ought to work together to achieve national aims and goals.

We have examined in detail the various stakeholders that corporations need to focus on including governments and regulators. We have looked at the challenges that corporations face when they attempt to set their strategic direction around government legislation. And while the challenge in the late twentieth century was for corporations to work with government policy there has been a marked shift since the beginning of the twenty-first century in the west that has altered the shape of the relationship between corporations and governments. In the early 1990s James Post observed the beginning of the shift towards an amalgamation of public and corporate policy with reference to the success of the Asian economies of Japan and South Korea (Post, 1991, p. 8). Post argued that corporations were beginning to become involved in meaningful policy issues; among them he included education, hunger, homelessness and crime (Post, 1991, p. 13). He named specific public policy challenges for corporations in the 'political process'.

Internal challenges were:

1 a shift from crisis management to issues management;
2 productivity enhancement; and
3 improved standards of ethics, responsibility and accountability.

External challenges were:

1 the cost of 'doing politics';
2 political fragmentation threatening established political affairs; and
3 temporary political coalitions attempting to resolve social problems.

Post added to the mix what he called 'mega challenges' – challenges to the corporate sector that had the potential to disrupt activity and to dominate the policy agenda. His prescience was evident.

The mega challenges were:

1 racial demographics in America that would transform power;
2 unpredictable internationalization increasing corporate and government risk; and
3 environmental concerns that would influence the actions of corporations and governments.

(Post, 1991, p. 18)

Post concluded correctly that a legitimate relationship existed between corporations and governments in the development of societies. The challenges raised, he argued, had the potential to increase co-operation between governments and corporations in the development of public policy.

Three of the meaningful policy issues identified by Post have altered in scale and gravity. Homelessness and crime have become a migration issue. Hunger has become an agribusiness issue. Education remains an education issue. The question of corporate investment in public policy issues such as migration, agribusiness and education is one of strategic communication. Do corporations communicate their concerns, their intent and their engagement in policy issues to their stakeholders? Do corporations have a role in the ever-expanding issue of global migration, especially that of asylum being sought by increasing numbers of people fleeing from civil wars in the Middle East and the failed states of North Africa? Do corporations have a role in the education of millions in developing countries? Do corporations have a role in the development of agribusiness to alleviate hunger in both the developing and developed world? (See the Syngenta case study in Chapter 6.)

## Migration

In late 2015 hundreds of migrants held in a registration camp in Serbia broke free of the camp and pushed through police lines. They headed towards Hungary. They walked along a motorway. Their objective was to reach Hungary's capital and then travel to Germany where they would seek asylum. The migrants – some seeking asylum from Syria and other Middle Eastern conflicts and others who were 'economic' migrants seeking better lives in Europe – were described by German chancellor Angela Merkel as having the potential to change Germany in the coming years (BBC, 2015b). Ms Merkel was not referring exclusively to the three hundred who had escaped Serbia. She was referring to the 'breathtaking' numbers of people leaving Africa and the Middle East, travelling through Turkey, Greece and by boat across the Mediterranean to reach western Europe, Scandinavia and Britain.

It was estimated that 350,000 asylum seekers arrived in Europe between January and September 2015. Germany expected to receive more than 800,000 asylum applications that year. (One-third of which were economic migrants from Balkan countries, most of whom were rejected.) Ms Merkel's remark that breathtaking numbers of people would alter the shape of Germany was evidence-based. While Ms Merkel's government had invested an additional €6 billion in aid to assist the migrant inflow the question was what had German or multinational corporations invested? And how were corporations communicating their involvement if they were engaged?

The United Nations High Commission for Refugees (UNHCR) identified a variety of organizations that had assisted in the location of thousands of asylum seekers in Germany and Austria in September 2105 – faith-based organizations, NGOs and individuals. It argued that assistance from the highlighted bodies was 'driving governments to change policies and rhetoric' (UNHCR, 2015). Its press matter was silent on the engagement of corporations or other businesses. The UNHCR is a supranational organization funded by the United Nations. It was established in 1950 to assist Europeans displaced after the Second World War. In 2012 the UNHCR published *'The State of The World's Refugees: In Search of Solidarity'* (UNHCR, 2012). It also published a guide for doing business with UNHCR:

> *In trying to help and protect some of the world's most vulnerable people in so many different places and types of environment, UNHCR must purchase goods and services worldwide. This might range from buying fleets of heavy duty vehicles needed in the most inaccessible parts of the African continent to purchasing needles and thread for a self-help project in Pakistan. UNHCR also hires consultants and specialized companies and their staff for projects.*
>
> *(UNHCR, 2016)*

It publishes a code of conduct for suppliers which states: 'The Global Compact is a voluntary international corporate citizenship network initiated to support the participation of both the private sector and other social actors to advance responsible corporate citizenship and universal social and environmental principles to meet the challenges of globalization' (UNHCR, 2013).

While individual German corporations were silent on the issue of migration the Confederation of German Employers' Association (BDA) claimed the waves of asylum seekers could benefit German industry. The chief of BDA, Ingo Kramer, called for 'efforts at all levels' – meaning government should act to ease the rules of access to employment – so corporations would have a guarantee that a trainee would not be deported. Similarly the head of the Federation of German Industries (BDI), Ulrich Grillo, argued that quick integration into employment would help the refugees and help German industry. Particular sectors including health and leisure needed qualified workers while engineers, programmers and technicians were also in demand (Grillo, 2015).

Migration was a global issue, a meaningful policy issue on the public agenda of every western country.

## Agribusiness

The nature of agriculture has altered globally since the end of the twentieth century. The challenge for governments has been the balance between the maintenance of small farm holdings run by families with corporate activity or agribusiness run by large corporations with global networks and supply chain systems. The issue is food and the question is how to feed a growing global population.

According to the Global Policy Forum, an independent NFP that claims to monitor the UN, companies such as Cargill, Nestlé, Monsanto, ConAgra and Archer Daniels Midland dominate the world's food system:

> They control very large shares of the international markets for grains, fertilizers, pesticides and seeds, and they are involved in the food system from the farm to the supermarket. Farm equipment manufacturers, such as Deere & Company, are also influential, as are the big food retailers. Hedge funds and other investment firms are rapidly creating a global market for agricultural land, bringing other powerful actors into the food system. These companies shape government food policy. They squeeze out small farmers, promote energy-hungry industrial agriculture and create an unsustainable system of production and distribution.
>
> (Global Policy Forum, 2012)

Greenpeace, an NFP organization, claims multinationals control the world's food industry. It claims five companies control the world's grain trade and 'determine what farmers sow and what we eat' (Greenpeace, 2016). It adds:

> Corporate control of agriculture has historical precedents. For example, four of today's dominant grain-trading players are the same as 100 years ago: Bunge, Cargill, Continental, and Louis Dreyfus. What is new is the emergence of multinational supermarkets consolidating distribution and retailing and the agrochemical giants controlling seeds. This represents a few powerful companies dictating industry protocols to millions of small farmers, small suppliers – and to consumers.
>
> (www.greenpeace.com)

Greenpeace cites the example of food scarcity in Mexico being the result of 'policies and global trade agreements that liberalize trade and promote a globalized food economy' (Greenpeace, 2016).

Unlike the issue of migration, corporations with direct interests in agribusiness communicate their engagement and investment.

Archer Daniels Midland (ADM) is one of the largest food processors in the world, headquartered in Chicago, Illinois and founded in 1902. Its aim is to 'serv[e] as a vital link between farmers and consumers, we take crops and process them to make food ingredients, animal feed ingredients, renewable fuels and naturally derived alternatives to industrial chemicals'. As part of its 'strong communities' rhetoric, ADM provided $32,000 to underprivileged Mexican families for finance, housing and education assistance (Archer Daniels Midland, 2014). The company exists, it claims, to 'earn and keep the admiration of investors and colleagues, peers and partners, customers, farmers and community members; create value from agriculture and for stakeholders; grow our Company—our results, our activities and operations around the world—in a responsible manner, and stay true to our purpose of serving vital needs' (adm.com).

Bunge, an agribusiness corporation, was founded in the Netherlands in 1818 as a trading firm. It is listed on the New York Stock Exchange and claims to be a 'leading agribusiness and food company with integrated operations that circle the globe, stretching from the farm field to the retail shelf'. Its challenge, it claims, is to 'ensure food security for a growing population in a sustainable way'. It claims to help farmers produce larger harvests and connects farmers to customers. The company publishes its code of conduct that guides 'all members of the Bunge community' on ethical and legal matters (Bunge, 2014).

It also publishes a document entitled *Setting a Global Table* in which it represents the challenge it faces as a global food supplier. Farmland, it argues, is not evenly distributed so people in Asia, the Middle East and North Africa rely on farmers in America and Eastern Europe. Its role it says is to 'get crops from where they are grown to where they are needed efficiently and safely, thereby ensuring a dependable source of affordable, high-quality food year-round' (Bunge, 2016). The future, it adds, is where its greatest challenge lies. In this it claims commodity markets are at the centre of global agribusiness.

## Education

In western countries, the education of children and adults is a given. They receive comprehensive schooling at least until the ages of fourteen or sixteen with options to continue. There are three levels of schooling: primary, secondary and tertiary. Schooling is associated with educating. Training is an additional form of educating. It is this form which is most often associated with private enterprise. Training may be undertaken as part of an employee programme. Or it may be the development of a new skills set.

In developing countries, according to the United Nations Educational, Scientific and Cultural Organization (UNECSO), 20 per cent of young people fail to complete primary education. UNESCO claims the vast majority of the world's least educated live in rural landscapes:

> *Many young farmers facing land scarcity and the effects of climate change, lack even basic skills needed to protect themselves and make ends meet. Women are the most in need. They need training in business and marketing to find opportunities beyond farm work and reduce the obligation of migrating to cities in search of a job.*
>
> (UNESCO, 2012)

It is normative for governments to invest in education of their stakeholder populations. It is also an important issue for corporations who seek skilled employees to sustain their activities.

Fortescue Metals, an Australian listed corporation, is located in the Pilbara region of Western Australia. It claims to be the world's fourth largest iron ore miner. Its corporate social responsibility claim is to aspire to be a corporate citizen welcomed by communities that host its activities. Its claim is to generate long-term value for stakeholders by 'empowering communities, providing economic opportunity, behaving with respect and caring for people and the environment'. As part of its community focus Fortescue has created what it calls A Five Star Program. The programme was conceptualized to assist indigenous Australians with the 'education skills and support to obtain sustainable employment.' It comprises an aboriginal high school scholarship scheme, school-based traineeships, work-based traineeships, an aboriginal cadetship scheme and apprenticeships. The corporation claims it is committed to 'the retention of our aboriginal employees and the Five Star program guarantees the individual a permanent job placement at the end of their chosen career pathway' (Fortescue, 2016).

In creating the programme the corporation insinuated itself into a meaningful policy issue on the Australian public agenda. It reinforced its reputation, image and brand with a variety of stakeholders. At the same time, Fortescue chairman Andrew Forrest was invited by the Australian government to lead an inquiry into disparity in indigenous employment. The resulting 2014 report was entitled *Creating Parity* (The Forrest Review, 2014). The report argued the need for 'wholesale' changes to community attitudes so that indigenous children would receive the same educational advantages of non-indigenous children. It asked parents, the community and leaders to demand the right of children to be educated to reach their full potential. It sought an end to paternalism so 'first Australians' could 'stand on their own feet' and be independent, and for governments and welfare agencies to remove impediments to independence.

## THE CHALLENGE OF CREATING PARITY AND SHARED PROSPERITY

We have invested deeply in this book in the idea that strategic communication creates an environment in which corporations that communicate effectively are more likely to be profitable across their range of stakeholders than those that focus solely on shareholders. An underlying principle is the development and sustainability of a relationship between the corporation and the society in which it lives. A report published by Harvard University Business School in September 2015 had as its focus the possibility that corporations or firms could be more profitable if they engaged more effectively with their societies. The report, entitled *The Challenge of Shared Prosperity*, examined specifically the challenge to American firms (Rivkin, Mills and Porter, 2015). It argued that while firms thrived and prospered, the results did not become distributed throughout society. The report's authors argued leading companies were thriving but the resultant prosperity was not shared among citizens. They argued further that 'shared prosperity is a hallmark of any truly competitive economy' (Rivkin, Mills and Porter, 2015, p. 1). The report indicated that entrepreneurship was vital to the future prosperity of American society and that policy makers and firms needed to be jointly more active in promoting a skilled work force and easier access to capital. It noted that immigration legislation may have constrained entrepreneurial activity given that immigrants were 'disproportionately more likely to start their own businesses (Rivkin, Mills and Porter, 2015, p. 13). Sixty-six per cent of those surveyed for the report placed above economic growth, the issues of inequality, middle-class stagnation, poverty and economic mobility. The causes of inequality attached to these issues were education (limited economic mobility and rising poverty), globalization, technological change (middle-class stagnation), taxes (slow economic growth and rising inequality), politics (slow economic growth) and regulation (slow economic growth). Further, the report indicated, the economy was not expected to recover if existing policies and institutions remained. One of the problems lay with the weakness of the political will of national administrations to reform or restructure economic institutions.

In 2014 the World Bank published a report entitled *Shared Prosperity: Paving the Way in Europe and Central Asia* (Bussolo and Lopez-Calva, 2014). Its content was defined by two strategies: end extreme poverty and boost shared prosperity. Its authors argued the goals of the strategies were sustainable from economic, social and environmental perspectives.

Shared prosperity it argued was 'an enormous challenge' that could be achieved through 'bold thinking and determined action'. It argued for a reconciliation between growth and equity which meant the establishment of better relationships between corporations and governments and corporations and the societies in which they were located. The World Bank shared prosperity goal urged new interventions and policies:

*The core of the two goals is an overarching concern for sustainability. The strategy estab-lishes explicitly that the pursuit of shared prosperity, measured through income growth among the bottom 40, must be economically, environmentally, and socially sustainable. Shared prosperity cannot be achieved through approaches that are self-defeating over time. An imprudent fiscal policy that involves redistribution to the bottom 40 (percent of income distribution), but undermines future financial solvency; a growth model that relies on the overexploitation of natural resources without a corresponding investment in the productive capacity of the economy through a strategy of diversification; and a social contract that systematically excludes some groups, inducing polarization and weakening social cohesion: all these would have to be ruled out. The concern with social sustainability and overall governance in the context of the growth process should trans-late into ensuring equality of opportunity among all citizens so that socioeconomic achievement is not associated with specific circumstances or particular social identities. Policies to promote economic growth should reflect the limited nature of non-renewable resources, as well as the impact of economic activity on the environment—with special emphasis on climate change—and the need to protect biodiversity. Environmentally sustainable policies are essential for economic growth.*

(Bussolo and Lopez-Calva, 2014, p. 68)

The World Bank advocated an asset-based approach to shared prosperity which focused attention upon the axis between the corporate entity and government:

*The level and accumulation of assets that people own (human capital, financial capital, physical assets, natural capital, and social capital) matter for income generation, as do the intensity with which they are used and the existing returns to these assets. In addition to market income, transfers (both public and private) either reinforce or offset the patterns determined by the market. In the medium and long term, the level and distribution of assets and their returns become key drivers behind growth and the incidence of growth.*

(Bussolo and Lopez-Calva, 2014, p. 90)

The decisions that affect the accumulation of assets, the World Bank claimed, are made by households and firms within societies. But, it added, variables that govern the income generated by the assets lie outside the control of households. The inference was that firms or corporations control income and were macro-economic in nature. It recommended countries look closely at boosting shared prosperity by moving away from policies that maximized growth but did not focus on where the growth came from.

From these reports we can deduce that the corporation in two of the world's largest economic zones – the United States of America and the United States of Europe – is iden-tified as both the evil and the good. At once it is the evil creator of the economic problems of modernity and the good creator of the social solutions to the economic problems of modernity. It is not surprising, therefore, that corporations are reticent about entering the sphere of pubic policy. The challenge of shared prosperity remains a rhetorical one.

# CONCLUSION

Throughout this book we have argued that corporations, using strategic communication, can achieve effective outcomes in a variety of stakeholder situations. In identifying themselves as part of the societies in which they are located corporations can make bold plans for long-run dynamic growth through the communication of determined action. But in doing so they must navigate a course that is increasingly more complex. Stakeholders are more sophisticated than ever before in information-seeking and information-disseminating. Issues and events are more complex and require more intelligent engagement. Societies are more diverse and more dysfunctional. To succeed in a multidimensional society which has disconnected from traditional, observable vectors, a corporation must conceptualize and operationalize a communication strategy that is identifiable and acceptable. It must be easily apprehended. Corporations must communicate intention by building relationships with the those civil society actors who are most likely to champion the investment of the corporation in society.

A theory of corporate strategic communication must anticipate fluctuations across different timescales of socioeconomic activity: short run, medium run and long run. It must anticipate human behaviour within a competitive global environment and an orthodox static economic environment. At the same time it must conceptualize the external forces which impact upon the core competences of its operational activities. It must anticipate a non-static environment – one with potential financial, economic or social turning points. It must triangulate reputation, image and brand to provide a competitive edge. It must use its prime artefact, its annual report, in a corporate communication strategy as tactical representation where content drives the corporate narrative. It must analyse stakeholders as three distinct groups: strategists (profit-seekers), non-strategists (employees and dependents) and anti-strategists (rent-seekers). It must be interested in the attributes of stakeholders so that communicative actions can be created or adjusted. It must abandon the idea of a vertical structure to represent stakeholders and look to the differential transmission of communication model. It must create a set of grand strategy principles that allow it to frame a persuasive corporate narrative. It must create a grand strategy and a narrative that can be clearly identified and interpreted by the greatest number of stakeholders. It must communicate its contribution to meaningful policy issues on the public agenda. It must provide normative and rhetorical appeals to attitudes that tap structures of solidarity and support effective responses to sociopolitical issues and events. It must provide opportunities for demands that claims be redeemed in discourse. And finally it must respond truthfully with straightforward answers to queries and objections within the wider community.

In the second decade of the twenty-first century many global corporations remain locked into mid-twentieth-century communication paradigms. They cannot grasp why the disruptive upstart is shifting the balance. They fail to recognize the relevance and sense of purpose that is playing out around them as societies alter rapidly in shape and texture. Others – like those included in this book as case studies of excellence in corporate strategic communication – have the flexibility and foresight to create powerful narratives aligned seamlessly with their societies.

Corporations have the potential to act in partnership with states to achieve societal goals and objectives. A measure of their future success will be identifiable in how they choose their strategic communication.

# REFERENCES

Airbus (2014). Airbus Industries, CSR report, www.airbus.com/company/corporate-social-responsi bility, date accessed 2 June 2016.

Alibaba Group (2016). www.alibaba.com.

ANZ (2016). www.anz.co.nz.

Archer Daniels Midland (2014). Annual Report, http://www.adm.com/en-US/investors/shareholder_ reports/2014AR/Pages/default.aspx, date accessed 6 March 2015.

Appear Here (2016). *If You Did A Popup, What Would It Be?*, www.appearhere.co.uk, date accessed 3 June 2016.

Bank of America (2014). CSR Report, about.bankofamerica.com/en-us/global-impact.html, date accessed 6 March 2015.

Bank of China (2014). 'Serving Society Delivering Excellence', Annual Report, pic.bankofchina.com/ bocappd/report, date accessed 3 June 2016.

Bank of China (2016). www.boc.cn/en.

Barclay's Bank (2016). www.barclays.com.

BBC (2015a). 'Can a Company Live Forever?', BBC News, New York, 19 January.

BBC (2015b). 'Migrant Crisis: Influx Will Change Germany, Says Merkel', BBC News, 8 September.

Bhagwati, G. (2004). *In Defense of Globalization*, Oxford University Press.

BHPbilliton (2014a). *Value Through Performance*, Annual Report, www.bhpbilliton.com

BHPbilliton (2014b). *Resourcing The Future*, Shareholder Circular, www.bhpbilliton.com.

Berg, C. (2014). 'Politics Not Policy Will Decide Who Gets Bailed Out', *The Drum*, 22 July, www.abc. net.au/news/thedrum.

Bice, S. (2014). 'What Gives You a Social Licence? An Exploration of the Social Licence to Operate in the Australian Mining Industry', *Resources*, vol. 3, pp. 62–80.

BMW (2014). BMW Group 2014 Annual Report, https://www.bmwgroup.com/content/dam/bmw-group-websites/bmwgroup_com/ir/downloads/en/2014/12507_GB_2014_en_Finanzbericht_Online.pdf, date accessed 3 June 2016.

Bonini, S., Court, D. and Marchi, A. (2009). 'Rebuilding Corporate Reputations', McKinsey Insights, *McKinsey Quarterly*, http://www.mckinsey.com/global-themes/leadership/rebuilding-corporate-reputations, date accessed 3 June 2016.

Booth, W. (1961). *The Rhetoric of Fiction*, University of Chicago Press.

BP (2014). British Petroleum 2014 Annual Report, http://www.bp.com/content/dam/bp/en/corpo-rate/pdf/bp-annual-report-and-form-20f-2014.pdf

BP (2016). British Petroleum, www.bp.com, date accessed 1 June 2016.

Botan C. and Hazelton V. (Eds) (2006). *Public Relations Theory*, Lawrence Erlbaum.

Box (2015). Annual Report, www.boxinvestorrelations.com.

Bowen, H. (2006). *The Business of Empire: The East India Company and Imperial Britain 1756–1833*, Cambridge University Press.

Bunge (2014). *Code of Conduct*, http://www.bunge.com/citizenship/files/code_conduct/code-of-conduct-eng.pdf, date accessed 1 June 2016.

Bunge (2016). *Setting a Global Table*, http://www.bunge.com/global-table.html, date accessed 1 June 2016.

Burke, K. (1966). *Language as Symbolic Action: Essays on Life, Literature, and Method*, University of California Press.

Bussolo, M. and Lopez-Calva L. (2014). *Shared Prosperity: Paving the Way in Europe and Central Asia*, World Bank.

Canadine, D. (2013). *The Undivided Past: History beyond our Differences*, Allen Lane.

Carswell, J. (1993). *The South Sea Bubble*, Alan Sutton.

Chartered Secretaries Australia (2011). (Renamed to: Governance Institute of Australia), www.governanceinstitute.com.au, date accessed 1 June 2016.

Chikofsky, E. and Cross, J. (1990). 'Reverse Engineering and Design Recovery: A Taxonomy', *IEEE Software*, vol. 7, pp. 13–17.

Chilton, P. (2004). *Analysing Political Discourse: Theory and Practice*, Routledge.

China Daily (2015). 'Luxury Goods Makers Sue Alibaba', *China Daily*, 18 May.

Clarke, T. and Clegg, S. (1998). *Changing Paradigms: The Transformation of Management Knowledge for the 21st Century*, HarperCollins.

Cornelissen, J. (2014). *Corporate Communication: A Guide to Theory and Practice*, Routledge.

Dahl, R. (1957). 'The Concept of Power', *Behavioral Science*, vol. 2, no. 3 (July).

Dahlgren, P. (2009). *Media and Political Engagement*, Cambridge University Press.

Dale, R. (2004). *The First Crash: Lessons from the South Sea Bubble*, Princeton University Press.

Diageo (2016). www.diageo.com.

Diasamidze, I. (2014). 'Point of View in Narrative Discourse', *Procedia Social and Behavioral Sciences* vol. 158, pp. 160–5.

Dolfsma ,W. (2009). *Institutions, Communication and Values*, Palgrave Macmillan.

Durkheim, E. (1964). *The Division of Labour in Society*, Free Press.

Edwards, B., Foley, M. and Diani, M. (2001). *Beyond Tocqueville: Civil Society and the Social Capital Debate in Comparative Perspective*, University Press of New England.

European Commission (2015). ec.europa.eu.

Exxon Mobil (2014). 'The Outlook for Energy: A View to 2040', http://corporate.exxonmobil.com/en/energy/energy-outlook, date accessed 2 June 2016.

Feaver, P. (2009). 'What Is Grand Strategy and Why Do We Need It?', *Foreign Policy*, 8 April.

Feaver, P. and Popescu, I. (2012). 'Is Obama's Foreign Policy Different From George W. Bush?', *E-International Relations*, 3 August 2012.

Federal National Mortgage Association (2015). (Fannie Mae) www.fanniemae.com.

Fenton, C. and Langley, A. (2011). 'Strategy As Practice and the Narrative Turn', *Organization Studies*, vol. 32, no. 9, pp. 1171–96.

Ferguson, N. (2008). *The Ascent of Money: A Financial History of the World*, Allen Lane.

Financial Conduct Authority (2014). www.fca.org.uk.

Financial System Inquiry (2014). www.fsi.gov.au.

Fishman, C. (2006). *The Wal-Mart Effect: How the World's Most Powerful Company Really Works and How It's Transforming the American Economy*, Penguin.

Forbes Global (2000). *The World's Biggest Public Companies*, www.forbes.com/global2000.

Fortescue (2016). Aboriginal Cadetships, Five Star Program, http://fmgl.com.au/community/five-star-program/aboriginal-cadetships/, date accessed 2 June 2016.

Fortune 500 (2014). www.fortune.com/fortune500.

Freeman, E. (1984). *Strategic Management: A Stakeholder Approach*, Cambridge University Press.

Freeman, E. (1994). 'The Politics of Stakeholder Theory', *Businees Ethics Quarterly*, vol. 4, no. 4, pp. 409–21.

Friedman, M. (1970). 'The Social Responsibility of Business Is To Increase Its Profits', *New York Times Magazine*, 13 September.

GE (2014). 'A New Kind of Industrial Company', General Electric 2014 Annual Report, https://www.ge.com/ar2014/assets/pdf/GE_AR14.pdf, date accessed 3 June 2016.

GE (2015). *Sustainability Priorities*, www.gesustainability.com/how-ge-works, date accessed 3 June 2016.

Global Policy Forum (2012). *Agribusiness Companies*, www.globalpolicy.org

Goertz, G. and Mahoney, J. (2012a). *A Tale of Two Cultures: Qualitative and Quantitative Research in the Social Sciences*, Princeton University Press.

Goertz G. and Mahoney J. (2012b). 'Concepts and Measurement: Ontology and Epistemology', *Social Science Information*, vol. 51, no. 2, pp. 205–16.

Gofee, R. and Jones, G. (1998). *The Character of a Corporation: How Your Company's Culture Can Make or Break Your Business*, HarperCollins.

Greenpeace (2016). Corporate Control of Agriculture, http://www.greenpeace.org/seasia/ph/What-we-do/Genetic-Engineering/agriculture/problem/Corporate-Control-of-Agriculture/, date accessed 2 June 2016.

Gregory, H. (2002). *Comparative Matrix Of Corporate Governance Codes Relevant To The European Union And Its Member States*, Weil, Gotshal & Manges.

Grillo, U. (2015). *German Industries Make Economic Case To Welcome Refugees*, BusinessWorldOnline, www.bworldonline.com

Grunig, J. and Hunt, T. (1984). *Managing Public Relations*, Wadsworth.

Habermas, J. (1989). *The Structural Transformation of the Public Sphere: An Inquiry into a Category of Bourgeois Society*, MIT Press.

Hackett-Fischer, D. (1996). *The Great Wave: Price Revolutions and the Rhythm of History*, Oxford University Press.

Hall, J. and Trentmann, F. (eds) (2005). *Civil Society: A Reader in History, Theory and Global Politics*, Palgrave Macmillan.

Hazleton, V. (1992). 'Towards a Systems Theory of Public Relations', in H. Avenarius and W. Armbrecht (eds), *Public Relations Als Wissenschaft: Grundlagen Und Interdisziplinare Ansatze*, Westdeutscher, 33–46.

Hazleton, V. (1993). 'Symbolic Resources: Processes in the Development and Use of Symbolic Resources', in H. Avenarius, W. Armbrecht and U. Zabel (eds), *Image and PR*, Westdeutscher, 87–100.

Hazleton, V. and Long, L. (1985). 'The Process of Public Relations: A Model', Paper presented to the International Communication Association, Honolulu, Hawaii.

Hazleton, V. and Long, L. (1988). 'Concepts For Public Relations Education, Research and Practice: A Communication Point of View', *Central States Speech Journal*, vol. 39, pp. 77–87.

Hobbes, T, [1651] (2012). *Leviathan The Matter, Forme and Power of a Common Wealth Ecclesiasticall and Civil*, Oxford University Press.

Johnson, G. and Scholes, K. (2001). *Exploring Corporate Strategy*, Prentice Hall.

Jones G. (2000). *Merchants to Multinationals: British Trading Companies in the Nineteenth and Twentieth Centuries*, Oxford.

Karabell, Z. (2009). *Superfusion: How China and America became One Economy and Why the World's Prosperity Depends on It*, Simon & Schuster.

Kering (2015). Annual Report, www.kering.com.

Kingfisher (2015). 'Kingfisher Holdings Ltd response to AP (Associated Press) news release', Kingfisher Holdings Ltd, 25 March 2015, http://www.kingfisher.co.th/announcement/abused_labor/001-2.pdf, date accessed 3 June 2016.

Kingfisher (2016). www.kingfisher.co.th.

Kueh, Y. (2008). *China's New Industrialization Strategy: Was Chairman Mao Really Necessary?* Edward Elgar.

Landes, D. (1969). *The Unbound Prometheus: Technological Change and Industrial Development in Western Europe from 1750 to the Present*, Cambridge University Press.

Langella, I., Carbo, J. and Dao, V. (2012). 'An Examination of the Symbiosis between Corporations and Society with Lessons for Management Education and Practice', *Global Virtue Ethics Review*, vol. 6, no. 3, pp. 51–82.

Leveson Inquiry (2011). www.levesoninquiry.org.uk.

Locke, J. (1963). *Two Treatises of Government*, Cambridge University Press.

Lucaites, J. and Condit, C. (1985). 'Reconstructing Narrative Theory: A Functional Perspective', *Journal of Communication*, vol. 35, no. 4, pp. 90–108.

Mall Secrets. (2014). www.mallsecrets.com.

Martinez, A. (2014). 'Storyworld Possible Selves and the Phenomenon of Narrative Immersions: Testing a New Theoretical Construct', *Narrative*, vol. 22, no.1, pp. 110–31.

Maruha Nichiro (2015). Maruha Nichiro financial statement for the year ended 31 March 2015, www.maruha-nichiro.co.jp.

Mauha Nichiro (2016). www.maruha-nichiro.co.jp.

Mayhew, L. (1997). *The New Public: Professional Communication and the Means of Social Influence*, Cambridge University Press.

McDowell, R., Mason, M. and Mendoza, M. (2015). 'AP Investigation: Are Slaves Catching the Fish You Buy?', Yahoo News, 25 March.

McFarlane J. (2005). *Challenging the Role of Corporations in Society*, Melbourne University.

Microsoft (2014). Microsoft Citizenship Report, www.microsoft.com/about/csr.

Miller, H. (2014). 'Narrative Competition in Public Discourse', *Administrative Theory & Praxis*, vol. 36, no. 3, pp. 287–307.

Millstein, I. (2002) *Comparative Matrix of Corporate Governance Codes Relevant to the European Union and its Member States*, Weil, Gotshal and Manges.

Mintzberg, H. (1994). *The Rise and Fall of Strategic Planning*, Free Press.

Mitchell R., Agle, B. and Wood, D. (1997). 'Toward a Theory of Stakeholder Identification and Salience: Defining the Principle of Who and What Really Counts', *The Academy of Management Review*, vol. 22, no. 4, pp. 853–86.

Moir, L. (2001). 'What Do We Mean By Corporate Social Responsibility?' *Corporate Governance*, vol. 1, no. 2, pp. 16–22.

Nathan, J. (1999). *Sony: The Private Life*, HarperCollins.

National Real Estate Investor (2010). *Retail Real Estate Review*.

New York Times (1999). 'Fannie Mae Eases Credit to Aid Mortgage Lending', *New York Times*, 30 September.

Nisbet, R. (1953). *The Quest For Community: A Study in the Ethics of Order and Freedom*, Oxford University Press.

NSW Government (2016). New South Wales Government, www.nsw.gov.au, date accessed 2 June 2016.

Nye, J. (2008). *The Powers to Lead*, Oxford University Press.

Nye, J. (2011). *The Future of Power*, Perseus Books.

OFA (2016). Ontario Federation of Agriculture, www.ofa.org, date accessed 3 June 2016.

Olson Zaltman (2015). Deep Metaphors, www.olsonzaltman.com.

Ontario Government (2016). www.ontario.ca/home/ontario-government, date accessed 2 June 2016.

Ontario Government Department of Community and Social Services (2015). www.ontario.ca.

Page, K. and Hazleton, V. (1999). *An Empirical Analysis of Factors Influencing Public Relations Strategy Selection and Effectiveness*, International Communication Association.

Peter Pan Seafoods (2014). *Ocean Watch*, http://www.ppsf.com/press/OceanWatch_2014.pdf, date accessed 4 June 2016.

Philippines Government (2016). www.gov.ph, date accessed 1 June 2016.

Post, J. (1991). 'The Corporation and Public Policy in the 1990s', *Journal of Organizational Change Management*, vol. 4, no. 1, pp. 7–21.

Potter, J. and Wetherell, M. (1987). *Discourse and Social Psychology*, Sage.

Porter, M. and Kramer, M. (1996). 'Strategy and Society: The Link between Competitive Advantage and Corporate Social Responsibility', *Harvard Business Review*, vol. 84, no. 12, pp. 76–92.

Prno, J. and Slocombe, D. (2012). 'Exploring the Origins of Social Licence to Operate in the Mining Sector: Perspectives from Governance and Sustainability Theories', *Resources Policy*, vol. 37, no. 3, pp. 346–57.

Putnam, R. (2000). *Bowling Alone: The Collapse and Revival of America Community*, Simon & Schuster.

PwC (2015). *Changing the Game: Outlook for the Global Sports Market to 2015*, www.pqc.com/industries/changing-the-game

PwC (2016). PricewaterhouseCoopers, www.pwc.com, date accessed 1 June 2016.

Reinhart, C. and Rogoff, K. (2009). *This Time Is Different: Eight Centuries of Financial Folly*, Princeton University Press.

Riddell, W. (2015). 'Slater + Gordon: A Lesson in Listed Law Firms', *Australian Financial Review*, (April).

Rivkin, J. W., Mills, K. G. and Porter, M. E. (2015). *The Challenge of Shared Prosperity: Findings on Harvard Business School's 2015 Survey on U.S. Competitiveness*, Harvard University Business School.

Rolls-Royce (2014). 'Better Power For a Changing World', Rolls-Royce Annual Report 2014, http://www.rolls-royce.com/~/media/Files/R/Rolls-Royce/documents/investors/annual-reports/2014-annual-report-v2.pdf, date accessed 1 June 2016.

Royal Dutch Shell (2014). Royal Dutch Shell plc Annual Report and form 20-F for the year ended 21 December 2014, www.royaldutchshell.com

Samuelson, P. and Scotchmer, S. (2002.) 'The Law and Economics of Reverse Engineering', *Yale Law Journal*, vol. 1575, pp. 1615–20.

Schlesinger, A. (ed.) (1994). *Running For President: The Candidates and their Images*, Simon & Schuster.

Serbian Government (2016). www.srbija.gov.rs, date accessed 2 June 2016.

Shamir, R. (2011). 'Socially Responsible Private Regulation: World Culture or World Capitalism?', *Law and Society Review*, vol. 45, no. 2, pp. 313–36.

Shen, D. (2013). 'Implied Author, Authorial Audience and Context: Form and History in Neo-Aristotelian Rhetorical Theory', *Narrative*, vol. 21, no. 2, pp. 140–58.

Simkovic, M. (2011). 'Competition and Crisis in Mortgage Securitization', *Indiana Law Journal*, vol. 88, pp. 213 –71.

Slater, R. (1999). *Jack Welch and the GE Way: Management Insights and Leadership Secrets of the Legendary CEO*, McGraw Hill.

Slater and Gordon (2014a). 'Code of Conduct', https://media.slatergordon.com.au/code-of-conduct. pdf, date accessed 3 June 2016.

Slater and Gordon (2014b). 'Brighter Outcomes', Annual Report 2014, https://media.slatergordon. com.au/annual-report-2014.pdf, date accessed 3 June 2016.

Slater and Gordon (2015). 'Foundations for Growth' Annual Report 2015, http://www.slatergordon. co.uk/media/5694130/slater-and-gordon-annual-report-2015.pdf, date accessed 3 June 2016.

Slovenian Government (2016). www.vlada.si/en, date accessed 1 June 2016.

Smith, A. (1776). *The Wealth of Nations: An Inquiry into the Nature and Causes of the Wealth of Nations*, Clarendon Press.

Snooks, G. (1998). *Longrun Dynamics: A General Economic and Political Theory*, Macmillan.

Stanton, R. (2007). *Media Relations*, Oxford University Press.

Stewart, T. (1998). 'America's Most Admired Companies: Why Leadership Matters', *Fortune*, 2 March.

Stiglitz, J. (2006). *Making Globalization Work*, W W Norton.

Stoll, P., Busche, J. and Arend, K. (2009). 'WTO: Trade-Related Aspects of Intellectual Property Rights', *African Development Review*, vol. 21, no. 3, pp. 589–90.

Tata Motors (2015). www.tatamotors.com.

The Crag (2015). *The World's Largest Collaborative Climbing Database*, www.thecrag.com.

The Forrest Review (2014). Creating Parity, www.indigenousjobsand trainingreview.dpmc.gov.au.

Tokoro, N. (2007). 'Stakeholders and Corporate Social Responsibility (CSR): A New Perspective on the Structure of Relationships', *Asian Business & Management*, vol. 6, pp. 143–62.

Toyota (2014). 'Aiming to Achieve Sustainable Growth and to Bring Smiles', Toyota Motor Corporation Annual Report, http://www.toyota-global.com/pages/contents/investors/ir_library/ annual/pdf/2014/p3_4.pdf, date accessed 6 June 2015.

Trenchard, J. and Gordon, T. (1720). *Cato's Letters: Essays on Liberty, Civil and Religious, and Other Important Subjects*, Cato Institute.

UFIP (2015). Union Française des Industries Pétrolières (French Union of Petroleum Industries), http://www.ufip.fr, date accessed 22 September 2015.

Ulhøi, J. and Madsen, H. (2013). 'New Patterns in Corporate Sustainable Development?', *Procedia Social and Behavioural Sciences*, vol. 99, pp. 46–56.

*Undercurrent News* (2013). 'Seafood Connection to Sell Peter Pan Products in Europe', 5 December.

UNESCO (2012). 'Twenty percent of young people in developing countries fail to complete primary school and lack skills for work', United Nations Educational, Scientific and Cultural Organization Press Release, http://en.unesco.org/gem-report/sites/gem-report/files/gmr2012-pressrelease_0. pdf, date accessed 3 June 2016.

UNHCR (2012). *The State of The World's Refugees: In Search of Solidarity*, United Nations High Commission for Refugees, Oxford University Press.

UNHCR (2013). UN Supplier Code Of Conduct, www.unglobalcompact.org, date accessed 3 June 2016.

UNHCR (2015). 2015 Global Appeal, United Nations High Commission for Refugees, 5 September, www.unhcr.org.

UNHCR (2016). Doing Business, United Nations High Commission for Refugees, http://www.unhcr. org/doing-business.html, date accessed 3 June 2016.

United Nations (2014). *World Urbanization Prospects*, www.esa.un.org.

United States Department of Housing and Urban Development (2002). www.hud.gov.

Wall, F. and Greiling, D. (2011). 'Shareholder Versus Stakeholder Orientation in Managerial Decision Making', *Review of Managerial Science*, vol. 5, no. 2, pp. 87–90.

Wallis Inquiry (1987). The Wallis Report on the Australian Financial System, www.aph.gov.au/About_Parliament/Parliamentary

Wal-Mart (2015). *Save Money, Live Better*, www.walmart.com.

Wang, J. (2011). 'China's Search for a Grand Strategy', *Foreign Affairs*, vol. 90, no. 2, pp. 68–79.

Weber, M. (1947). *The Theory of Social and Economic Organization*, Free Press.

Wehrfritz, G. (2008). 'Lured Into Bondage', *Newsweek*, 4 December.

Weil, Gotshal and Manges (2002). *Comparative Matrix of Corporate Governance Codes Relevant to the European Union and its Member States*, www.weil.com.

Wolfe M. (2008). *Fixing Global Finance*, The Johns Hopkins University Press.

Zaltman, G. and Duncan, R. (1977). *Strategies For Planned Change*, Wiley.

Zaltman, G. and Zaltman, L. (2008). *Marketing Metaphoria: What Deep Metaphors Reveal About the Minds of Consumers*, Harvard Business School Press.

# INDEX